DIALOGUES ON THE ETHICS OF ABORTION

What happens when two intelligent and highly informed fictional college students, one strongly pro-choice and the other vigorously pro-life, are asked to put together a presentation on abortion? Their conversations over five days – friendly but lively, charitable but clear – are captured in this book.

Through these dialogues, students and other interested readers are introduced to the difficult moral issues of abortion. In Chapter 1, readers learn about *Roe v. Wade* and other relevant legal cases. Chapter 2 covers basic, philosophical issues such as: What is a person? Are fetuses persons? Is fetal potential morally relevant? How shall we define the moral community? Chapter 3 introduces students to Don Marquis's "Why Abortion is Immoral" and also the metaphysical issues of personal identity and its relevance to abortion. Chapter 4 covers Judith Jarvis Thomson's "A Defense of Abortion", including objections and responses to the argument from bodily autonomy. Finally, Chapter 5 looks at abortion in hard cases, such as in cases of rape, fetal disability, non-viable pregnancies, and sex-selection; the chapter also includes a conversation on fathers and abortion.

With a Foreword by Laurie Shrage, topics headings in the margins, and an annotated bibliography, *Dialogues on the Ethics of Abortion* is an easy-to-use volume and valuable resource for anyone interested in a fair and clear-headed approach to one of the most contentious moral issues of our time.

Bertha Alvarez Manninen is Professor of Philosophy at Arizona State University, West Campus. She is the author of the book, *Pro-Life, Pro-Choice: Shared Values in the Abortion Debate* (2014) and the co-editor of the book *Being Ethical: Classic and New Voices on Contemporary Issues* (2017). She is also the co-author of *A Civil Dialogue on Abortion* (2018), published by Routledge.

Philosophical Dialogues on Contemporary Problems

Philosophical Dialogues on Contemporary Problems uses a well-known form – at least as old as Socrates and his interlocutors – to deepen understanding of a range of today's widely deliberated issues. Each volume includes an open dialogue between two or more fictional characters as they discuss and debate the empirical data and philosophical ideas underlying a problem in contemporary society. Students and other readers gain valuable, multiple perspectives on the problem at hand.

Each volume includes a foreword by a well-known philosopher, topic markers in the page margins, and an annotated bibliography.

Titles in series:

Dialogues on the Ethical Vegetarianism
Michael Huemer

Dialogues on the Ethics of Abortion
Bertha Alvarez Manninen

Dialogues on Climate Justice
Stephen M. Gardiner and Arthur R. Obst

Forthcoming:

Dialogues on Free Will and Responsibility
Thomas A. Nadelhoffer

Dialogues on Gun Control
David DeGrazia

For more information about this series, please visit: www.routledge.com/Philosophical-Dialogues-on-Contemporary-Problems/book-series/PDCP

DIALOGUES ON THE ETHICS OF ABORTION

Bertha Alvarez Manninen

Routledge
Taylor & Francis Group

NEW YORK AND LONDON

Cover image: © Getty images

First published 2022
by Routledge
605 Third Avenue, New York, NY 10158

and by Routledge
4 Park Square, Milton Park, Abingdon, Oxon, OX14 4RN

Routledge is an imprint of the Taylor & Francis Group, an informa business

Library of Congress Cataloging-in-Publication Data
A catalog record for this title has been requested

ISBN: 978-0-367-62438-5 (hbk)
ISBN: 978-0-367-61656-4 (pbk)
ISBN: 978-1-003-10945-7 (ebk)

DOI: 10.4324/9781003109457

Typeset in Bembo
by KnowledgeWorks Global Ltd.

CONTENTS

Foreword by Laurie Shrage *ix*

Preface *xi*

Acknowledgements *xviii*

Day 1: *Roe v. Wade* and Other Legal Concerns 1

 (a) *Does the Bible prohibit abortions? 2*

 (b) *The thalidomide scare. 3*

 (c) *Does* Roe v. Wade *legalize abortion on demand? 4*

 (d) Roe v. Wade *does not legalize abortion on demand. 6*

 (e) *What's included in the right to privacy? 7*

 (f) Planned Parenthood v. Casey *asserts viability as the point where abortion can be restricted. 8*

 (g) *Many states do restrict abortion access at some point in pregnancy. 9*

 (h) *New York's* Reproductive Health Act. *9*

 (i) Doe v. Bolton, *and how to define maternal health. 10*

 (j) *Making abortions illegal won't stop them. 11*

 (k) *The effectiveness of laws prohibiting abortion. 12*

 (l) *Women sentenced to prison over a miscarriage and the case of Savita Halappanavar. 12*

 (m) *The role of contraception in reducing abortion rates. 13*

 (n) *The role of sex education in reducing abortion rates. 13*

 (o) *Do our tax dollars fund abortion? 14*

 (p) *Personhood Amendments. 15*

(q) *Embryos and fertility treatments.* 16
(r) *Killing abortion doctors.* 17
(s) *Does abortion harm women?* 18

Day 2: Abortions as Murder, Fetal Personhood, and
Arguments from Potential   26

(a) *Viability and quickening as times when abortion becomes murder.* 26
(b) *Abortion kills an innocent child.* 27
(c) *Can "innocence" apply to embryos?* 28
(d) *Is killing all human life wrong?* 29
(e) *What is a person?* 30
(f) *Is genetic humanity sufficient for personhood?* 30
(g) *The cognitive traits of personhood.* 30
(h) *Persons who are not genetically human.* 31
(i) *Genetic humans who are not persons.* 32
(j) *Embryos and fetuses lack all the mental traits of personhood.* 33
(k) *The relationship between rights and desires.* 34
(l) *Do infants have a right to life?* 35
(m) *The argument from potential.* 36
(n) *What does "potential" mean?* 36
(o) *Do potential persons have the same rights as actual persons?* 40
(p) *The right to life protects persons from harm.* 42
(q) *Sentience as a prerequisite for being able to be harmed.* 42
(r) *Harm as the setting back of interests.* 43
(s) *Must you be sentient in order to have interests?* 44
(t) *When do fetuses become sentient?* 45

Day 3: Fetal "Future-Like-Ours" Arguments, and
Considerations of Personal Identity   51

(a) *Sanctity of life arguments.* 51
(b) *Sanctity of life arguments and euthanasia.* 53
(c) *Abortion and religious diversity.* 55
(d) *Future-like-ours arguments.* 56
(e) *Future-like-ours arguments, contraception, and arguments from potential.* 58
(f) *Alternative accounts of the wrongness of killing.* 59
(g) *Do fetuses have futures of value?* 62
(h) *Is the fetus the same being that will later enjoy a future?* 63
(i) *A fertilized egg is not an individual human being.* 65

(j)   *Personal identity consists in the persistence of a human organism. 65*

(k)   *Personal identity consists in the continuation of mental contents. 66*

(l)   *Personal identity consists in the continuation of a conscious mind. 67*

(m)   *Does death harm a fetus to the same degree as it harms a person? 70*

Day 4: The Bodily Autonomy Argument   78

(a)   *Abortion and the security persons. 78*

(b)   *Is the right to life a positive right? 79*

(c)   *The violinist example. 82*

(d)   *Is the violinist example too weird? 83*

(e)   *The violinist example's relevance to abortion. 85*

(f)   *Kant's principle of humanity and its relation to pregnancy and abortion. 88*

(g)   *The violinist example as analogous to rape. 91*

(h)   *The responsibility objection. 91*

(i)   *The tacit consent objection. 94*

(j)   *The special relationship objection. 96*

(k)   *The killing vs. letting die distinction. 98*

(l)   *Restricting abortion after viability. 100*

(m)   *Can we compel using someone's body to save another? 102*

(n)   *The compensation objection. 103*

Day 5: Abortion in Hard Cases   108

(a)   *Pro-choice and feminism. 109*

(b)   *Early feminism and pro-life advocacy. 109*

(c)   *Does abortion allow for the sexual exploitation of women? 110*

(d)   *Abortion and pro-family support policies. 110*

(e)   *Areas where pro-choice and pro-life feminists agree. 111*

(f)   *Abortion due to Sex-selection. 113*

(g)   *Virtue theory and abortion. 115*

(h)   *Later abortions 118*

(i)   *Abortion for non-viable pregnancies. 119*

(j)   *Abortion due to fetal disabilities. 121*

(k)   *Is there a duty to have the "best" child? 122*

(l)   *Subjective stories of families with disabled children. 122*

(m)   *The expressivist argument against selective abortion. 123*

(n)   *The parental attitude argument against selective abortion. 124*
(o)   *Fathers and abortion. 125*
(p)   *The right of refusal. 126*
(q)   *Men and grief over abortion. 129*
(r)   *Can a man force a woman to gestate? 129*
(s)   *Abortion in cases of rape. 130*
(t)   *Final thoughts. 133*

Annotated Bibliography   *139*
Index   *161*

FOREWORD BY LAURIE SHRAGE

As we near the 50th anniversary of *Roe v. Wade*, the cultural and intellectual divisions over abortion appear deeper than ever and less yielding to reasoned discourse. In this many-decade battle, we have witnessed the murder of abortion providers, while opponents of abortion claim they are daily witnesses to the murder of unborn persons. The two major political parties in the U.S. have taken opposite policy positions and they recognize that, for many voters, this single issue can be decisive when evaluating candidates for office. The "pro-life" and "pro-choice" movements continue to attract money and new adherents, while scholars research the demographics and ideologies of each side. New laws restricting abortion are passed every year in most U.S. states, and then challenged in court, including laws that challenge *Roe*'s basic regulatory scheme and justifying arguments.

It is critical that we try to understand the increasing polarization around the issue of abortion, and how it may be part of the increasing political polarization in the U.S. and other parts of the world. Some scholars attribute the division over abortion to political manipulation and groupthink, which are fairly resistant to rational reflection and dialogue. Yet, even if we believe that voters' views on abortion are often the result of misinformation about abortion and pregnancy, or irrational fears, prejudice, and misplaced sympathies, it can be useful to explore how people on different sides of this issue justify their views to themselves and to others. Depolarization requires that we try to understand the perspectives of our political opponents, but not necessarily to win them over to our side. We do this in order to comprehend the thinking behind our diverse views, and to evaluate the evidence and reasons that each side presents. While we may never agree about many aspects of the abortion issue, sincere and honest dialogue can show us how we can live together peacefully despite our deep moral and political differences. In the case of abortion, respectful conversation can help us imagine and develop social policies that each side finds minimally acceptable.

Dialogues on the Ethics of Abortion illustrates how productive dialogue can proceed on one of the most contested issues of our day, while also providing an important tool for facilitating wider conversations on the issue of abortion. With two smart and resourceful characters representing each side, Bertha Manninen gives us an up-to-date distillation of the critical issues and tenets behind the pro-life and pro-choice positions. The dialogue format offers a lively and accessible way to get up to speed on the best arguments and evidence each side has to offer. Over the space of several days, each discussant raises difficult issues and challenges to the other, and there is no easy way to decide who has gained the upper hand on any issue. With great respect for her readers, Manninen leaves room for them to decide which discussant has made the strongest case.

While very relevant to the present moment, *Dialogues on the Ethics of Abortion* helps us break through the limits of our current thinking in order to reimagine the rules or practices that can respect the critical concerns of all sides. Can we balance society's interest in protecting the health of women and girls with society's interest in protecting human life by developing rules and practices that give substantial weight to both interests? After reading this book, you and your interlocutors will be in a better position to answer this question, and to contribute to engaged and civil debate about access to abortion.

Laurie Shrage
Winter Park, FL 9/16/21

PREFACE

My Story

Throughout my life, I have believed many things, and have held many perspectives, on the moral permissibility of abortion. I was raised in the Catholic Church, much like "L" in the dialogue you're about to read, and so I believed what many Catholics believe: abortion was murder, embryos and fetuses were morally equivalent to infants, and I should vote for political candidates who espoused pro-life views in the hopes of one day overturning *Roe v. Wade*. I was proudly pro-life, and I wanted to see abortion ending in the United States sometime in my lifetime.

When I was a junior in college, I took a class called Biomedical Ethics. The class covered many issues often found in the field of medicine and biology, and it included a section on abortion ethics. It was in that class that I was first introduced to Judith Jarvis Thomson's essay "A Defense of Abortion", which is the primary text under discussion in Chapter 4 of this book. The crux of Thomson's argument is that assuming fetal personhood is not sufficient for rendering abortion morally impermissible. In order to make her argument, Thomson asks you, the reader, to imagine that you are hooked up to a famous violinist for nine months, while your kidneys work to extract poisons from his kidneys. If you unplug yourself, the violinist will die. Are you morally required to stay connected to the violinist? Thomson argues that you are not so required, and that no person has a right to forcibly use the body of another, even for life itself. Pro-life advocates argue that once the fetus is considered a person, with the same right to life as you or me, this immediately renders abortion immoral, on a par with killing any other person. Thomson's argument contradicts this view, and offers a new (at least it was to me) way of critically analyzing the issue of abortion. If Thomson is right, pro-life advocates aren't arguing that fetuses have the same rights as you or me or any other person, they are arguing, instead, that fetuses have *even more* rights than a person, for they want to bestow on the fetus a right that no other person possesses – the right to use someone else's body for sustenance. Reading Thomson's argument changed my views on abortion – by the time Biomedical Ethics was over, I had become pro-choice.

However, it wasn't just Thomson's essay that challenged my beliefs about abortion. In Biomedical Ethics we read an essay from another philosopher, Mary Anne Warren, entitled "On the Moral and Legal Status of Abortion." In this essay, Warren argues that embryos and fetuses are not persons because they lack the cognitive capacities of persons, such as sentience, self-consciousness, the ability to communicate, and engaging in self-motivated activities. Over the years I read similar views from philosophers Peter Singer and Michael Tooley, and became convinced by all three that fetuses were not persons after all. In her essay, Warren states that embryos and fetuses are less person-like than fish, and for years after that, I was convinced she was right. In a few years I had swung the pendulum way back – I went from proudly pro-life to proudly pro-choice. I held on to these beliefs throughout the rest of my undergraduate and graduate years. By the time I wrote my dissertation on the moral permissibility of abortion (and stem cell research), I still held on to the beliefs engendered in me by both Thomson and Warren. But then, something important changed me.

In 2008, on Mother's Day, I learned I was pregnant with my first child, who is now 13 years old. During my first sonogram, I was able to see my daughter, about 10 weeks into the pregnancy. She was moving up a storm. She did somersaults in my uterus, and was just extremely active. I thought it was amazing that all that could be going on inside my body and I could not feel a thing (at least not yet). Driving home that day, I was still in awe of what I had seen, but then also disturbed. What I saw on the sonogram screen was not just a clump of cells. There was a beating heart, limbs that were already being exercised, a formed body and head, and a face. While there was no sentience or consciousness yet – I could not shake the feeling that what I saw on the screen was a very little baby, but a baby nevertheless. Over the next few days, I re-read Warren's argument, and found myself completely turned off from her saying that a fetus was morally equivalent to fish (and, as it turns out, many of my students, when I teach Warren's essay, often reject or express disdain at this part of Warren's argument as well – even amongst students who are otherwise pro-choice). What I saw on the sonogram screen was not a fish, was not just a clump or cells, or products of conception. Was the being a person, with the same moral rights as any other person? If not a person, did it have at least *some* moral status? For reasons I will explain below, I think granting fetuses personhood would entail many undesirable consequences for women. Nevertheless, as "L" says in Chapter 2, I do think fetuses are worthy of some moral status, even if it is not personhood. How could I still call myself pro-choice if I was having such a change of heart? I still believed women had a right to an abortion, but I could no longer defend that view by adhering to the belief that fetuses lacked moral status.

I struggled for a few years with the tension between what I wanted to argue (that women have a right to an abortion) with what I now had come to believe about fetuses (that they had some moral value). Four years later, I became pregnant with my second child, who is now 9 years old. My first pregnancy was quite easy in comparison to other women's pregnancies, but this second pregnancy was fraught with more complications. I had a heart condition that made pregnancy more dangerous, and was later diagnosed with gestational diabetes. Being pregnant while dealing with medical issues cemented my view that pregnancy must be voluntarily – I could never argue in favor of putting a woman through such a precarious physical state without her consent. So this is where I was; my first pregnancy left me with the belief that fetuses have some degree of moral value, while my second pregnancy left me with the belief that pregnancy should always be voluntary, and that women always have a right to decide if they wish to put their body and mind through pregnancy.

These appear to be two irreconcilable beliefs, but I have spent the last few years of my research and scholarship arguing that these beliefs can, indeed, be harmonized. Thomson's argument here is critical. Granting fetuses moral status, even full personhood, does not yield the conclusion that abortions are impermissible. No person has a right to use someone's body without their consent, even to save their lives. Fetuses, like all other persons, do not have that right either. This is the argument that has allowed me to retain my pro-choice views for the past 25 years. Yet I also believe that striving for a society with fewer abortions is a worthwhile goal, and much of my work has been devoted to researching how we can achieve this goal. As it turns out, criminalizing and prohibiting abortions does not do much to reduce abortion rates (this is discussed in Chapter 1 of this book). Countries with restrictive abortion laws have about the same rate of abortion as countries with more liberal abortion laws. What does seem to minimize abortion rates is having a stronger social safety net. For example, universal healthcare so women can medically care for themselves and their children without resulting in bankruptcy, affordable and quality childcare so that women do not have to choose between continuing their education, or career, and motherhood, monetary assistance to lessen the poverty in which many single mothers find themselves. Pro-life advocates need to care as much about the resulting baby and child than they do about the fetus. This is a point where pro-choicers and pro-lifers can come together: we can strive to build a society where abortions will become less common.

Abortion in Contemporary Society

Roe v. Wade was decided in 1973, and almost 50 years later, the United States is still arguing over the morality of abortion rights. For years, several states have attempted to pass Personhood Amendments, which would grant personhood to embryos and fetuses upon their conception. None have yet to pass, but pro-life advocates continually introduce the amendments during election years, with the goal of going all the way to the Supreme Court, in the hopes that *Roe v. Wade* would be overturned. The most recent incarnation of abortion restrictions in the United States has come from Texas. In what is the most restrictive abortion law in the country, Texas now bans abortions after six weeks of pregnancy, often before a woman even realizes she is pregnant. In order to enforce the law, Texas is relying on private citizens rather than the government. Any person in the state of Texas can sue anyone who performs or aids in an abortion, and they stand to receive $10,000 if the case is successful. On September 1, 2021, the United States Supreme Court declined an emergency request to block the law from going into effect. This has emboldened other states, who are now seeking to enact their own restrictive abortion laws. For example, Republican Arkansas Senator Jason Rapert has stated that he has "ordered a bill to be filed in Arkansas to update our law to mirror the Texas SB8 bill."[1]

While some states work to enact restrictive abortion laws, other states are doing the opposite. For example, in 2019, the state of New York enacted the *Reproductive Health Act*, which solidifies a woman's right to obtain an abortion up until 24 weeks gestational age, in addition to legalizing third trimester abortions in situations where the pregnancy is non-viable (meaning the fetus has some sort of an affliction that is incompatible with life), or if the abortion is necessary to protect the woman's life or health. The bill also reaffirms abortion, as well as contraception, as a "fundamental component of a woman's health, privacy and equality."[2] The law also removes abortion from the state's criminal code and renders it a public health issue, thereby protecting any medical professional who performs abortions from prosecution. Texas's and New York's respective abortion laws highlight the deep divide that exists in the United States when it comes to abortion, and that division does not appear to be healing any time soon.

Granting fetal personhood has implications that extend beyond abortion, as "C" points out in Chapter 1. For example, El Salvador has one of the most restrictive abortion laws in the world – there is a near total ban on all abortions except when necessary to save the pregnant woman's life. In 1999, El Salvador's constitution was amended to recognize embryos and fetuses as persons from conception onward. One result from this is that women who suffer miscarriages have been jailed. There is the case of Teodora del Carmen Vásquez, who was sentenced to 30 years in prison for homicide when her pregnancy ended in a stillbirth. Eventually, the Salvadorian Supreme Court ruled that there was not an enough evidence to conclude that Vásquez deliberately killed the fetus, and she was released.[3] However, many women remain in prison for the "crime" of miscarrying their fetus. While this may seem extreme, it is the natural consequence of granting embryos and fetuses personhood. If they are entitled to the same rights as any other person, and individuals who kill persons go to prison, it follows that deliberately killing a fetus would bring with it a prison sentence. This leaves women who experience miscarriages vulnerable.

Other consequences that arise from granting embryos and fetuses personhood would be that embryos leftover from In vitro fertilization treatments cannot be destroyed, as they routinely are now, which leaves open the question of what to do with them. Should they be forcibly implanted in women's (particularly the genetic mother's) bodies? Can they be put up for adoption, regardless of whether the genetic parents agree to it? Another disturbing consequence of granting embryonic and fetal personhood is that it renders violence against abortion doctors permissible. In 2009, George Tiller, an abortion provider known for conducting late abortions, was murdered by Scott Roeder, who confessed to the killing on the grounds that he was saving the lives of innocent children. This may sound extreme, but it is, once again, the natural consequence of bestowing fetal personhood. After all, violence is allowed in either self-defense or in defense of the life of an innocent third party. If I saw someone holding an axe over a baby's head, and the only way to stop him is through the use of lethal force, no jury would convict me if I killed the man in order to save the baby. If fetuses are persons, morally and legally akin to infants and children, killing abortion doctors becomes permissible for the reason Roeder gave in defense of his killing of George Tiller.

Aims and Audience

So much has been written about the ethics of abortion that it seems redundant to publish yet another book on the issue. My hope it to reach an audience that does not typically read the articles in academic journals. This book assumes no background in philosophy, and is meant to be accessible to either beginning philosophy students, or just readers who want an introduction to the many issues at stake when discussing abortion. The book also introduces readers to other philosophical issues that, while tied in with abortion ethics, are also worth exploring in their own right. Issues such as personal identity over time, the definition of "potential", what it means to be a "person", what kinds of beings are part of the moral community; all these topics, on their own, are worthy of reflection and conversation. This is yet another goal for this book: to illustrate to readers how the ethics of abortion is connected to other philosophical issues – issues that we do not, typically, discuss much in society outside of a classroom. I hope this book demonstrates that one reason that pro-life and pro-choice advocates are constantly arguing with each other is that they share different foundational philosophical beliefs. Without conversing about these beliefs, we remain where we are – a standstill about an important moral issue that sometimes turns contentious, and sometimes even violent.

It may have been easy for me, a pro-choice advocate, to give the clear "win" here to "C", who represents the pro-choice side. Instead, I decided to make "C" and "L" evenly matched because I genuinely believe that both sides have strong moral arguments. While I think that, ultimately, the pro-choice arguments are stronger, there are many pro-life arguments that are worthy of reflection and discussion. When I was pro-life as a young adult, I thought all pro-choicers were baby killers. When I switched to being pro-choice after college, I thought all pro-lifers were religious zealots (I know I was). After many years of studying the ethical dimensions of abortion, I have concluded that I was wrong about both of my stereotypes. Pro-choice advocates, generally, do not support infanticide (and I say "generally" because some pro-choice philosophical arguments do entail that infanticide is permissible; see Warren, Singer, and Tooley again). Rather, they do not believe that a fetus is a person and morally equivalent to a baby. Moreover, when it comes to a choice between the life of the fetus or the pregnant woman's bodily autonomy, pro-choice advocates often believe that the latter takes precedence. Pro-life advocates, on the other hand, believe that the life of the fetus is more pressing than the woman's bodily autonomy, and they also fully believe that fetuses are equivalent to infants. While some may have religious grounds for opposing abortion, secular pro-life arguments exist, and they can be rather compelling. Both "C" and "L" make strong arguments in this book, and I leave it up to the reader to decide which one is the strongest.

Finally, I wrote this book as a dialogue for three reasons. First, as above-mentioned, this renders the book more accessible to readers who have no previous philosophical background. Second, it makes the book more interesting and entertaining than it would be to read a traditional academic essay. Finally, I hope that the book serves to highlight the importance of civil dialogue and philosophical reflection. Discussion of topics as contentious as abortion often devolve into a shouting match with both sides engaging in ad hominem attacks. As a society, it seems like we have lost the capacity to listen and learn from others who disagree with our political, religious, or ethical views. In this book, both interlocutors listen to each other, debate each other civilly, and even highlight some areas of shared values and commonalities. I hope that this book will serve as a model for what a more fruitful conversation on abortion ethics can look like.

When I was a philosophy student, and even now as a philosophy professor, I was often asked what is the use of a philosophy degree, especially on the job market. It is more difficult to make a case for the importance of studying philosophy when the purpose of a higher education has gone from overall intellectual and spiritual growth, to just securing employment. But philosophy is not just about getting a job (though many studies have found philosophy majors fare well on the job market in comparison to other humanities degrees), it is about cultivating and honing your critical thinking and writing skills and to learn how to argue and debate in productive ways (all of which will benefit you on the job market). It is also about exploring issues that underlie the human experience. My hope is that you, my reader, will come to appreciate the value of philosophical reflection as you work your way through this book. Who knows – maybe you, like I did in college, will fall in love with philosophy.

Notes

1 Oren Oppenheim. "Which States' Lawmakers Have Said They Might Copy Texas Abortion Law." ABC News (2021). https://abcnews.go.com/Politics/states-lawmakers-copy-texas-abortion-law/story?id=79818701
2 State of New York. "S. 240 Reproductive Health Act" (2019). https://legislation.nysenate.gov/pdf/bills/2019/S240
3 Elisabeth Malkin. "They Were Jailed for Miscarriages. Now, Campaign Aims to End Abortion Ban." *The New York Times* (2018). https://www.nytimes.com/2018/04/09/world/americas/el-salvador-abortion.html

ACKNOWLEDGEMENTS

I would like to thank Andrew Beck, who first approached me about writing this book, and has been a supportive editor throughout the whole process. I would also like to thank Marc Stratton for his role in helping this book come to fruition. Thank you to an anonymous reader for their very helpful comments that facilitated making this book so much better, and to Dr. Laurie Shrage for agreeing to write the foreword. I would also like to thank Arizona State University for granting me a sabbatical that allowed me to focus on finishing this book. Finally, I would like to thank my husband, Tuomas, and our two girls, Michelle and Julia, for their patience as I worked long hours, and for always being there for me with hugs and kisses when I get home.

1

DAY 1

Roe v. Wade and Other Legal Concerns

Day 1 – Scene: Two college-aged women, C and L, have been assigned as partners for a class presentation on Abortion in America.

C: This is an important topic, even though it's one that people have been debating for decades now, to no avail it seems.

L: I agree it's a very important topic, especially since I think we need to do away with state-sanctioned killing in all of its forms, which includes abortions.

C: Talk about hitting the ground running!

L: It's something I am pretty passionate about.

C: Well, we have different opinions on this issue. I guess that's why the professor paired us up. I am worried about the state of *Roe v. Wade*. With a conservative Supreme Court, I believe it is only a matter of time before an abortion case hits their desks. Already in 2020, 200 members of congress asked the Supreme Court to "revisit" *Roe v. Wade* with the hopes of overturning it.

L: You fear *Roe v. Wade* may be overturned, and I hope very much that it is overturned one day. This should be a fun project to do together. Let's look at the directions.

C: So according to the directions the professor gave us, we have to explain our position in regards to abortion and consider and respond to two objections from an opposing perspective. That must be why she paired us up, so we can respond to each other's concerns. I can start. You can already anticipate my perspective. I am a feminist

DOI: 10.4324/9781003109457-1

and a big supporter of women's reproductive rights in all its forms. I have been studying the abortion issue for the past few years, doing a lot of reading from a lot of different perspectives. And because of that all studying, I am proudly unequivocally pro-choice. I think abortion should be legal, accessible, and safe.

(a) Does the Bible prohibit abortions?

L: Well, you already know where I stand. I am proudly pro-life. I think murdering babies, which is all that abortion is, is morally wrong and should be illegal. One main reason I believe this is that I am a devout Catholic. My Biblical beliefs lead me to the conclusion that all life is sacred, from the beginning of a person's existence, which is at conception, until the time she dies.

C: You know, I hear a lot that abortions are against the will of God, or that they are not Biblical, but it's never been clear to me where in the Bible God prohibits abortions.

L: Well one of his commandments is "thou shalt not murder."

C: But that assumes that abortion is murder.

L: Of course it's murder. You're killing an innocent baby. What else could it be?

C: Well I am sure we will get to that topic, but is abortion specifically prohibited in the Bible?

L: God specifically talks about unborn children having moral value. He talks about how he started His individual relationship with each of us while still in the womb. In Jeremiah 1:5 He tells Jeremiah: "before I formed you in the womb I knew you, before you were born I set you apart."

C: But that seems to be referring specifically to Jeremiah.

L: If He knew Jeremiah, He knows all of us.

C: But there are other points in the Bible where He does not seem to regard fetuses as having equal value. Let me look up the quote I have in mind.

(C looks up quote on her smartphone)

C: In Exodus 21:22-25 it reads: "When men strive together, and hurt a woman with child, so that there is a miscarriage, and yet no harm follows, the one who hurt her shall be fined, according as the woman's husband shall lay upon him; and he shall pay as the judges determine. If any harm follows, then you shall give life for life, eye for eye, tooth for tooth, hand for hand, foot for foot, burn for burn, wound for wound, stripe for stripe." Does that not show that the life of the fetus is not worth as much as the life of a person? The price for the loss of fetal life is a fine, whereas the price for the loss of a life is much higher.

L: I am familiar with this quote. It depends on the translation used. In other translations, the word is not "miscarriage" but "premature birth." So if the woman gives birth early, but there is no additional harm, then there's just a fine to be paid.

C: Well, at least it shows that it's not clear. A lot can be left up to interpretation. Aren't there other parts of the Bible where God commands the death of the unborn as well?[1]

L: There are many places in the Old Testament where God commands the death of all kinds of people, born and unborn, for varying reasons. But that still does not mean, for us, that human life has no value. We can't legalize killing adult human beings because God commands that some adult human beings be killed in the Bible.

C: Fair enough. But if your belief is religious, can you really impose those beliefs on others? I don't share your religious views, so why should there be a law based on religion that I, and other people, have to follow?

L: Well, I think there are good reasons to prohibit abortions that are not religious in nature that we can talk about, but it is not possible for me to be in favor of a law that I see as violating God's will. It's the same reason I reject the whole "if you don't like abortions, don't have one" reasoning. I am not ok with people committing murder no matter who does it. It's like saying "if you're not in favor of having slaves, don't have one." I can't be in favor of a law or policy that would allow the owning of a human being, no matter who does it.

C: Well, slavery and abortions are hardly the same thing.

L: For me, there are equally awful.

C: But you know that before abortion was legal, many women still got one, and many women who should have had easy access to one were often denied abortions. Are you familiar with the case of Sherri Finkbine and thalidomide babies?

L: I am not.

(b) The thalidomide scare.

C: Sherri Finkbine was the host of the kids' TV show *Romper Room*. In 1961, Finkbine took medication that contained the chemical thalidomide, which was given to many women as a way of relieving morning sickness. Well, it turns out that thalidomide caused severe birth defects in fetuses. Many babies were born with either shorter arms or legs, which looked like flippers, or sometimes no arms or legs at all.[2] Finkbine's baby was one of them. She scheduled her abortion in Arizona but it was cancelled after Finkbine's identity was released to the press and the hospital could not get assurance that it wouldn't be prosecuted. She even received death threats. Finkbine had to travel to Sweden to get her abortion. The thalidomide tragedy pushed abortion back into the limelight in the United States. Now, should Finkbine had to have gone through all that?

L: I acknowledge that what she went through was hard. But I can't agree that the life of a baby is worth less because he is missing his limbs.

C: It's not about the fetus's life being worth less. It's about parents having a choice regarding whether they want to bring such a baby into the world.

L: Once a baby is conceived it is already in the world. A baby with no limbs has the same right to live as any other baby.

C: Ok, so let's switch gears a bit and talk about your opposition to *Roe v. Wade*.

(c) Does *Roe v. Wade* legalize abortion on demand?

L: Ok. I oppose *Roe v. Wade* and its legalization of abortion on demand. I think it's one of the worst Supreme Court decisions in our nation's history.

C: Do you believe abortions are bad at any time during pregnancy? Or are early abortions acceptable? According to the Centers for Disease Control, 91% of abortions take place in the first trimester, at less than 13 weeks gestation. Are even those abortions unacceptable?[3]

L: I believe all abortions, with the exception of when it is necessary to save the mother's life, are immoral no matter when in pregnancy the abortions take place.

C: Well, I think abortion should be legal, safe, and easily attainable.

L: At all points during pregnancy?

C: At the very least in early to mid-pregnancy, but in some cases, yes even later abortions are acceptable. I *do* think that obtaining later abortions require more pressing moral reasons than early abortions, and perhaps *some* restrictions on later abortions can be justified. But in some cases, I do believe the reasons for obtaining a later abortion are valid ones. Early abortions, however, where 91% of them happen, are completely morally justifiable.

L: I cannot imagine a single good reason why it would be permissible to kill a fetus that is close to being born. Even if you don't think early fetuses have value, certainly late gestation fetuses are pretty much babies. I mean, we see in premature births that the being that is born is a baby and not a clump of cells. Saying that even babies at a later stage in pregnancy can be aborted is completely unjustified.

C: Well, we can talk about this throughout our conversation if you'd like. Let me start our debate by asking, what you mean when you say that *Roe v. Wade* legalizes "abortion on demand?"

L: I mean that, because of *Roe v. Wade,* women can have an abortion for whatever reason at whatever time in pregnancy, even until the birth of the baby.

C: So you think women can walk into an abortion clinic at any time during her pregnancy for any reason at all and get an abortion?

L: Yes, that's what *Roe v. Wade* legalized.

C: Ok, well, let's look up and read the text from the case and see where it allows for that.

Both women turn to their books and start reading the text of Roe v. Wade. *As they are searching …*

L: Incidentally, did you know that "Roe", who's real name was Norma McCorvey, changed her mind afterwards and became pro-life? She championed a lot of pro-life causes and even tried to get the Supreme Court to overturn her case.

C: I actually did not know that.

L: If she changed her mind maybe you can too.

C: I doubt that very much. Anyways, let's look at the text. First, the Justices who decided *Roe v. Wade* found that a woman's right to privacy, guaranteed by the 14th Amendment's appeal to personal liberty, secures a right to terminate a pregnancy for several reasons. On page 137 it reads: "The detriment that the State would impose upon the pregnant woman by denying this choice altogether is apparent. Specific and direct harm medically diagnosable even in early pregnancy may be involved. Maternity, or additional offspring, may force upon the woman a distressful life and future. Psychological harm may be imminent. Mental and physical health may be taxed by child care. There is also the distress, for all concerned, associated with the unwanted child, and there is the problem of bringing a child into a family already unable, psychologically and otherwise, to care for it. In other cases, as in this one, the additional difficulties and continuing stigma of unwed motherhood may be involved."[4]

L: Those are some pretty broad reasons. Almost any reason could count under these.

(d) *Roe v. Wade* **does not legalize abortion on demand.**

C: Maybe, but look here right under the passage we just read: "On the basis of elements such as these, appellant and some *amici* argue that the woman's right is absolute and that she is entitled to terminate her pregnancy at whatever time, in whatever way, and for whatever reason she alone chooses. *With this we do not agree.*"

L: Well maybe they *say* that, but the decision functionally allows women to seek an abortion whenever in pregnancy they want and for whatever reason.

C: But look here *(C points in L's book).* Here we clearly see what the decision did and did not legalize. "(a) For the stage prior to approximately the end of the first trimester, the abortion decision and its effectuation must be left to the medical judgment of the pregnant woman's attending physician. (b) For the stage subsequent to approximately the end of the first trimester, the State, in promoting its interest in the health of the mother, may, if it chooses, regulate the abortion procedure in ways that are reasonably related to maternal health. (c) For the stage subsequent to viability, the State in promoting its interest in the potentiality of human life may, if it chooses, regulate and even proscribe abortion except where necessary, in appropriate medical judgment, for the preservation of the life or health of the mother." So the Justices clearly wrote that abortion "on demand" applies only to the first trimester. During the second trimester, abortions may be limited due to concerns over maternal health. During the third trimester, a state can regulate abortions after a fetus becomes viable.

L: What exactly does "viable" mean?

C: It denotes the period in pregnancy where a fetus is able to survive outside the womb, even with medical aid.

L: So how premature could a baby be and still be viable?

C: I remember a couple of years ago reading that a baby born at 23 weeks, here in the United States, within the second trimester, survived and was eventually allowed to go home. She is considered the youngest preterm baby to survive.[5]

L: I am assuming you'd think such a baby was entitled to medical attention when she was born, right?

C: Yes, of course.

L: Well how can you think a 23-week-old baby deserves medical attention but that a later fetus can be aborted? Isn't the later fetus, who is more developed than the preterm baby, a baby as well?

C: Like I said, we can talk about these hard cases in due time. But what I wanted to show is that there is no such thing as abortion on demand throughout all stages of pregnancy. The Supreme Court did say that states can proscribe abortions after the fetus achieves viability.

L: You mentioned that the right to an abortion is predicated upon a constitutional right to privacy.

(e) What's included in the right to privacy?

C: Yes, and at the same time as *Roe v. Wade* was decided in 1973, there was another Supreme Court case, *Doe. v. Bolton*, that overturned Georgia's anti-abortion laws (*Roe* overturned Texas's). There the Justices reiterated that the right to privacy applies to (*reads from her book*) "family, marriage, and sex ... [and] the right to choose whether to bear children."[6]

L: But the Constitution does not mention a right to privacy. It's not even clear where that came from.

C: The 14th Amendment does talk about preserving personal liberty (along with life and property). Before *Roe* and *Doe*, the Supreme Court was already leaning to asserting that a right to liberty entailed a right to privacy, especially with matters such as sex and procreation.

L: What do you mean "before"? Where there other abortion cases?

C: Not abortion, but did you know that just 57 years ago contraception was illegal in the United States? *Griswold v. Connecticut* in 1965 made it legal for married persons to obtain contraception. And then 7 years later, *Eisenstadt v. Baird* extended it to unmarried people. Both cases are in our book. In the latter case, the judge wrote: (*reading from her book*) "if the right of privacy means anything, it is the right of the individual, married or single, to be free from unwarranted governmental intrusion into matters so fundamentally affecting a person as the decision whether to bear or beget a child."[7] So these cases can be seen as precursors to *Roe v. Wade*.

L: Even if I were to agree that there is a right to privacy in the Constitution (I am still on the fence about that)...

C: You're in good company. Not even all the Justices agreed that there was such a right.

L: Right, well, even if I agreed, the right to privacy extends to a decision whether or not to have children, or create children. But once you have a child, you can't claim that your right to privacy entails that it's ok to kill her. Once you have the child, her right to life trumps your right to privacy.

C: Only if you think that abortion kills an already existing child.

L: Which I do …

C: I want to talk about this issue, whether fetuses are persons, I do. But I think it would take us too far off track right now, even though we keep coming back to it.

L: Ok, we can put it on hold. I want to go back to the issue of fetal viability. During 1973, fetuses were generally considered viable in the third trimester, but technology has gotten a lot better, and as your example shows, babies can now be born in the second trimester and survive.

C: About that, I want to emphasize this baby was a unique case. Most babies born at 23 weeks gestation do not survive. So I am not sure we can say that viability is now attainable during the second trimester because of one case. Technology would need to be able to routinely save babies this young in order for me to agree that viability now takes place in the second trimester.

L: Fair enough. But technology is only going to improve right? One day it will get good enough to be able to routinely save fetuses at 23 weeks, and even earlier. Maybe even one day we would be able to fully artificially gestate a fetus from conception.

C: Eventually, maybe.

L: But wouldn't this pose a problem for *Roe*'s decision? Can states restrict abortion in the third trimester, or during viability, since these two do not necessarily occur at the same time anymore?

(f) *Planned Parenthood v. Casey* **asserts viability as the point where abortion can be restricted.**

C: That's a great question and it's actually been dealt with by the Supreme Court as well. Look on page 151 – the case is *Planned Parenthood v. Casey*, 1992. There the Justices overturned the "trimester" framework and confirmed that the State has the "power to restrict abortions after viability, if the law contains exceptions for pregnancies endangering the woman's life or health."[8]

L: But wait a minute – these cases say that a state *may* restrict abortions if they choose to. It does not say that they *must* restrict abortions. So it's possible still that a state decides to not put any restrictions at all.

(g) Many states do restrict abortion access at some point in pregnancy.

C: You're right that the court decisions don't *require* states to put any restrictions on abortion. But, it so happens that many states *do* put such restrictions. *(C searches on her smartphone)*. Here look according to this, as of 2021, 43 states prohibit abortions after some point in pregnancy, unless it is necessary to protect the woman's life or health.[9]

L: What states would those be?

C: The vast majority of states restrict abortions after viability. Some states restrict it after a certain week in gestation. For example, Florida, Nevada, and Massachusetts prohibit abortions after 24 weeks, and Georgia, Indiana, Iowa, Kansas, and Kentucky prohibits them after 20 weeks, of course with exceptions for the mother's life or health.

L: You said 43 states have restrictions. That leaves 7 states that have no restrictions. I recently heard that New York legalized abortions into the third trimester in 2019.

C: Let's look it up. *(C searches her smartphone again)*. Yes, it's called the *Reproductive Health Act*. It doesn't just legalize certain cases of third trimester abortions.

L: What else does it do?

(h) New York's Reproductive Health Act.

C: The law removes abortion from the state's criminal code and renders it a public health issue. This protects any medical professional who performs abortions from prosecution.

L: They *should* be prosecuted. Murder should always be prosecuted.

C: Well, we're going to get to that soon. Let's stick to abortion laws for now.

L: Ok. From what I heard, New York's law legalizes abortion into the third trimester, after fetal viability.

C: It does, but only under certain circumstances. Abortions are legal in New York in the third trimester only if, one, the pregnancy is actually deemed non-viable.

L: Which means the baby cannot survive outside the womb?

C: Right. This is for cases of severe fetal abnormalities that are incompatible with continued life, for example anencephaly.

L: I read about this in one of my biology classes. This is a condition when the baby's brain does not grow properly, so that only the brain stem and lower brain develops.

C: Right. Those babies cannot survive outside the womb. They often die during childbirth or shortly after birth. The *Reproductive Health Act* would make it easier for women to secure a safe abortion into the third trimester if the fetus is not expected to live. Second, abortions are allowed in the third trimester when it is necessary to preserve the mother's life or her health.[10]

(i) *Doe v. Bolton*, and how to define maternal health.

L: But what counts as "life or health"? If we go back to *Doe v. Bolton,* the Justices defined "health" really broadly. They wrote *(L reads from her book):* "medical judgment may be exercised in the light of all factors – physical, emotional, psychological, familial, and the woman's age – relevant to the wellbeing of the patient. All these factors may relate to health."[11]

C: That sounds about right. They were trying to cover as many bases as possible. "Health" can mean many things.

L: Right, but that's my worry. It can mean so many things that a woman could just come up with any reason to abort in the third trimester, and that would be covered under "health."

C: I guess it boils down to our views about what women would or would not do. I don't think a woman would gestate a fetus for two-thirds of a pregnancy and then just decide willy-nilly to abort for any reason at all.

L: I don't have that assurance as much as you.

C: Ok, fair enough. We can talk about this some more later. But you will at least agree that there are *some* restrictions on abortion – at least in 43 states, which is most all of the states in the U.S.

L: Ok, so maybe there are some restrictions after all, though in my mind there are not enough. And I am not really sure how I feel about viability being a cut-off point for when abortion can be restricted. It makes the fetus's right to life contingent on developing technology. 30 years ago, when viability occurred in the third trimester, fetuses had no right to life until then. Now they may have a right to life into the end of the second trimester. Doesn't it seem odd to base someone's right to life on the changing state of technology?

C: I don't think it's odd. Say someone falls into an irreversible coma – they are never going to have a second of conscious life ever again. Most people would approve of "pulling the plug" on that person, though we wouldn't be in favor of "pulling the plug" on a person who has a good chance of recovery and only needs assistance for some time.

L: I can see that.

C: Ok, but let's say that in 50 years we've developed technology that allowed us to "wake" people up from what used to be irreversible comas. Now the same coma that used to be permanent is temporary. Wouldn't it then become wrong to "pull the plug" on someone we could easily revive?

L: That sounds about right.

C: Well then this is an example of someone who's right to life is contingent upon evolving technology. If it works in this example, it can work for fetuses as well.[12]

L: I suppose I can see why that would work. But I reject the viability criterion anyway. It's not relevant for me if we're talking about when in pregnancy we should restrict abortions.

C: So that brings me to another question: what do you think are the ideal abortion laws?

L: Well, viability is irrelevant, as I think abortions should be illegal throughout all points in pregnancy unless it is necessary to save a woman's life. So say that she experiences an ectopic pregnancy, or if she is suffering from dangerously high blood pressure and the only way to stop it is to end the pregnancy. In those cases, I would be ok with abortion. In these cases the baby is going to die either way, so we may as well save one life. Otherwise no.

C: Not even in cases of rape?

L: I know it may make me sound like a monster, but no. I don't think the baby should be faulted for the actions of his father. The man should be prosecuted to the furthest extent of the law, but the baby shouldn't pay.

C: So that means almost all abortions should be illegal. So here's my question: what do you hope to get out of that? That is, what do you think such abortion laws would effectively do?

L: Well hopefully it will prevent abortions and save the lives of innocent babies.

(j) Making abortions illegal won't stop them.

C: But you, as much as me, have heard the stories of what life was like before abortion was legalized. Back alley-abortions, and clothes hanger abortions, or women drinking dangerous chemicals in the hopes of inducing a miscarriage, and such. Laws against abortions don't stop abortions, they just make it so that women who get them do so under perilous circumstances.

L: But that's not a good argument in favor of allowing abortions. You're saying that outlawing abortions would be wrong because women are going to get them anyways, and often in ways that may jeopardize their health. But just because one may get in trouble for doing a bad action doesn't make the action any less wrong. I understand that you don't think abortion is a bad action, but for someone who does, this argument doesn't work.

C: I am less concerned, for now, with proving that abortions are morally permissible. We can devote the rest of our conversation to that issue. I am more concerned now with the *effectiveness* of abortion laws.

L: Making something illegal won't stop all instances of it, but it will significantly save some babies from abortion.

(k) The effectiveness of laws prohibiting abortion.

C: I don't think the evidence shows that at all. In some studies, countries with restrictive abortion laws had about as much incidences of abortion as countries with more liberal abortion laws.

L: I find that hard to believe. Making it illegal will deter some people.

C: Here look at this study (*shows L smartphone*): "women living under the most restrictive laws (i.e., where abortion is prohibited altogether or allowed only to save a woman's life) have abortions at about the same rate as those living where the procedure is available without restriction (37 and 34 abortions per 1000, respectively)."[13] There was also a massive 2016 study that shows that while abortion rates are declining in developed countries with liberal abortion laws, they are not declining, and are slightly increasing, in developing countries, many of which have restrictive abortion laws.[14] So it's actually somewhat higher in countries with restrictive abortion bans. Plus, countries with restrictive abortion laws also have some more dire consequences for women. Did you know that in some of those countries, women have been held legally liable for miscarriages?

L: That's awful! How did that happen?

(l) Women sentenced to prison over a miscarriage and the case of Savita Halappanavar.

C: There was a case in El Salvador where a woman experienced a stillbirth and was sentenced to 30 years for aggravated homicide. She was eventually released because their Supreme Court ruled there was not enough evidence that she intended to kill her baby, but she was initially sentenced.[15]

L: Well I am definitely not in favor of that.

C: All making abortion illegal would do is harm women and save very little, if any, babies. Have you heard of the case of Savita Halappanavar in Ireland?

L: I have not.

C: Ireland used to prohibit almost all abortions before 2018. She died in 2012 from septicemia, after she was denied an abortion while she was miscarrying. They only removed the fetal remains after they had died in the womb, but by then she developed blood poisoning and died.

L: That's awful. That seems to be a case where the mother's health is on the line, so I would be ok with an abortion in those cases, especially since the baby was dying anyway. And I certainly am against jailing women for miscarriages.

(m) The role of contraception in reducing abortion rates.

C: Good! At least we agree on that. I think we can also agree that, if we really want to reduce abortion rates, we should be looking at what actually works. The abortion rates in the United States have been continually declining. One possible reason for this is wider use of, and access to, contraception.[16] If you prevent unplanned pregnancies, you prevent abortions.

L: Well I think that's something else we agree on. I have no problems with increasing access and education behind contraception. In this I stray from more conservative Catholic beliefs.

C: There are some philosophers who actually argue that all women of childbearing years (and men too once the technology allows for it) should be fitted with some sort of reversible contraception, that this should be the "default" option. In these cases, having a child would then become a deliberate choice, since you would have to go and get the contraception removed in order to get pregnant. Think what that would do to overpopulation and to abortion rates! It would reduce them drastically.[17]

L: Well, I don't know about that. It would have to be a choice, not mandatory. I think increasing access to contraception and sex education would get us pretty far.

(n) The role of sex education in reducing abortion rates.

C: I am glad you brought up "education" because that's important as well. It's not enough to just have contraception available, you have to teach people how to use it correctly. States that endorse abstinence-only education, or no sex education at all, like Mississippi and New

Mexico, have higher teen pregnancy rates than states that endorse medically accurate and comprehensive sex education, like New Hampshire and Massachusetts, which includes knowledge on the use of contraception, alongside of abstinence.[18]

L: Well I do think abstinence should be taught as a good, if not the best, choice when it comes to pre-marital sex, but we don't live in a utopian world where all people are going to wait until marriage. So I agree with you that we should have medically accurate sex education and access to contraception. I much rather my tax dollars go to funding these than funding abortions.

C: What do you mean when you say that your tax dollars fund abortion?

(o) Do our tax dollars fund abortion?

L: Well some of our tax dollars go to Planned Parenthood, which is the number one abortion provider in the country.

C: But Planned Parenthood does so much more than just abortions. They test for sexually transmitted diseases (STDs), give out birth control (which we both agreed was a good thing), offer screening for certain kinds of cancers (like breast cancer and cervical cancer), and provide Papanicolaou (PAP) exams for women. They are especially important for lower-income women who don't have medical insurance.

L: But they also do abortions, and some of our tax dollars fund those abortions.

C: Less tax money goes to abortions than you may think. In 1976, the United States congress passed the Hyde Amendment, which prohibits using federal funds to pay for abortions, except when the abortion is necessary to save the woman's life, or if the pregnancy is a result of rape or incest. This mostly affects poorer women on Medicaid, since Medicaid cannot cover most abortions.

L: I've heard about this amendment, but there are still some ways abortions are funded. It hasn't stopped some states from covering abortions anyway. 17 states use their own Medicaid money to fund abortion beyond the limitations of the Hyde Amendment.[19]

C: But that's not the majority. Millions of women on Medicaid do not have their abortions covered.

L: Tax dollars shouldn't cover any abortions, unless it is necessary to save the mother's life. It forces those of us who are pro-life to fund something we consider murder.

C: How far would you take that logic? I am against my tax dollars being used to fund wars I don't agree with, but I still have to pay those taxes. And in many of those wars, actual innocent persons are killed.

L: But national security benefits all of us. Abortion has no benefit other than killing innocent babies.

(p) Personhood Amendments.

C: So I am assuming from what you've said that you're in favor of Personhood Amendments? The state attempts to classify embryos and fetuses as legal persons from conception onwards. So far states like Colorado, Alabama, Oklahoma, and Mississippi have attempted to pass them and have failed due to voter rejection.[20]

L: Yes, I am absolutely in favor of those laws. Protection under the law should begin the second a new person begins to exist.

C: But let's go back to something we agreed on. You agreed with me that women jailed for miscarriages is a bad thing.

L: Absolutely. Miscarriages are tragic, and the last thing a woman needs when experiencing that is the fear they're going to be prosecuted.

C: Agreed! But here's the thing, if you think fetuses are equivalent to babies, and should have the same rights as born babies, doesn't it follow that all fetal deaths *should* be investigated, just like the deaths of babies are investigated?[21]

L: But miscarriages are not deliberate acts, you can't help them. They aren't abortions and should not be treated as if they are.

C: But that's not the point. When a child dies, their death is always investigated, right? At least until it can be proven that they weren't murdered. *Some* level of investigation always takes place. So wouldn't this mean that women who miscarry would be investigated as well to some extent, especially since the causes of miscarriages are not always clear?

L: Maybe. I had not thought of it that way.

C: And what about women who have physically exacting jobs, like being police officers? Should such women be fired, or have her work otherwise altered, in order to make sure the fetus is safe?

L: I am not comfortable with saying that she should get fired or removed, no.

C: And it's not just that, think about the effects for other areas as well. Consider what happens during In vitro fertilization (IVF).

L: That's when couples who are having trouble getting pregnant fertilize embryos outside the womb and then transfer them back into the womb in the hopes of becoming pregnant.

C: Right, but the thing is that sometimes more embryos are created than are implanted. Sometimes the procedure works the first time around, and there are leftover embryos frozen in those clinics.

L: What happens to them?

C: They can be donated to other couples. But many embryos are discarded. There was a case in 1992 in Tennessee, *Davis v. Davis*, involving a formerly married couple who had embryos frozen in a fertility clinic. At first, the woman wanted to implant them herself to try to have a baby, but then she sought to donate them to a childless couple. The man stated that he didn't want to be a parent to those embryos, and wanted them destroyed instead. The courts ultimately agreed with the man that his right to privacy meant he couldn't be forced to become a father against his will, especially since his ex-wife could undergo fertility treatments later if she really wanted to be a mother.[22]

L: I think that was a bad decision. The reverse should have been what happened – the person who wanted the embryos to live should have won.

C: Even though it would have made the man a father against his will?

L: He was already a father. As soon as those embryos began to exist, he was a father to them. And even if you don't consider him a father, the embryos' right to life was more important than his "right" to not be a father.

C: What about leftover or surplus embryos at fertility clinics? What should happen to them if no one wants to gestate them?

L: Well, I suppose if Personhood Amendments passed, and legal protection begins at conception, then even frozen embryos would be protected.

C: So what do you do with all the frozen embryos? Should women be forcibly impregnated with them? Is discarding them equivalent to murder?

L: We should probably stop creating more embryos in a lab than we would be willing to implant.

C: Maybe so, but what do we do with currently existing embryos?

L: I really don't know. Encourage embryo adoption as much as possible.

C: You're dodging the question. Let's say that no one wants to adopt them and the genetic parents don't want to implant them. They get destroyed or thrown away. Do you really think that this is equivalent to murder?

L: Yes, I do think that. In cases such as these, I think I'd want to say that the genetic parents have an obligation to implant them in the hopes of having them grow into infants.

C: So women should have embryos forcibly implanted in them?

L: I know that sounds bad, but I can't think of anything better to do with those embryos.

(r) Killing abortion doctors.

C: Ok, well, here's another question for you: do you believe it is morally permissible to kill another human being in order to save an innocent life?

L: I mean, I'm not comfortable with the idea of killing anyone.

C: But let's say someone was about to kill an innocent person and the only way to stop them is by lethal force. Would it be acceptable to use the lethal force?

L: I mean, I guess. If that's the only option.

C: Then would it be permissible to kill abortion doctors, if fetuses were to be considered persons? In 2009, Dr. George Tiller, who was famous for performing late abortions, was killed by anti-abortion activist Scott Roeder. Roeder's defense was that he felt it was the only way to stop him from continuing to kill what he considered to be innocent babies.

L: I am definitely not in favor of that. Lethal force should always be the last option, when there are no other recourses to saving innocent life. I feel that abortions should be protested against, but always peacefully, without violence. Politicians should continue fighting for pro-life laws and causes, but, again, peacefully.

C: I am glad we agree on that as well.

L: But here's one thing we have not brought up that I think is important. I assume that you are in favor of abortion access because you think of it as a matter of healthcare, right? To not have abortion access, you think, is harmful to women?

c: Yes, I do think limited abortion access is harmful to women. I think all women who are feminists (and that should be all women) should support abortion rights and access to safe and legal abortions.

(s) Does abortion harm women?

l: I want to talk later about your assertion that to be a feminist necessitates being pro-choice. Let's come back to that. But what about the concern that it's abortion itself that is harmful to women? That's a common pro-life concern; not just that abortion harms the baby, but that it harms women as well.

c: Well, what do you mean by "harm"? Access to safe and legal abortion is what reduces harm for women. A legal abortion performed in a clean environment by a medical professional does not harm women.

l: There are some concerns in the pro-life community that abortion threatens future fertility and that there is a link between abortion and breast cancer.

c: From the studies that I have read, there is no link between abortion and breast cancer. A 2003 study from the National Cancer Institute concluded that there was no such connection. There is also no evidence that abortion affects women's future fertility.[23]

l: What about mental health? There are concerns that having an abortion is tied into depression and mental illness. There is even a name for it: post-abortion syndrome.

c: I have heard about this claim. Here's something interesting. In 1987, then President Ronald Reagan put together a committee, headed by the Surgeon General at the time, C. Everett Koop, aimed at showing that abortion was harmful to women. Koop himself was anti-abortion, and so he was certainly eager to find such connections. You know what happened?

l: I am thinking by your reaction that he didn't find any connection.

c: That's right. Not only did he not find any connection between abortion and women's physical or mental health, he wrote a letter to President Reagan to that effect, and regrettingly so, since he *wanted* to find such connections.[24]

l: But there are women who do get depressed after getting an abortion.

c: It doesn't surprise me that some women feel sadness after getting an abortion, but that's different than saying that there is some mental illness that is intrinsic to abortion.

In 2008, the American Psychological Association conducted an extensive study on whether there is any such thing as "post-abortion syndrome" and they concluded that all the evidence suggested there is no such mental illness.[25]

L: Ok, but what do we do with women who do feel sadness. How do you explain that if abortion isn't a big deal?

C: Well, first, I didn't say abortion was not a big deal. I said it should be legal, accessible, and safe. There are women who have abortions and never give it a second thought, and there are women who do feel some amount of grief or sadness afterwards. For those women, I think, first, we have to see what they're really upset about.

L: What does that mean? They're clearly upset about the abortion itself.

C: I don't think that's clear at all. From what I have read on this topic, many women who feel sadness after an abortion typically feel unsupported about their decision, or feel like their decision wasn't really their own to make. They feel coerced into the decision by their parents or their partners. Sometimes they have pre-existing mental conditions. It's not the abortion itself that made them feel this way, it is other things that were embedded in the decision. Those other factors can be difficult to untangle from the abortion itself, since they are all present at the same time, but that's different than saying that it's the abortion itself that lead to these negative emotional feelings.[26]

L: OK, but if a woman does feel sadness after an abortion, doesn't that mean that she regrets the procedure? And doesn't that regret point to abortion being something that's morally wrong?

C: There's a lot to unpack here in what you said. Have you heard of the Turnaway Study?

L: No, I haven't.

C: Let's look it up. *(looks up on smartphone)*. It was a recent study where over 1000 women who sought abortions, some received them and some did not, were interviewed and followed for five years. The study concluded that women are not harmed by abortions. Here's a direct quotation: "abortion does not increase women's risk of having suicidal thoughts, or the chance of developing PTSD [post-traumatic stress disorder], depression, anxiety, low self-esteem, or lower life satisfaction. Abortion does not increase women's use of alcohol, tobacco or drugs."

The study also found that "95% of women said abortion was the right decision for them. Women who received a wanted abortion were more likely to have a positive outlook on the future and achieve aspirational life plans within 1 year." [27]

L: What about the women who didn't receive the abortions? And why didn't they?

C: Well, first let me note that the fact that there were women who didn't receive the abortion shows that there is no right to "abortion on demand" through all points during pregnancy, like you said at the start of this conversation.

L: Ok, that's noted.

C: Of the women who were denied an abortion, many cases were because it was too late in their pregnancy. They didn't even realize they were pregnant before 20 weeks gestation, and after that they were limited by financial concerns and other logistical obstacles. But it is actually women who were denied abortions who seemed to have the most trouble adjusting. Here it reads that "women denied an abortion had almost 4 times greater odds of a household income below the federal poverty level and 3 times greater odds of being unemployed. There was an increased likelihood that women didn't have enough money to pay for basic family necessities like food, housing, and transportation if they were denied an abortion. Women unable to terminate unwanted pregnancies were more likely to stay in contact with violent partners, putting them and their children at greater risk than if they had received the abortion. Continuing an unwanted pregnancy and giving birth is associated with more serious health problems than abortion."

L: But none of this is to deny that some women feel sadness after an abortion.

C: It does not surprise me that *some* women do, but that does not mean that the decision was wrong, or that they regret it. I was really sad when my family signed off on my grandfather's Do Not Resuscitate order when he was really sick. And when he died, I even felt a little bit of guilt thinking that we had allowed him to die. But I am still confident that the decision was the best one, and I don't regret it. Women who feel sad after an abortion should receive any and all support that they need to feel better. But sadness is not a mental illness, and there is no evidence that abortions lead to mental illness. There also isn't any evidence that it harms women physically.

L: I mean, I guess I just don't understand how women can't feel bad that they willfully killed their unborn babies.

C: I think that's an important distinction that we should make here. No pro-choice person I know thinks it's ok to kill babies. We just don't agree that a fetus is equivalent to a baby. We don't think that fetuses are persons yet, or that they should have rights equal to that of women. So we don't disagree that you shouldn't kill babies; we just disagree about what constitutes a baby.

L: That seems to be the issue on which there is the most disagreement, yes.

C: So here's something to consider given that disagreement. I know you, and millions of others in the U.S., strongly believe that abortions are morally reprehensible. Still, that alone is not grounds for making the action illegal. There are many actions that are considered morally reprehensible by some that are still legal. For example, there are many people who believe that eating meat is morally reprehensible, and they may believe that as strongly as you believe that abortions are morally wrong. Yet, eating meat is still legal. Many people strongly oppose U.S. involvement in certain wars or conflicts, but not only are those wars and conflicts legal, they are sanctioned by the United States government. The important point here is that we live in a liberal democratic society, and such a society permits some amount of moral and religious diversity, especially on issues where there is substantial disagreement.

L: But that's only some issues, and not others. Many people think recreational drug use is perfectly moral, but recreational drug use is still mostly illegal.

C: Well, many more states are legalizing cannabis use, so not all recreational drug use is illegal. And alcohol use is still perfectly legal if you're over 21.

L: Well, right, but what I am trying to say here is that there are indeed some issues where there is moral disagreement in society but that the government has still declared the content of those issues illegal.

C: I think a lot of it comes back to whether you think the government should be involved in the private lives of its citizens. For example, many of us believe that infidelity is immoral, yet it is not illegal. Mostly because we also believe that the government should largely stay out of our private and sexual lives. Whether or not a woman wants to remain pregnant is also part of her private and sexual life, and as such the government should stay out of it. There is also the issue relating to the separation of church and state. You said earlier that you believe abortions are wrong because of your religion, but there are many of us who do not agree with your religious viewpoints, and there are many other religious viewpoints out there besides Catholicism. As such it is good to have a government where there is a separation of church and state and where no one religion has a say on how other people in other religions, or lack thereof, should live.

L: While I agree that there is some merit to living in a society with diverse religious and moral points of view, I don't think abortion is one issue where we should be tolerant of differing views, regardless of whether those views are religious in nature. It is not just related to a woman's private or sexual life, it involves the life of a wholly distinct human being. Once our decisions potentially involve harming a third party, the government has every right to get involved. From a pro-life perspective, abortion is murder, and we cannot be tolerant of different views that allows us to commit murder.

C: But some people in our society believe vehemently that eating meat is murder. Should they push for laws making meat-eating illegal?

L: Killing a cow or a pig is not the same thing as killing a baby.

C: Only if you believe abortion does kill a baby. Once again, we're back to issues of fetal personhood.

L: It seems that we always come back to that question. Should we consider fetuses persons or not. If they are persons, then we have to revise our laws and practices to reflect that.

C: Well that's not just a legal question, it's also a moral and a philosophical one. I think we've put off the fetal personhood question for too long. Let's talk about it.

L: Well, it's getting late and I don't think we have the time to get into that now.

C: Alright. It is getting kind of late. I'm getting hungry. You want to go get something to eat with me? We don't have to talk about class. We can meet on Friday and continue the conversation for our presentation.

L: Sounds good! Let's go.

Notes

1 For example, in Hosea 9:14, God causes the death of the unborn by giving women "a miscarrying womb and breasts that are dry." (New International Version.)
2 See: James H. Kim and Anthony R. Scialli. "Thalidomide: The Tragedy of Birth Defects and the Effective Treatment of Disease." (2011). *Toxicological Sciences*, 122.2: 1–6.
3 According to the Centers for Disease Control, in 2016: "91.0% of abortions were performed at ≤13 weeks' gestation; a smaller number of abortions (7.7%) were performed at 14–20 weeks' gestation, and even fewer (1.2%) were performed at ≥21 weeks' gestation." https://www.cdc.gov/reproductivehealth/data_stats/abortion.htm
4 United States Supreme Court. *Roe v. Wade* (1973). https://www.law.cornell.edu/supremecourt/text/410/113
5 BBC News. "World's Smallest' Surviving Premature Baby Released from U.S. hospital." (2019). https://www.bbc.com/news/world-us-canada-48458780
6 United States Supreme Court. *Doe v. Bolton* (1973). https://www.law.cornell.edu/supremecourt/text/410/179
7 United States Supreme Court. *Eisenstadt v. Baird* (1972). https://supreme.justia.com/cases/federal/us/405/438/
8 United States Supreme Court. *Planned Parenthood v. Casey* (1992). https://www.law.cornell.edu/supremecourt/text/505/833
9 Guttmacher Institute. "An Overview of Abortion Laws" (2021). https://www.guttmacher.org/state-policy/explore/overview-abortion-laws
10 State of New York. *S. 240 Reproductive Health Act.* (2019). https://legislation.nysenate.gov/pdf/bills/2019/S240
11 United States Supreme Court. *Doe v. Bolton.* (1973). https://www.law.cornell.edu/supremecourt/text/410/179
12 This example appears in: David Boonin. *A Defense of Abortion.* (2003). Cambridge University Press, p. 131.
13 Guttmacher Institute. "Abortion Worldwide 2017: Uneven Progress and Unequal Access" (2018). https://www.guttmacher.org/report/abortion-worldwide-2017
14 Gilda Sedgh, Jonathan Bearak *et al.* "Abortion Incidence Between 1990 and 2014: Global, Regional, and Subregional Levels and Trends." (2016) *The Lancet.* http://www.thelancet.com/pdfs/journals/lancet/PIIS0140-6736%2816%2930380-4.pdf
15 New York Times. "They Were Jailed for Miscarriages. Now, Campaign Aims to End Abortion Ban." (2018). https://www.nytimes.com/2018/04/09/world/americas/el-salvador-abortion.html
16 Guttmacher Institute. "The U.S. Abortion Rate Continues to Drop" (2019). https://www.guttmacher.org/gpr/2019/09/us-abortion-rate-continues-drop-once-again-state-abortion-restrictions-are-not-main
17 Margaret P. Battin. "Sex and Consequences: World Population Growth vs. Reproductive Rights." (1997). *Philosophic Exchange*, 27.1: 19–31.
18 Kathryn Kost and Stanley Henshaw. "U.S. Teenage Pregnancies, Births and Abortions, 2010: National and State Trends by Age, Race and Ethnicity." (2014). https://www.guttmacher.org/sites/default/files/report_pdf/ustptrends10.pdf
19 Guttmacher Institute. "Medicaid Coverage of Abortion" (2021). https://www.guttmacher.org/evidence-you-can-use/medicaid-funding-abortion
20 For example, in Colorado in 2010 a proposed constitutional amendment appeared in the ballot stating: "An amendment to the Colorado Constitution applying the term 'person' as used in those provisions of the Colorado Constitution relating to inalienable rights, equality of justice and due process of law, to every human being from the beginning of the biological development of that human being." The amendment failed to pass, with 70% of Colorado voters rejecting it.
21 See: Bertha Alvarez Manninen. "Beyond Abortion: The Implications of Human Life Amendments." (2012). *Journal of Social Philosophy*, 43.2: 140–160.

22 Tennessee Supreme Court. *Davis v. Davis* (1992). https://law.justia.com/cases/tennessee/supreme-court/1992/842-s-w-2d-588-2.html. The court ruled that "disputes involving the disposition of preembryos produced by in vitro fertilization should be resolved, first, by looking to the preferences of the progenitors. If their wishes cannot be ascertained, or if there is dispute, then their prior agreement concerning disposition should be carried out. If no prior agreement exists, then the relative interests of the parties in using or not using the preembryos must be weighed. Ordinarily, the party wishing to avoid procreation should prevail, assuming that the other party has a reasonable possibility of achieving parenthood by means other than use of the preembryos in question. If no other reasonable alternatives exist, then the argument in favor of using the preembryos to achieve pregnancy should be considered."

23 Susan Cohen. "Abortion and Mental Health: Myths and Realities." (2006). *Guttmacher Policy Review*. 9.13. https://www.guttmacher.org/gpr/2006/08/abortion-and-mental-health-myths-and-realities "In 2003, the National Cancer Institute (NCI) convened more than 100 of the world's leading experts on the topic of abortion and breast cancer. After a lengthy and exhaustive review of all of the research, including a number of newer studies that avoided the flaws of their predecessors, they concluded that 'induced abortion is not associated with an increase in breast cancer risk', noting that the evidence for such a conclusion met NCI's highest standard. In 2004, an expert panel convened by the British government came to the same conclusion … The preponderance of evidence from well-designed and well-executed studies shows no connection between abortion and future fertility problems. Several reviews of the research conclude that first-trimester abortions pose virtually no long-term fertility risks – not only for premature and low-birth-weight delivery but for infertility, ectopic pregnancy, miscarriage and birth defects as well."

24 Excerpt from Koop's letter to Reagan: "… the available scientific evidence about the psychological sequelae of abortion simply cannot support either the preconceived beliefs of those prolife or those prochoice … I regret, Mr. President, that in spite of a diligent review on the part of many in the Public Health Service and in the private sector, the scientific studies do not provide conclusive data about the health effects of abortion on women." Throughout his career, Koop continued to deny the existence of post-abortion syndrome, even though he remained pro-life. In 1988, he wrote: "… the people who would like to see a report that the health effects of abortion are so devastating that abortion should be stopped, use as one of their weapons the fact that there is such a thing as a postabortion syndrome …. As we have talked to various groups, there is no doubt that there are people who experience a postabortion syndrome, but there are people who have a post-death-of-my-child syndrome, post-death-of-my-mother syndrome, post-lost-my-job syndrome." (cited in: Bertha Alvarez Manninen. *Pro-Life, Pro-Choice: Shared Values in the Abortion Debate*. (2014). Vanderbilt University Press, p. 138).

25 The APA 2008 study concluded that: "the best scientific evidence indicates that the relative risk of mental health problems among adult women who have an unplanned pregnancy is no greater if they have an elective first trimester abortion than if they deliver that pregnancy" (cited in Manninen, 2014, p. 138).

26 Manninen (2014): "Nevertheless, there are some women who do suffer negative emotional and mental consequences after procured abortion, much of which can be attributed to other aspects independently from the abortion. These risk factors include events that occur after the abortion, perceived lack of support for the abortion decision, ambivalence concerning the decision to abort and difficulty coming to that decision, compromised coping capacities in general, the quality of the relationship with the woman's male partner, and feeling coerced into the

abortion. One study found that women who felt pressured into the abortion, rather than coming to the decision purely as a product of their own free will, were more likely to experience post-abortion maladjustment. The same study also found that women who did not receive emotional support after the abortion were more likely to suffer in its aftermath. Moreover, many women who experience psychiatric disorders after an abortion likely suffered from psychiatric disorders before the abortion as well" (pp. 138–139).

27 University of California San Francisco's Bixby Center for Global and Reproductive Health. "Turnaway Study" (2019). https://www.ansirh.org/sites/default/files/publications/files/turnaway_study_brief_web.pdf

2

DAY 2

Abortions as Murder, Fetal Personhood, and Arguments from Potential

Day 2 – Scene: In a university coffee shop, L and C have come back together to further discuss their presentation.

C: Ok, so to repeat something you said last time: you believe that abortion is murder. That the Bible's prohibition of murder applies to embryos and fetuses at all points in gestation.

L: That's right.

C: And when does that begin for the fetus? When does it become murder to kill them?

L: At conception, of course. That's when the embryo begins to exist.

(a) Viability and quickening as times when abortion becomes murder.

C: But conception wasn't always thought to be the time when abortion becomes murder. Like we talked about last time, some people think it's at viability when abortion becomes murder.

L: Yes, but I don't see why it becomes immoral to kill a fetus only after they no longer need the woman's body. You're still causing their death regardless of whether they are dependent on her body or not.

C: Well, I think the reasoning is that once you no longer need to live off a person's body, you become an independent being. Before then, you're dependent on someone else's body for your life.

L: But being dependent doesn't mean you don't have a right to life. What if your child gets into a car accident and

DOI: 10.4324/9781003109457-2

now is so injured they are dependent on you for continued survival – does that now mean that they lack a right
to life?

C: I think that's different than a being who is essentially
parasitic on another human being.

L: It seems rather dehumanizing to refer to the embryo or
fetus as a parasite.

C: Well, scientifically at least, they are.

L: But the term "parasite" has really negative connotations.
I am not comfortable referring to any human being in
such a way.

C: Ok, I won't use it anymore. Let's consider some other
possibilities. What about quickening? When the woman
can first feel the fetus move inside her. The Catholic
Church used to say, hundreds of years ago, that this is
when the fetus first gained its soul.

L: We know better now, don't we? A fetus is moving long
before a mother feels it. Quickening is an outdated concept and it's irrelevant for the embryo's right to life.
Killing the embryo is murder when it first begins to exist.

C: Well it's not murder legally speaking, right? Murder is
the illegal and premeditated killing of a person. Abortion
is legal, and fetuses are not considered persons under the
law.

L: Just because something is legal doesn't mean it's morally
permissible. It was legal to keep, beat, and kill slaves pre-
Civil War, but that doesn't mean it should have been that
way, or that it wasn't murder. It was murder even then.
The law isn't always the best arbitrator of morality.

C: Fair enough. So what you mean is that abortion is murder morally, and that, therefore, it should also be murder
legally. We're talking about *moral* rights, not just legal
rights.

**(b) Abortion
kills an
innocent child.**

L: I am talking about both. I think we can give moral arguments that abortion is wrong, and this should have implications for whether abortion should legally be considered
murder. If the fetus has a moral right to life, that moral
right should be recognized under the law and translate
to also having a legal right to life. And fetuses should
have legal rights, as well as moral rights, because killing a
fetus, like killing a born child, is murder.

C: The problem with that argument is that it is
question-begging.[1]

L: What does that mean?

C: Well, there's a couple of ways an argument can "beg the question." One way is arguing in circles. Something like: "I know that the Bible is the word of God because it says so in the Bible."

L: That's not what I am doing.

C: No, but another way of begging the question is assuming the very conclusion you're trying to prove. You're assuming that abortion is wrongful killing, and you're assuming that fetuses are morally equivalent to infants and children. You need to provide *arguments* for that conclusion, not just assume it.

L: Ok, let's start with why abortion should be called "murder." Any taking of innocent life should be considered murder.

C: It's only murder if it is wrongful killing. You're assuming again.

L: Ok. Any instance of killing an innocent life is wrongful killing. All wrongful killings are murder. Abortion involves the taking of an innocent life, so abortion is wrongful killing. Because it's wrongful killing, it is also murder.

(c) Can "innocence" apply to embryos?

C: Ok. That's a good set up of your argument. One question: what do you mean by "innocent"?

L: I mean that the life in question is not guilty of any crime or wrongdoing. A fetus is not guilty of anything.

C: Would you consider a plant, for example, an innocent life?

L: I am not sure the concept of "innocence" applies to a plant.

C: I don't think it does either. "Innocence" can only apply to entities who are capable of doing wrong and choose not to. Plants aren't innocent. Insects aren't innocent. They aren't guilty either. They aren't anything in this regard, because they can't act morally either way.[2]

L: That's right. But what does that have to do with our conversation?

C: Well, fetuses are like plants and insects in this way. They aren't capable of acting autonomously. They don't understand good and bad. They don't act in any which way, innocent or guilty.

L: But we use that terminology to describe babies too don't we? Don't we say babies are innocent? And they too aren't capable of acting wrongly or rightly.

C: True enough. Maybe we shouldn't be using that terminology either in reference to babies.

L: But we agree that killing babies is murder, right? Regardless of whether the term "innocence" can apply to them.

C: Right, but now you're assuming, not arguing, that embryos and fetuses are morally equivalent to babies. Let's go back to your claim that it is wrong to take innocent life. Do you believe that *any* taking of innocent life is wrongful killing? What about killing plants, or killing insects? Plants and insects are alive aren't they? And they're at least as innocent as embryos.

(d) Is killing all human life wrong?

L: They are biologically alive, yes, but they aren't human lives. Embryos and fetuses, like babies, are living humans.

C: So it is only wrongful killing to take innocent *human* life?

L: Maybe not "only." I think it's morally wrong to kill some animal life for no good reason too. Like it would be wrong to kill a dog or a cat for no good reason.

C: But is it murder?

L: I don't know. That's a good question. My inclination is to say that it is not as bad as killing a human life, but may still be bad. But taking all innocent human life is definitely morally wrong.

C: Well now we're getting into animal rights, which is an important topic, but not our topic. So it's wrongful killing, and therefore murder, to take all innocent human life. What about sperm? Or ova? They are biologically alive. They are human too. They are innocent in that they have done nothing wrong. Is it wrongful killing to destroy sperm and ova? What about human cancer cells? Those cells are biologically alive, and they are human cells. But clearly we wouldn't say that it is morally wrong to kill cancer cells.

L: It's clearly not murder, or wrongful killing, to destroy sperm or ova, or cancer cells. That would make radiation and chemotherapy murder!

C: Right. But they are biologically alive, and they are human cells. This is something they all have in common: babies, embryos, fetuses, cancer cells, sperm, ova ... they are all biologically living human life. It is impermissible to kill babies, but it is permissible to destroy sperm or ova or cancer cells. Are embryos more like babies in this regard, or are they more like sperm and ova?

L: I am not clear what your point here is.

C: My point is that it is not always morally wrong, and not always murder, to destroy biologically living human life. So it is not enough to say that what makes killing an embryo or fetus morally wrong is that they are biologically living human lives.

L: But sperm and ova and cancer cells are not human *beings*. They are not persons.

(e) What is a person?

C: Ah, there's the magic word! "Persons." That's what we're really talking about here, right? What do we mean by "person" here?

L: A person is a human being. A living organism that is a member of our species. Persons are also members of the moral community. They are the kind of beings who deserve moral and legal rights. Part of these rights is the right to life, making it morally (and legally) wrong to kill them.[3]

(f) Is genetic humanity sufficient for personhood?

C: You seem to be saying that personhood is a biological category. That the only requirement necessary for personhood is that you are a member of our species. All members of the species *Homo sapiens* are persons?

L: Yes. Think about what made slavery wrong, or what made the Holocaust wrong. It was the denial of personhood to human beings that made possible two of the greatest human rights violations in history.

C: But is what made them persons their genetic humanity, or something else?

L: What else could there be?

C: Well, go back to the animal example. You said that taking animal life is morally wrong, but not as wrong as taking human life. Why is that? What makes human life different than animal life?

L: Well, human beings have different mental capacities. We are more intelligent. We are self-aware.

(g) The cognitive traits of personhood.

C: Let's make a list of all the mental traits that a being must have in order to be a person and "count" morally. What separates things that matter morally from things that don't. If I kick a soda can down the street that would be fine, but it wouldn't be ok to kick a kitten down the street. How come?

L: Clearly it's because kittens can feel pain. They are sentient. Same reason it would be morally bad to kick a dog, or any other living creature.

C: Be careful with that. Not all living creatures are sentient. It's permissible to pull weeds from the ground right? Remember we noted that being biologically alive is not sufficient for moral status.

L: Ok, so any kind of conscious life has some level of moral status.

C: So, we have sentience – the ability to feel pain and pleasure. That's what separates, say, animal life from soda cans. But that's not enough right? You don't count kittens as persons. It may be wrong to kill them sometimes, but we don't think killing them is murder. So what more do we need? What separates human life from animal life?

L: Well, like I said above, humans have reasoning abilities. We are self-aware. We can act autonomously, which means we have self-motivated activity. We're more intelligent than animals. We can do math and science. Create music, appreciate art, understand philosophy. All sorts of stuff.[4]

C: So what makes human beings morally significant, what makes them persons, is that they have certain mental, or cognitive, capacities that other animals do not. So it's not their *genetic* humanity that is important, it's their *mental life*.

(h) Persons who are not genetically human.

L: I am not sure we can separate the two. Genetic humanity and the mental life in question go hand-in-hand.

C: Not quite. Think of all the science fiction movies with robots or aliens that are intelligent. We look upon them as persons, in the context of the film. E.T. was a person because he was an intelligent being, even though he wasn't human. Superman is an alien, but he's a person because he is has all the mental traits you mentioned. You believe in God, right?

L: Yes, like I said last time I am a devout Catholic.

C: One important thing that differentiates Western religion from some Eastern religions is that for Christianity, Judaism, and Islam, God is a person. He is intelligent, self-aware, is capable of self-motivated activity, and He desires a relationship with humans.

L: Right, but why is all this relevant?

C: Because I want you to see that it is conceptually possible to separate genetic humanity and personhood. There are examples of non-humans who are persons. So being human is not necessary for ascribing personhood to something or someone.

(i) Genetic humans who are not persons.

L: Fair enough. But there are no examples of humans who are non-persons. That is, there are persons who are not human, but there are no humans who are not persons.

C: That's not right. There are many genetic humans who do not have the mental abilities you described. Humans who are severely mentally disabled do not have the self-aware-ness you are describing, at least not as robustly. Infants are sentient, but not yet self-conscious. Someone in the advanced stages of dementia becomes less self-aware and they lose their capacity for self-motivated activity.

L: Right, but you wouldn't say they aren't persons right? They are still members of our moral community. They still have rights.

C: All that I want to show you is that genetic humanity and those mental capacities don't always go hand-in-hand. There are non-humans who have robust mental capacities and there are humans who do not have robust mental capacities. So we're back to the question of what makes someone a person: their membership into a certain biological species, or their possession of certain mental capacities?

L: Wait, wait, I want to go back to the question I just asked. Infants, the elderly with dementia, the mentally disabled, they are still part of our moral community right? Just because they lack some of the mental capacities that we have does not make them less worthy of care.

C: I think we need to distinguish two different ways that the term "person" is being used here. We're collapsing those two definitions into one, and I think it's the source of some of our disagreements.

L: Ok, what are the two ways the term is being used?

C: There is "person" in the strict sense – a being that has all the cognitive traits we have flagged as being part of per-sonhood: self-awareness, self-motivated activity, ration-ality, autonomy, and sentience. Then there is "person" in the moral sense of the term, to denote members of the moral community. This includes all persons in the strict sense, but can also include beings who are not persons in the strict sense, but who have at least some of the men-tal traits we've been highlighting. So infants, the elderly with dementia, and the mentally disabled may not be persons in the strict sense, since they lack robust mental capacities, but they are persons in the moral sense – they are part of the moral community and have moral (and therefore legal) rights.

L: So all persons in the strict sense are also persons in the moral sense, but there could be some beings who are not persons in the strict sense, but could still be persons in the moral sense. So what determines if they are persons in the moral sense, if they are not persons strictly speaking?

C: I think it's important that they, at least, possess *some* of the mental traits we have highlighted. Infants, the dementia patient, and the severely mentally disabled are, at the very minimum, sentient, and they may also have some of the other mental traits as well, even if they don't have them very robustly.

L: Ok, I can agree to that.

C: But I can think of living humans who have *none* of those capacities. Humans in persistent vegetative states, in permanent comas, with machines keeping them alive, for example. They might still be biologically alive, but we often remove whatever is keeping them alive and we let them die, and that's not considered murder.

L: That's because they have lost all their potential for life. They aren't "coming back" so to speak. But that's different than the cases we're talking about.

C: That's fair. Here is what I am open to granting you so far. I am willing to admit that it may not be necessary to have *all* the mental traits we talked about in order to be a person in the moral sense – part of our moral community. That is, I am willing to admit that one can be a moral person without being a person in the strict sense. But what makes all these individuals members of the moral community from the infant, to the adult, to the elderly, or mentally disabled, is not that they are genetic humans, but that they have *some* of the cognitive traits we listed as being morally relevant for personhood.

L: I am not convinced you can separate the two as much as you want. Genetic humanity makes those mental states possible.

C: Not always...

L: But generally...

(j) Embryos and fetuses lack all the mental traits of personhood.

C: But here is one category of genetic humans who have *none* of the mental traits you mentioned as being morally significant: embryos and early fetuses. Embryos and early fetuses don't have the mental capacity for even basic consciousness. In this sense, dogs and cats approximate personhood more than embryos and early fetuses.

L: But embryos and fetuses are still members of our kind. It is within our nature to be rational beings, and that nature exists in an embryo and a fetus from the moment they start to exist. If there were another species where their very nature lead to them being rational, autonomous, and self-aware, I'd be in favor of protecting them too.[5]

C: See, I believe that species membership is irrelevant. What matters is *actually* having those mental capacities, even to a very minimal extent. A being who possesses *some* of those mental capacities may be a person in the moral sense, even if they are not persons in the strict sense, but a being that lacks *all* those mental capacities is not a person either in the strict or in the moral sense. They are not part of the moral community, and have no moral or legal rights.[6]

L: I disagree. Why is *actually* having those traits relevant, especially if you're going to possess those traits later on?

(k) The relationship between rights and desires.

C: I'll answer the first part now, and the second part later. Why is *actually* having those traits relevant for being a person and therefore a member of the moral community? Let's have a conversation about rights, specifically about the moral right to life. If I violate your rights, I have typically frustrated a desire that you have. If you have a car, and you desire that car, it would violate your rights to take it from you. But if you don't desire the car, and you let me have it, then I haven't violated your rights.[7]

L: Ok…

C: Or look at it this way: animals may have a right to not be tortured because they have the capacity to feel pain, and this certainly creates a corresponding desire to not feel pain. But they have no right to, say, an education because they do not have the capacity to desire any of the benefits that comes from obtaining an education.

L: I'm following you.

C: What would the corresponding desire be for having a moral right to life? You need to have the capacity to desire continued existence right? What makes killing you morally wrong is that I frustrate your desire for continued life. But in order for you to have the capacity to desire continued existence, you need to be able to conceive of yourself as a distinct entity who can exist over time. And you can only do that if you *actually* possess self-consciousness, that is, if you're *actually* a person in the strict sense.[8]

L: So what you're saying is that no being who is not self-conscious has the moral right to life because without self-consciousness you lack the relevant corresponding desire necessary for having a right to life? So embryos and fetuses lack a right to life because they lack self-consciousness and therefore are incapable of desiring continued existence.

C: They're incapable of desiring *anything*. They lack all the mental capacities of personhood. So they are not the kinds of beings who can have any rights at all.

(I) Do infants have a right to life?

L: Well by that logic infants would lack a right to life as well, since they too are not sufficiently self-aware to desire continued life.

C: Some philosophers have agreed with that conclusion. They have argued that infants do not have the same claim to life as actual persons with the capacity for self-consciousness.[9]

L: Well that's a pretty appalling point of view. I mostly certainly do not agree with that. And I thought you didn't either.

C: You're right, I don't. But when we disagree with an argument, we have to explain where the argument goes wrong.

L: Ok, here is where I think your argument goes wrong. I don't agree with tying up rights with desires. Let's go back to the car example. If I don't desire my car, but haven't given you permission to take it, to take it would still be stealing. What makes it not a violation of a right is not that I don't want it, but that I gave it to you.

C: Ok, I can see that.

L: But more importantly, there are clear examples of having a right to something even if you lack the capacity to desire it. Wouldn't you agree that infants and young children have a right to medical care were they to get sick?

C: I do believe that – but that's because I believe in universal healthcare and that all persons have a right to medical care when they're sick.

L: Ok, but infants and young children lack the mental capacities to actively desire medical care. Suppose there was a child with a mental disability and there was an educational program that would help her develop her cognition. Wouldn't the child have a moral right to access that educational program, even if she lacks the cognitive capacities to desire it?[10]

C: That sounds right to me.

L: Ok, then, so having the capacity to desire something is irrelevant as to whether someone has a right to it. And if that's the case, then it doesn't matter that an infant lacks the capacity to desire continued existence – he still has a right to life. By the same token, it does not matter that embryos or fetuses lack the capacity to desire continued existence because they lack self-awareness. They can still have a right to life.

C: Ok, I can concede that you bring up a good point here. But I am still not convinced that a being that lacks all cognition can have rights. So let's back track a bit. We need to ask two questions here: What kinds of things have a right to life, and why think that embryos and fetuses are those kinds of things?

(m) The argument from potential.

L: Go back to my claim that a fetus's nature is important. Our human nature is what underlies the mental capacities that make us persons. So even if a fetus doesn't have those mental capacities *now*, it will, barring any unfortunate event, develop those capacities in the future. So I can concede that a fetus may not be a person in the strict sense of the term, but their potential to develop those capacities is significant enough to warrant regarding them as persons in the moral sense of the term.

C: So, to recap what you said: Persons are beings with certain mental traits, and it is those traits that make human life valuable. It is part of our human nature to develop those capacities, to become rational beings. Embryos and fetuses may lack personhood in the strict sense, in that they lack the mental capacities in question, but their potential for developing those characteristics is sufficient for regarding them as members of the moral community, as persons in the moral sense. That was part of your claim above when you said that it is important that fetuses will possess the relevant mental states "later on."

L: Right. So embryonic and fetal potential matter. They deserve a place in our moral community in general, and, in particular, they also have a right to life, because of that potential.

(n) What does "potential" mean?

C: What do you mean by "potential" in this context?

L: Well, as far as I can see, there are two ways we can understand "potential." First, y is a potential x if it has the innate capacity to develop into x. That is, it is part of y's nature to grow into x. The embryo and the fetus will grow into a person in the strict sense if allowed to be gestated, born, and grow up. The attainment of personhood is part of their innate nature.

C: When does this potential start?

L: It starts right when the fetus is first conceived.

C: Does it though? Quite a bit of fertilized eggs don't implant in the uterus. I've read that about 2/3 of fertilized eggs fail to successfully implant in the womb. That means most fertilized eggs lack the potential to grow into a person.[11]

L: The fact that they failed to implant doesn't take away from the fact that embryos and fetuses are the kinds of beings who have the innate potential to become a person. It's part of their design, so to speak.

C: Even if they don't implant?

L: The failure to implant does not change their nature. But this isn't immediately relevant for abortion anyways. By the time the pregnancy test is positive, the embryo has successfully implanted and has begun to grow.

C: What about IVF embryos, like we talked about last time. Do they have potential?

L: Yes, it is also part of their innate nature to grow into persons. This potential will be realized if they are allowed to successfully gestate for nine months.

C: But that's the key word, right? – *if* they are gestated. Embryos and fetuses do not have potential on their own. They need a deliberate human act, gestation, to grow into a person. IVF embryos need even a more deliberate act – they need to be transferred into a uterus and successfully implant and then gestated for nine months.[12] Without the woman willing to gestate, the embryo and the fetus has no potential to grow into anything.

L: It's true that embryos and fetuses need the proper environment to realize their potential, but that doesn't mean they lack potential. Acorns are potential trees, are they not? They can't grow into actual trees without being planted in the right kind of environment, but that doesn't take away their potential. An acorn has, as part of its innate nature, the potential to grow into a tree. The embryo and fetus have, as part of their innate nature, the potential to grow into persons.

C: If an acorn existed in some sort of barren wasteland with no soil, I would not still consider it a potential tree. Without the environment, there is no potential.

L: But if you plant something totally different, say a leaf, it wouldn't grow into a tree. This is because an acorn has the innate potential to grow into a tree, and a leaf doesn't. Similarly, the embryo has an innate potential to grow into a person – into the kind of being that has the kind of cognition that makes their life significant. That alone should be sufficient for being part of the moral community.

C: Ok, how about this. How far are you willing to take considerations of potential? Aren't sperm and ova potential persons too? Considered together they have as much potential as an embryo to grow into a person. Should we give sperm and ova a right to life as well based on their potential?[13]

L: That's different. The sperm and ovum together create the embryo, but they are more like ingredients. Neither of them, by themselves, can grow into a person.

C: I don't see the difference between that kind of potential and the potential of an embryo.

L: If we followed your life in reverse, from adulthood, back to childhood, and infancy, we would go all the way back to when you were an embryo. You came into existence at that point; you were never a sperm or an ovum. The potential of an embryo was *your* potential to grow into a person. There is an identity relation between an embryo and the person the embryo becomes; they are the same individual. Sperm and ova are the ingredients to make the embryo but they are not the embryo itself.[14]

C: Maybe I can see that difference.

L: This question is a good segue for understanding the second sense of the term "potential" – when we're talking about probabilities. There are millions of sperm when a man ejaculates. That means there's, like, a one in a million chance of a particular sperm joining with an ovum to become an embryo. But once you have the embryo, you have a being who is a member of our species and whose genetic code makes it so that they will acquire morally significant cognition. At this point we have a being with a much higher chance of becoming a rational being.[15] So in this second sense, an embryo being a potential person means that the embryo has a high probability of developing into a person.

C: Can you clarify the difference between these two kinds of potential again?

L: Sure. In the first sense of the term "potential", we are talking about something's innate nature. Embryos and fetuses are potential persons in that it is part of their very nature as biological human beings to grow into a person. In the second sense of the term "potential" we are talking about probabilities. In this sense, embryos and fetuses are potential persons given that, if they are gestated and live long enough, they have a high probability of becoming a person. Once a woman finds out she is pregnant, that means that the embryo in question is a potential person in both senses of the term. They are potential persons both because it is in their nature to become persons and because they probably will become persons so long as the pregnancy is successful.

C: But what if the fetus miscarries, or the infant the fetus becomes dies? Doesn't that mean it is no longer a potential person?

L: It is no longer a potential person in the probabilistic sense of the term, but its nature is unaffected. If an infant dies that doesn't change the fact that it was part of its nature to become a person. Same with a fetus. A miscarried fetus is no longer a potential person in the probabilistic sense, but that doesn't change the fetus's innate nature.

C: Still, embryonic and fetal potential do not exist in a vacuum. Without the woman allowing them to gestate, they have no potential by themselves. It is the woman's decision to gestate that gives the embryo their potential.

L: No, it is the woman's decision to gestate that allows the embryo's potential to thrive, but the potential was always there. If you implant a random cell into a woman's uterus, it wouldn't grow into a baby because a single random cell has no potential. But if you successfully implant an embryo, it grows into a fetus, and then a baby, because of its potential.

C: Ok, how about this related question. You are saying that, even though the embryo and fetus lack the relevant mental properties, even though they are not persons in the strict sense, we should still regard them as persons in the moral sense because of their potential.

L: That's right.

C: But you're saying more than that, right? You're not just saying that they should be included in the moral community, you're saying that we should regard them as if they are persons in the strict sense because you want to give them the rights of persons in the strict sense. You think a kitten is part of the moral community, but you don't think it's murder to kill it (even though it may still be wrong to a lesser extent), because it is not a person in the strict sense. But you're saying that it *is* murder to kill an embryo or a fetus. You want to give them *more* rights than you would a kitten, even though they lack all cognition, because of their potential to be persons in the strict sense.

(o) Do potential persons have the same rights as actual persons?

L: I guess that's right. I believe that all persons in the strict sense *and* potential persons have the same right to life.

C: But that doesn't seem right to me. We don't give beings rights or status based upon what they may be in the future, only what they actually are in the present. Children are potential adults; it is in their innate nature to become adults, like you say it is in the embryo's and fetus's innate nature to become persons. But that doesn't mean we give them the same rights as actual adults. Prince Charles and Prince William are potential kings, but they are not given the rights of kings while they're princes. I may be a potential doctor, were I pre-med, but that doesn't give me the rights of actual doctors.[16]

L: Your examples here help in further clarifying the two definitions of "potential" that we are working with. Human children have it in their innate nature to become human adults. Pre-med students don't become doctors because of their innate nature (they could have become teachers or lawyers or actors instead), but because their schooling makes it probable that they will become doctors in the future.

C: Ok, but neither sense of the term "potential" means that we should give a potential x the same rights as an actual x.

L: Let me clarify what I mean to say. The rights you've just listed are rights that only belong to someone once they have achieved or attained certain properties. It is necessary to have a medical license in order to have the rights of a doctor, for example.

C: Right. And it is necessary to *be* a person in the strict sense in order to have the rights of a person in the strict sense. Potential does not cut it.

L: But that's the very point I am disputing. You are saying that one must be a person in the strict sense to have a right to life. I am saying that it is *not* necessary to be a person in the strict sense in order to have a right to life. Embryos and fetuses have the innate potential to be persons in the strict sense, and that potential endows them with a robust moral personhood. They have rights that even kittens or puppies don't – the right to life – based on that potential. So you're right that I do think embryos and fetuses have more rights than dogs and cats, because their innate potential for higher-order cognition makes them a different kind of being than a dog or a cat.

C: But dogs or cats have at least *some* cognition. I don't understand how something with some cognition can have less rights than something with no cognition at all. I guess I am not clear on why you think that embryonic or fetal potential grounds inclusion into the moral community, or any rights whatsoever. I can see why being a rational being, a self-conscious, autonomous being, gives one a right to life. I can even see why sentience alone can ground certain rights, like the right to avoid pain. I do not see why mere potential does.

L: Well, let's think about why we would give someone a right to life. I think one reason is because all human life is valuable, and to kill someone is to take away something valuable in the world.

C: But the thing that makes human life valuable, according to you, its mental properties, are not something an embryo has!

L: But it has the innate potential to gain those mental properties. That makes their life valuable. Imagine we lived in a society that was really in need of trees, and so really valued them. Wouldn't acorns also be valuable in that society, because of what it can become?

C: We're back to the acorn example. In a society where trees are un-growable, acorns wouldn't have any value because it cannot become anything. It's only when its coupled with the proper environment that it has any real potential.

L: The proper environment raises the probability that an acorn becomes a tree, but it doesn't take away from the acorn's innate nature. Similarly, gestation raises the probability that an embryo or fetus will grow into a person, but not gestating them does nothing to change their innate nature.

C: Ok, we appear to be at a standstill here. How about this? Earlier I said that what gives persons a right to life is their capacity to have the relevant desires, and to kill someone is to thwart their desire to continue living.

L: I think that's one thing that may make killing wrong, but it's not the only thing. I think a suicidal person's life has value, even if they do not desire living.

(p) The right to life protects persons from harm.

C: Agreed. But in both cases I think death is a bad thing because death harms them in some way – either by thwarting their desires or depriving them of their life. And the right to life exists in order to protect people from that harm.

L: Agreed.

C: So here's my question: are embryos harmed by death?

L: It seems clear to me that they are. They are harmed by not being allowed to realize their potential.

C: Why think that?

L: Well, we both agree that rational lives are valuable, right? It must be because we believe that the mental life of persons are good things.

C: Agreed.

L: Well I think it would harm embryos to deprive them of the conscious goods that is innate in their nature to realize. If it is a good thing to be a rational person, and the embryo's nature is one that leads to them becoming a rational person, it is a good thing for the embryo to be allowed to realize their innate nature. It's the same reason it would harm an infant if you killed her – you've also deprived her of all the goods that come with being a rational person.[17]

C: You keep comparing embryos to infants, but it seems like there are significant differences between them that makes it so that infants are the kinds of beings that can be harmed, but embryos are not.

L: Both are deprived of their lives.

(q) Sentience as a prerequisite for being able to be harmed.

C: But they are not the same kind of beings. I think only conscious beings can be harmed because only conscious beings have interests. Let's go back to the soda can example. Can you harm a soda can?

L: No, it's clear that a soda can cannot be harmed.

C: And why not?

L: Well, it has no capacity to feel pain.

C: Not just pain, it has no capacity to feel *anything* at all.

L: That's right.

C: What about other non-conscious objects? Cell phones, computers – can they be harmed?

L: No, for the same reason.

C: Right, so it seems like sentience is necessary in order to be the kind of being that can be harmed. But it isn't just sentience that matters, it's not just the capacity to feel pain that matters, it's the *consciousness* that comes with sentience.

L: What about it?

C: Well think about what it means to harm someone or something. It's to go against their interests, right?

(r) Harm as the setting back of interests.

L: What do you mean by "interests?"

C: An interest is something that you have a stake in, something that contributes to your well-being, something that matters to you.[18] You have an interest in continued life because continued life contributes to your well-being. Your life is also something that matters to you.

L: Ok.

C: To harm someone is to set back, or go against, those interests.[19] There seems to be two ways we can do this. There are your foundational interests. Things like your health, your life, some material resources. When you set back these interests you have very seriously harmed a person, since without these interests being realized, you can't really have any other interests at all.[20]

L: So something like the right to life exists in order to protect a person's foundational interests in continued existence.

C: Right, but there are other kinds of interests too. These are the most related to your personal goals and aspirations. Your interest in receiving an education is an example of this kind of interest, or landing that job you've been wanting.[21] To thwart these interests harms you too, though not in the same way as the harm that comes with thwarting the first kind of interests.

L: It seems like thwarting the first kind of interests are much more harmful, since without those interests you wouldn't be able to attain any of the other ones in the second category.

C: Right. But notice that all these things *matter* to the person in question. Nothing that you do to a soda can, or a cell phone, or a computer *matters* to them because they can't be affected in any way. They are non-conscious, inanimate beings.[22]

L: That sounds about right.

C: In order to have any kind of moral status, it must be possible to harm you in some way. If it is possible to harm you, it's because you have some interests that have been thwarted, whether it be the more foundational interests, like your life and health, or other interests, like your job and your education. Soda cans have no moral status because they cannot be harmed. And the reason they cannot be harmed is because they have no interests. And the reason they have no interests is because they aren't sentient nor conscious beings.[23]

(s) **Must you be sentient in order to have interests?**

L: What about plants and trees? It seems like you can harm them even though they aren't sentient or conscious. To rip a tree out of the ground harms it, doesn't it? To feed it plant food benefits it, right?

C: But plants don't care what happens to them. Whether you pull them out of the ground or feed them plant food, neither matters to them. Plants have no desires, plans, goals, or anything that can ground an interest.[24] We may not want to harm them because their existence matters to other people – say that it matters to all of us given that they produce oxygen – but nothing matters *to the plant*.

L: But we seem to attribute a welfare to many things that aren't conscious. Plants are one thing, but we say, for example, that you should have a good diet and get exercise for the "sake of your heart" and hearts are not conscious beings.

C: Right, but in that case what we really mean is that you should have a good diet and exercise for *your* sake. Your heart has no sake of its own over and above the interests of its owner.[25]

L: I think I see where you're going with this. Embryos are not conscious so they have no interests.

C: Right. Nothing at all matters to an embryo or an early fetus. Because they aren't sentient, and because they aren't conscious, there is nothing that can affect an embryo's or an early fetus's well-being. They don't even *have* a well-being of their own yet. There are things that can be done to enhance their growth, via continued gestation, or to thwart their growth, via abortion, but this is the same as it is with plants or trees. Neither have interests of their own. And because they have no interests, they cannot be harmed. Since they cannot be harmed, they have no claim to rights, since rights exist to protect people from harm.

L: Let's say, for now, that I agree with this. How does this affect abortion? Embryos may not be sentient, but certainly later fetuses are sentient. When a baby is born, she comes out crying and feeling cold and hunger. So she can clearly feel. We know that fetuses can hear in the womb and remember voices once born.

C: I think that this points to a substantial difference between early and late abortions. Early abortions *prevent* the existence of a conscious entity. Late abortions are more ethically problematic because we are dealing with a viable, sentient, and conscious being. Though I say that tentatively because I think some late abortion may be justifiable for other reasons.

**(t) When do
fetuses become
sentient?**

L: So it seems that we need to determine when an embryo
or fetus becomes sentient. When do they cross the threshold from being a being without interests, according to
your argument, to a being with interests who can now
be harmed?

C: This is a good question. Let's look it up.

Both women look to their smartphones.

L: So what is crucial to conscious awareness is a functioning
cerebral cortex.[26] There also needs to be a connection
between the spinal cord and the thalamus. This article
here states that this "starts to develop from 14 weeks
onwards and is finished at 20 weeks."[27]

C: This article describes the onset of consciousness as "cortical birth" and that "it is so gradual that it might seem
more accurate to speak of functional evolution rather than
birth." [28] In other words, consciousness doesn't just happen
all at once. It also says that if the beginning of consciousness is taken to be when fetuses first experience sleep/wake
cycles analogous to more mature human beings, then this
"varies from fetus to fetus, but occurs somewhere between
30–35 weeks of gestation. This is also the time when cortical functioning in the fetus begins to resemble mature
cortical functioning in other important respects."[29]

L: Those are significantly different times. It seems that the
earliest we can maybe have consciousness is in the beginning of the second trimester, but it may not happen until
even later.

C: Yes, I don't think we're going to find a definitive answer
here, but that doesn't mean we don't have some kind of
answer. Like I told you last time, 91% of abortions take
place in the first trimester, so that means the vast majority of abortions, almost all of them, happen before the
earliest time a fetus can be conscious. And if that's true,
and if it is also true that we need consciousness to have
any moral status at all, the earliest a fetus can have moral
status is during the second trimester of pregnancy.

L: I acknowledge that there seems to be a significant moral
difference between conscious and non-conscious beings.
But here's a question for you. Let's say I agree with you that
fetuses don't have robust moral status because they lack interests of their own. Still, does that mean that fetuses are completely disposable beings? Aren't there other things to which
we give moral standing or legal protection even though they
are not persons in either the strict or moral sense?

C: Give me some examples of non-persons who have moral standing or legal protection.

L: Well, some people think that non-human animals have rights, even though they aren't persons (as in, they don't have the same moral status as you and I do). There are animal cruelty laws, for example, so animals enjoy some legal protection.

C: True, but non-human animals are still sentient and conscious, and so they can still be harmed. Looking at it this way, a non-human animal should have more rights than a pre-sentient fetus, since the former can be harmed in ways the latter cannot. So yes they have legal protection even if they aren't persons, but it is because of their sentient nature. Non-human animals have interests.

L: Going back to the plant example, don't some people believe that trees and plants and ecosystems are worth protecting, that they have some moral standing? If so, these are examples of non-sentient, non-conscious beings that still has some degree of moral status and legal protection.

C: I would say that ecosystems have moral status only insofar as their well-being affects sentient and conscious creatures. Ecosystems are important to protect because doing so protects the life and welfare of other beings who are sentient, animals and humans alike. It's in animals' and humans' interests to protect these ecosystems.

L: There are other things, though, that have legal protection even though they are not persons. Some legal protections are given to things that aren't even alive – like certain works of art, or historic buildings. When the Notre Dame cathedral burned in France, many people believed that something of great worth had been destroyed, even though the Notre Dame cathedral is not a person, and it is a non-sentient, non-living thing.

C: Ok, I see what you're saying. I can concede that there are some examples of non-sentient, non-living beings are worthy of some legal protection. But I would still argue that their moral worth stems from the effects it has on others who are sentient and who have interests. The Notre Dame cathedral is valuable because humans give it value, because they appreciate it as an exquisite work of art. Such is also the case with other pieces of art, or historic buildings. It's not the thing itself that has value, its value comes from the fact that other people, for a variety of reasons, value it.

L: Couldn't we argue that something similar is the case with fetuses?

C: What do you mean?

L: Like buildings and ecosystems, couldn't fetuses have moral value even though they are not persons? If we can bestow legal protection onto trees and historic buildings, why couldn't we bestow legal protection onto fetuses on similar grounds? Fetuses are valuable to other persons, even if I were to grant that they are not persons themselves.

C: In the case of trees and historic buildings, bestowing legal protection on them does not interfere with anyone else's rights or well-being. Heck, in some cases we give them rights *in order to* protect the well-being of others (like the animals that are hurt when their habitat is destroyed). But bestowing legal protection onto fetuses directly opposes the rights of pregnant women. More rights for fetuses means less rights for them. So yes, I acknowledge that fetuses may be valuable to other people, but recognizing that value with legal protection means that the rights of actual persons – women – are compromised. It is hard to make the case that legal protection should be given to a being that lacks all interests when doing so directly conflicts with beings who clearly have interests.

L: Even so, I find it hard to conclude that fetuses are completely disposable beings, even if they aren't persons. And even so, I am still not convinced that an embryo or fetus lacks interests.

C: But you agree that only conscious beings can have interests?

L: Ehh … maybe? I mean, I can see why you say so, and I agree that there seems to be a level of harm we can bestow on a conscious being that we can't bestow on a non-conscious being. Still, I can't shake the belief that embryos are still harmed by being deprived of their life, even in early pregnancy, and even though they are not conscious beings. I'm wondering if maybe we can break for today and you give me a chance to look up some other articles that might help me out?

C: Sure that's no problem. We've covered a lot of bases today, so it would be good to take a break here. Same time next week? Maybe Monday morning?

L: That works, I'll meet you at this very table then.

Notes

1 See: Nathan Nobis and Kristina Grob. *Thinking Critically About Abortion: Why Most Abortions Aren't Wrong and Why All Abortions Should Be Legal.* (2019). Open Philosophy Press. https://www.abortionarguments.com/p/full-text.html#bad

2 Nobis and Grob (2019).

3 The second definition of "person" can be found in: Mary Anne Warren. "On the Moral and Legal Status of Abortion." (1973) *The Monist*, 57.1: 43–61. Warren does not equate biological humanity with personhood. She instead argues that persons are beings who have certain cognitive capacities and are, therefore, members of the moral community who are deserving of moral rights, including a right to life.

4 See: Warren, 1973 for a list of the cognitive traits of personhood. This includes: "(1) consciousness (of objects and events external and/or internal to the being), and in particular the capacity to feel pain; (2) reasoning (the developed capacity to solve new and relatively complex problems); (3) self-motivated activity (activity which is relatively independent of either genetic or direct external control); (4) the capacity to communicate, by whatever means, messages of an indefinite variety of types, that is, not just with an indefinite number of possible contents, but on indefinitely many possible topics; (5) the presence of self-concepts, and self-awareness, either individual or racial, or both" (p. 55).

5 See: Francis Beckwith. *Defending Life: A Moral and Legal Case Against Abortion Choice* (2007). Cambridge University Press: "… the pro-life position is based on the *personal nature* of human beings and the presence of that nature from the moment a human being comes into existence regardless of whether it has the present exercisable capacity for, or is currently engaging, in person acts. Consequently, if another species exists, whether in this world or in another … which possess a personal nature from the moment any of its individual members come into being, then pro-lifers would seek to have these creatures protected from unjustified homicide as well" (p. 162).

6 See: Warren, 1973; Michael Tooley. "Abortion and Infanticide." (1972) *Philosophy and Public Affairs*, 2.1: 37–65; and Peter Singer. *Practical Ethics*, 2 ed. (1993). Cambridge University Press. Warren writes: "Can it be established that genetic humanity is sufficient for moral humanity? I think that there are very good reasons for not defining the moral community in this way … the suggestion is simply that the moral community consist of all and only people, rather than all and only human beings … all we need to claim, to demonstrate that the fetus is not a person, is that any being which satisfies *none* [of the mental traits of personhood] is certainly not a person … a fetus is a human being which is not yet a person, and which therefore cannot coherently be said to have full moral rights" (pp. 54–56).

7 Michael Tooley "Abortion and Infanticide" (revised version), quoted in Singer, 1993: "the basic intuition is that a right is something that can be violated and that, in general, to violate an individual's right to something is to frustrate the corresponding desire. Suppose, for example, that you own a car. Then I am under a prima facie obligation not to take it from you. However, the obligation is not unconditional: it depends in part upon the existence of a corresponding desire in you. If you do not care whether I take your car, then I generally do not violate your right by doing so" (p. 96).

8 Singer, 1993: Singer writes "… the desire relevant to possessing a right to life is the desire to continue existing as a distinct entity. But only a being who is capable of conceiving herself as a distinct entity existing over time – that is, only a person – could have this desire. Therefore, only a person could have a right to life" (p. 97). Tooley, 1972: Tooley writes: "An organism possesses a serious right to life only if it possesses the concept of a self as a continuing subject of experiences and other mental states, and believes that it is itself such a continuing entity." (p. 44).

9 See: Warren (1973), Tooley (1972), and Singer (1993). Tooley (1972), for example, writes: "a newborn baby does not possess the concept of a continuing self … If so, infanticide during a time interval shortly after birth must be morally acceptable" (p. 63).

10 See: Bertha Alvarez Manninen and Jack Mulder Jr. *A Civil Dialogue on Abortion* (2018), Routledge: "while we can debate, in general, whether anyone possesses a moral right to healthcare or education, certainly one reason we *wouldn't* argue against someone possessing such a right is because they lack the cognitive capacity to desire it." (written by Manninen, p. 17).

11 Science News. "Which Fertilized Eggs Will Become Human Fetuses? Researchers Predict With 93% Accuracy." (2010). https://www.sciencedaily.com/releases/2010/10/101003205930.htm

12 Singer, 1993: "the process of IVF, however, leads to the creation of embryos that cannot develop into a person unless there is some deliberate human act (the transfer to the uterus) and that even then, in the best circumstances, will most likely not develop into a person" (p. 159).

13 Peter Singer and Deane Wells. *The Reproduction Revolution: New Ways of Making Babies.* (1984). Oxford University Press: "what can be said about the potential of the embryo can also be said about the potential of the egg and the sperm when separate but considered jointly. If we have the egg and we have the sperm what we have also has the potential to develop into a normal human being …" (p. 91).

14 Jim Stone. "Why Potentiality Matters." (1987). *Canadian Journal of Philosophy*, 17.4: 815–829. Stone distinguishes between two kinds of potential: weak and strong potential. A has the weak potential to become B if A is an "element in a causal condition that produces a B and, further, the matter of A will be (or will at least help produce) the matter of the B" (p. 818). Strong potentiality, on the other hand, entails an identity relationship between A and B: "the strong reading adds the requirement that A will produce a B if A develops normally and the B so produced will be such that it was once A" (p. 818). Stone argues that sperm and ova have the weak potential to grow into a person in that they are causal elements in producing an embryo, but the embryo, being the same individual as a future person, has the strong potential to become that person.

15 John Noonan. "An Almost Absolute Value in History" in *The Morality of Abortion: Legal and Historical Perspectives*, edited by John Noonan (1970). Harvard University Press: 51–59: "if a spermatozoon is destroyed, one destroys a being which had a chance of far less than 1 in 200 million of developing into a reasoning being … if a fetus is destroyed, one destroys a being … which had an 80% chance of developing further into a baby who, in time, would reason" (p. 57).

16 Singer, 1993: "There is no rule that says that a potential X has the same value as an X, or has all the rights of an X. There are many examples that show just the contrary. To pull out a sprouting acorn is not the same as cutting down a venerable oak. To drop a live chicken into a pot of boiling water would be much worse than doing the same to an egg. Prince Charles is the potential King of England, but he does not now have the rights of a king" (p. 153).

17 Stone, 1987: "What the fetus is finally, is something that makes itself self-aware; that good is the fetus's good – this is its nature. Anything benefits from having the good which it is its nature to make for itself. I submit that we have a prima facie duty to all creatures not to deprive them of the conscious goods which it is their nature to realize" (p. 821).

18 Joel Feinberg. *The Moral Limits of the Criminal Law, Volume 1: Harm to Others* (1984). Oxford University Press: "one's interests … consists of all those things in which one has a stake … these interests, or perhaps more accurately, the things these interests are in, are distinguishable components of a person's well-being … what promotes them is to his advantage or *in his interest*; what thwarts them is to his detriment or *against his interest*" (p. 34).

19 Feinberg, 1984: Feinberg defines harm as "the thwarting, setting back, or defeating of an interest" (p. 33).

20 Feinberg, 1984: Feinberg calls these kinds of interests "welfare interests" and defines them as: "they are the very most important interests a person has, and cry out for protection, for without their fulfillment, a person is lost ... when they are blocked or damaged, a person is very seriously harmed indeed, for in that case his more ultimate aspirations are defeated too" (p. 37).

21 Feinberg, 1984: Feinberg calls these kinds of interests "ulterior interests" and defines them as: "such aims as producing good novels or works of art, solving crucial scientific problem, achieving high political office, successfully raising a family, achieving leisure for handicraft or sport, building a dream house, advancing a social cause" (p. 37).

22 Bonnie Steinbock. *Life Before Birth: The Moral and Legal Status of Embryos and Fetuses* (1992). Oxford University Press: "It is this notion of *mattering* that is key to moral status. Beings that have moral status must be capable of caring about what is done to them. They must be capable of being made, if only in the rudimentary sense, happy or miserable, comfortable or distressed" (p. 5).

23 Steinbock, 1992: Steinbock calls this "the interest view" of moral status: "... without conscious awareness, beings cannot have interests. Without interests, they cannot have a welfare of their own. Without a welfare of their own, nothing can be done for their sake. Hence, they lack moral standing or status." (p. 5).

24 Steinbock, 1992: "Plants, like body parts and mere things, lack conscious awareness. Without conscious awareness, they cannot have interests – desires, plans, hopes, goals. They cannot take an interest in anything, including their own health, lives, or well-being" (p. 20).

25 Steinbock, 1992: "... one's heart does not have a sake of its own. The expression 'Do it for your heart's sake' makes sense only in context where proper cardiac functioning contributes to the well-being of the owner" (p. 19).

26 Rodrigo O. Kuljis. "Development of the Human Brain: The Emergence of the Neural Substrate for Pain Perception and Conscious Experience" in *The Beginning of Human Life*, edited by F.K. Beller and R.F. Weir. (1994). Kluwer Academic Publishers: 49–56. Kuljis writes that the cerebral cortex is responsible for "conscious experience, pain perception, and voluntary movements... an intact, normally functioning cerebral cortex is indispensable for human cognitive abilities" (pp. 49–50).

27 P.N.A. Van Scheltema, S. Bakker, F.P.H.A. Vandenbussche, D. Oepkes. "Fetal Pain." (2008). *Fetal and Maternal Medicine Review.* 19:4: 311–324, at p. 320.

28 J.A. Burgess and S.A. Tawia. "When Did You First Begin to Feel It? – Locating the Beginning of Human Consciousness." (1996) *Bioethics*, 10.1: 1–26, at. p. 19.

29 Burgess and Tawia, 1996, p. 23.

3

DAY 3

Fetal "Future-Like-Ours" Arguments, and Considerations of Personal Identity

Day 3 – Scene: After a few days off, L and C have come back together at the university coffee shop to discuss some pro-life arguments.

L: We're back!

C: We are. I've been looking forward to our conversation. Did you look up what you wanted to?

L: I did! I think I got some good material that allows me to better explain why I am pro-life.

C: Let's get to it then.

(a) Sanctity of life arguments.
L: You asked me earlier whether there was anything specifically in the Bible about abortion and we went back and forth with some passages. I found another one that I think helps my case. Genesis 9:6 reads that "whoever sheds human blood, by humans shall their blood be shed; for in the image of God has God made mankind." This shows, I think, that human life is special or sacred because it is the only life that is made in God's image.

C: But what does it mean to be made in God's image? God is a non-corporeal being right? So it can't be that we look like God, since God doesn't have a body or a face or eyes.

L: That's right.

C: So it must be that we are mentally similar to God in some way. Like God, at least the Western conception of God, we are persons with the capacity for self-awareness, sentience, we have moral agency, and the ability to form

DOI: 10.4324/9781003109457-3

meaningful relationships. So we are right back where we were last time: it's having certain cognitive capacities that underlies the moral status enjoyed by humans. It is in our personhood, then, that we are "like God."

L: I think we've argued the significance of personhood enough. Regardless of who or what is a person, this quote applies to all human life. And then I also looked up this quote from Pope John Paul II on the value of fetal life: "Some people try to justify abortion by claiming that the result of conception, at least up to a certain number of days, cannot yet be considered a personal human life. But in fact, from the time that the ovum is fertilized, a life is begun which is neither that of the father nor the mother; it is rather the life of a new human being with his own growth. It would never be made human if it were not human already. This has always been clear, and ... modern genetic science offers clear confirmation. It has demonstrated that from the first instant there is established the program of what this living being will be: a person, this individual person with his characteristic aspects already well determined. Right from fertilization the adventure of a human life begins ..."[1] And in another part of the book he also writes that human life has "sacred value ... from its very beginning until its end, and can affirm the right of every human being to have this primary good respected to the highest degree."[2] So all human life is sacred and has value. Taking any human life is always morally wrong and an affront to that inherent value. These are called "sanctity of life" arguments.

C: So taking human life is *always* wrong? What about self-defense?

L: I would think that this is one exception, and even then, we should strive to defend ourselves as non-violently as possible and use violence as a last resort.

C: What about the death penalty?

L: Even that as well. Criminals should be punished for their crimes, but even state-sanctioned killing should be avoided. Pope John Paul writes: "It is clear that, for these purposes to be achieved, the nature and extent of the punishment must be carefully evaluated and decided upon, and ought not go to the extreme of executing the offender except in cases of absolute necessity: in other words, when it would not be possible otherwise to defend society."[3]

C: What about war, and collateral damage in war?

L: Killing innocents in war should also be avoided as much as possible. There is a "just war" doctrine supported by the Catholic Church that outlines clearly when a war is deemed "just." Many of our wars don't meet those criteria, sadly.

C: Well I have to say that I admire your consistency very much. Many people I have talked to who claim to be pro-life don't apply it beyond abortion.

L: I appreciate you saying that.

C: But you know, many of the world's best thinkers disagree with the stance that all human life is sacred. Plato advocated infanticide for children born from incest, and euthanasia for people with certain disabilities.[4] Aristotle also argued in favor of euthanasia for any infant born with a deformity, and that abortions should be obtained for any couple that has too many children.[5]

L: Not to take anything away from them, but wasn't Aristotle also a supporter of slavery?[6] They aren't exactly the pillars of morality, are they?

C: Fair enough, then. I suppose the reason that I feel uncomfortable with this view is that it assumes that humans have some special spot amongst creation, one that is apart and different from other animals.

L: Well, didn't we agree that the capacity for reason sets human life apart from other animals?

C: Yes but we also noted that some non-human animals, like primates, may be more person-like than some human beings, like embryos or even newborns. I still don't think species membership by itself is all that is necessary in order to have moral status. But we've talked enough about that. Let me ask you something. What about end of life care? Don't we think it is permissible to take away life-sustaining treatments from people who are permanently vegetative?

L: Can you give an example?

(b) Sanctity of life arguments and euthanasia.

C: I read about a case in England, a young man named Anthony Bland, who was crushed by a mob of people at a soccer game. He wasn't brain dead, but he had enough brain damage to be in a persistent vegetative state. He was being kept alive by feeding tubes, and the parents asked the courts for the tubes to be removed so he could die.[7]

L: I think there is a distinction between killing someone who is alive and has a future ahead of her and removing life sustaining treatment from someone to allow his condition to run its course.

C: What about killing someone who is suffering from a terminal disease by prescribing a lethal medication? That's called physician assisted suicide, and it's legal in some states, for example, Oregon, California, Colorado, Maine, Vermont, and Montana. There was a woman named Brittany Maynard, who was diagnosed with brain cancer who moved to Oregon in order take advantage of their physician assisted suicide laws. She took medication prescribed by her doctor, and died surrounded by her loved ones.[8] Is that an affront to human dignity?

L: I would say so. Pope John Paul II also condemns euthanasia in his writings.

(L looks through the pages of her book)

Here it is: "On a more general level, there exists in contemporary culture a certain Promethean attitude which leads people to think that they can control life and death by taking the decisions about them into their own hands. What really happens in this case is that the individual is overcome and crushed by a death deprived of any prospect of meaning or hope. We see a tragic expression of all this in the spread of euthanasia-disguised and surreptitious, or practiced openly and even legally."[9]

C: I guess what I am saying is that I find a blanket condemnation of all forms of taking human life problematic. There seems to be some cases where death is what is in the patient's best interest. Anthony Bland wasn't living any kind of real life at all, and Brittney Maynard, it seems to me, had a right to decide for herself what kind of death she wanted.

L: I believe that only God can make that choice.

C: Let's go back to abortion. I actually looked this up in preparation for today. It's a story written by a mother named Emily Rapp about her son Ronan, who had Tay-Sachs disease, a disorder that progressively destroys your neurons, and eventually this leads to paralysis, loss of muscle control, and blindness, and then death. About her son's condition, she writes: "If I had known Ronan had Tay-Sachs ... I would have found out what the disease meant for my then unborn child; I would have talked to parents who are raising (and burying) children with this disease, and then I would have had an abortion. Without question and without regret, although this would have been a different kind of loss to mourn and would by no means have been a cavalier or uncomplicated, heartless decision. I'm so grateful that Ronan is my child. I also wish he'd never been born; no person should suffer in this way – daily seizures, blindness, lack of movement, inability to swallow, a devastated brain – with no hope for a cure. Both of these statements are categorically true; neither one is mutually exclusive."[10]

L: I can't imagine the pain of watching a child go through all that, or dying of brain cancer. But in the end, I can't justify killing a human being, even to avoid pain and suffering. We should try to minimize their pain as much as possible, but death needs to occur on its own, not by anyone's hands.

C: I don't disagree with you that human life is valuable, I just disagree that respecting that value can never coincide with approving of, or causing, death. When my grand-father was sick and slowly dying, my family signed a Do Not Resuscitate order. Not because we didn't love him and thought he had no value, but *because* we loved him and didn't want him to continue to suffer. Emily Rapp would have aborted her son for his own sake, so that *he* would avoid suffering.

L: Let me grant you, for the sake of argument, that it would be permissible to end the life of a terminally ill person who is experiencing pain and suffering. This doesn't really apply to most cases of abortion.

C: Later abortions, when they do occur, typically do so because the fetus has been diagnosed with some condition that is either lethal, or impacts their quality of life.

L: But let's skip that for now. We can come back to it later. Most abortions are not performed for these reasons. Most embryos and fetuses who are aborted are otherwise healthy. Even if I grant you that taking life may be morally permissible in cases of a terminal affliction (which I don't believe), this does not apply to most abortions.

(c) Abortion and religious diversity.

C: That's true enough. But I would like to note, like I did on our first day, that your opposition to abortion (and euthanasia and the death penalty) is due to your religious beliefs. And although you are allowed to have those beliefs, of course, the government should not be making laws favoring one set of religious beliefs over others. That's why we have a separation of church and state. Religious diversity, including having no religion, needs to be respected.

L: In general, I don't have a problem with making laws that respect religious diversity.

C: Then you may have a problem arguing against abortion on religious grounds. Not only do we have church and state separation, not all religions oppose abortion the way Catholicism does. Take for example Japan, which has many Buddhist citizens. Abortion is legal in Japan. The public and vehement debate surrounding abortion that we have in this country is largely absent in Japan. Nevertheless, there is a practice in Japan called *mizuko kuyo*, which is sort of like a grieving ritual for miscarried or aborted fetuses. Many women in the West have adopted some version of it in order to grieve pregnancy loss, whether that be unintentional, like a miscarriage, or intentional, like abortion.[11]

L: I did not know that. This actually relates to what we talked about yesterday. According to such a ritual, miscarriages and abortion still constitute the death of something with moral value, if not moral rights. Fetuses are not viewed as just disposable masses of cells, which is the language I hear a lot from the pro-choice side here. I can get behind making such grieving rituals more commonplace here in the U.S.

C: But that's just one differing view. It's not just Eastern religions that differ over abortion. Even here in the West there are differing religious views. Some Jewish persons have come out in defense of the pro-choice side by arguing that a Biblical defense of abortion restrictions is misguided. Many Jews don't believe that fetuses have souls until birth.[12] The National Council of Jewish Women defends abortion rights and has come out against laws that are designed to restrict abortion.[13] A PEW Research Center study illustrated that (*reads from phone*): "83% of Jews support abortion rights, as does 82% of Buddhists, 68% of Hindus, and 55% of Muslims."[14] So which religion's views ought to take precedence when deciding on abortion laws?

(d) Future-like-ours arguments.

L: Ok, I see your point. But what if we did away with religious considerations altogether? Let's argue against abortion purely on secular grounds. The argument that I found in the literature that I want to talk about today is secular. No religion at all. It's called the "future-like-ours" argument against abortion. It begins by asking a more general question: what is wrong with killing me or you?

C: Well, there's the impact it would have on our loved ones, for starters.

L: Yes, but that can't be *the* thing that makes killing wrong, since it wouldn't account for why it's wrong to kill someone with no loved ones or a hermit. So while the pain of loved ones is a horrible consequence of killing, it can't be what makes killing wrong.[15]

C: I agree.

L: Another possible answer to consider is that killing is wrong because of the effect it has on the killer; because it "brutalizes the one who kills." That is, killing has an adverse effect on the murderer himself.

C: Oh like in Harry Potter when killing breaks your soul into parts!

L: Or Aristotle's account of vice and virtue; that is, that doing vicious things (like killing) makes it so that your character devolves into something vicious as well.

C: But that doesn't seem to be the reason it is wrong to kill.

L: No it doesn't. That may be another consequence of killing, just like the effects on loved ones is a consequence of killing, but it cannot be *the* reason killing is bad. Besides, if it is true that killing has adverse effects on the killer's soul or character, it has to be because killing is wrong in the first place.[16]

C: Agreed. So what's left?

L: Well, obviously what's wrong with killing is the effects it has on the victim herself: "The loss of one's life deprives one of all the experiences, activities, projects, and enjoyments that would otherwise have constituted one's future. Therefore, killing someone is wrong, primarily because the killing inflicts (one of) the greatest possible losses on the victim ..."[17]

C: That seems obviously true. The person who suffers most is the victim.

L: Right but *why* does the victim suffer? Because they are deprived of all the valuable experiences that come with their future. The same kind of future that we would lose if we were killed; that is, the kind of future typically possessed by human beings. One full of experiences, projects, hopes, goals, friendships, love, self-affirmation – all these things.

C: I'm following you.

L: Well if this is true, then "it would seem that what makes killing *any* adult human being ... seriously wrong is the loss of his or her future."[18] This applies to children and infants also, wouldn't you say? Don't they too lose their future if killed?

C: That seems right to me too.

L: Ok, then, aren't embryos and fetuses deprived of *their* future when they are aborted? Here's another way of looking at it. If there is a property that makes killing morally wrong for adults, and that property is also possessed by a fetus, doesn't that mean it is morally wrong to kill the fetus for the exact same reason that it is morally wrong to kill the adult?[19]

C: I have to admit that this is a much better argument than the sanctity of life views you were first espousing.

L: I thought you would like it better. This view leaves open the possibility that certain kinds of euthanasia are morally permissible, which you seemed concerned with. Specifically, if the person in question does not have a valuable future ahead of her, it would be permissible, if she requested it, to euthanize her. So what happened with Brittany Maynard would be acceptable under this view.[20]

C: I'm surprised that you endorse it then.

L: Well, not completely. I still think it's wrong to kill even people who are sick and want to die, but I thought that this argument, at least, would be a good argument for why killing fetuses is morally wrong, at least to the same extent than killing any human being is morally wrong.

C: Well, not all abortions. Aborting a fetus that is sick and will likely suffer once born would be permissible under this view for the same reason euthanasia is. So aborting a fetus like Ronan wouldn't be immoral.

L: True enough, but you admit that the argument covers most abortions.

C: Well…

L: Ah! I should have known you have a comeback.

(e) Future-Like-ours arguments, contraception, and arguments from potential.

C: Well my immediate question is: doesn't this view mean contraception is immoral? When you use contraception, aren't you preventing the existence of a person with a future of value?

L: There is a distinction between killing an already existing individual who has a future of value, and *preventing* a possible person who would have a future of value had he existed. In one case, there is an actual subject of harm, and not in the other case. There is no individual who is harmed when contraception is used. The combination of sperm and egg would form an individual who has a future of value, but to avoid that potential combination does no one any harm.[21]

C: But contraception prevents a valuable future from being actualized, doesn't it?

L: It does, but we are under no moral obligation to create beings with valuable futures. Otherwise, women should be having babies every nine months to maximize the creation of valuable futures. No – we don't have an obligation to create beings with valuable futures, but once a being with a valuable future comes into existence, we have a moral obligation to not kill that being and deprive them of their valuable future.

C: Another question: isn't this just a rehashing of the argument from potential? That we should treat a potential person as if it were an actual person based on their potential? This argument seems to be saying that a fetus's potential for having a valuable future is the basis for grounding a prohibition against killing them. But didn't we see why that argument was problematic? A potential x does not have the same rights as an actual x.

L: Well I am not convinced that the argument from potential is as flawed as you think. Nevertheless, that is not relevant here. There is an important distinction between this argument and the argument from potential.

C: Explain the difference.

L: The argument from potential, as you stated it, relies not on what the fetus is now, but on what they will become in the future. Since it will become a person later, we should treat them as if they were a person now. Their potential personhood is a placeholder until the being becomes a person in their own right.

C: Right.

L: The future-like-ours argument is different from the argument from potential. In this argument, we are not looking towards what a fetus will *later* possess, we are looking at something an embryo or fetus *actually now* possesses. Embryos and fetuses actually now possess a future of value. Their potential is not a placeholder for the value they will come to acquire later. The possession of a valuable future is something they *now* have, something abortion deprives them of, therefore making them subjects of harm.[22]

(f) Alternative accounts of the wrongness of killing.

C: I am not yet convinced that a fetus has the same property that makes killing an adult wrong. Most people *want* to live; they desire continued life because they desire that their experiences continue. Someone like Brittany

Maynard did not desire that her life continue, and so euthanizing her was not morally wrong. So what I would say is that what makes killing wrong is not so much the deprivation of a valuable future, but the fact that killing frustrates someone's desire to continue living.[23]

L: I see where you're going with this. Since the fetus can't desire continued existence, killing them doesn't interfere with anyone's desire.

C: Right.

L: Well, I want to push back a bit here. Wouldn't we consider it wrong to kill someone who is suicidal and therefore does not desire continued existence? If someone is in a temporary coma, say a medically induced coma, and cannot desire their continued life at that moment, that does not mean it would be permissible to kill them while they're in that coma. What makes killing someone like Maynard permissible, under this theory, is not that she no longer desires life, but that her future is fraught of pain and suffering before her inevitable death.[24]

C: I guess that's right.

L: Plus, the reason we desire our lives is *because* of the valuable experiences that our future has in store for us. If someone was facing death at a young age, and we could somehow configure his brain so that he no longer desires his life, this does not make his death any less of a tragedy.[25]

C: I suppose that's right too.

L: Also this account, relying on the desire to live as the wrong-making feature of killing, would make killing infants permissible, since they do not yet have the mental capacity to desire continued existence. And while there are some philosophers who agree with that, we both agreed that was not something either of us could support.

C: True enough.

L: Well then it is possible that the death of a fetus is equally tragic, even though the fetus cannot desire continued existence. Their future is still full of all the experiences and activities that makes their life valuable. We could say that desiring your life adds to the reasons why it is morally wrong to kill someone, but it is not *the* main wrong-making feature of killing.

C: Ok, how about this one? What if what is wrong with killing is the *discontinuation* of valuable experiences? People value the experience of living and want that experience to continue.[26] But fetuses have not yet started experiencing anything. They have no experiences to continue or discontinue. The capacity to experience anything at all, as we discussed before, doesn't happen until, the very earliest, the second trimester of pregnancy.

L: But, again, what is wrong with discontinuing experiences, activities, goals, etc. is that those things are valuable in their own right. It would not be wrong, under this view, to discontinue a life such as Brittany Maynard's, because it is a life that is full of pain and suffering. So, again, what's doing the "heavy lifting" here, so to speak, is the value of the actual future, not just the discontinuing of experiences.[27] So it makes no difference whether one has past experiences or not – if their future is a valuable one, killing them is morally wrong.

C: But what if the fetus's future isn't valuable? What if it is a future where the child-to-be will grow up in poverty, or in foster care, or in an abusive home?

L: Those are definitely difficult circumstances for a baby to be born into. But difficult circumstances do not mean that life is devoid of value. Are you saying that it is better to not be born at all than to be born poor, or be in the foster care system, or in an abusive home? I bet if you talked to people who grew up poor, or in foster care, or in abusive homes, many of them will say that they are still glad that they were born. What we should be working for, as a society, are anti-poverty measures, or measures to reduce child abuse, rather than killing fetuses because they would be born in such circumstances.

C: Yeah, I guess you're right about that. I don't want to say that it is better not to be born than to be born poor. I never looked at it that way. But I will say that I find it funny that politicians who consistently argue against abortion also consistently argue against the social welfare programs that would help care for and sustain these children.[28]

L: You're not going to get any argument from me on that account. I am dismayed by this as well.

C: Hooray! Another area of agreement!

L: So have I convinced you that fetuses have futures of value of which abortion wrongly deprives them? Do you agree that the same thing that makes killing you and me wrong makes killing fetuses wrong?

(g) Do fetuses have futures of value?

C: I am not sure I am ready to commit to that. I still don't think fetuses *have* futures of value the same way you and I have futures of value.

L: What would be the relevant differences between our future of value and a fetus's future of value?

C: When I think about my future, I have a representation of my self enjoying the fruits of that future. Killing me deprives me of a future that I can represent to myself: it dashes my hopes, my dreams, my goals. It robs me of a future that I have created for myself. But in order to be able to do this, I must be self-aware or self-conscious. I have to be able to picture myself as an individual who will live in the future. So we're back to self-consciousness being necessary again. Fetuses don't have futures of value the same way you and I do. You aren't depriving a fetus of their hopes and dreams and goals because they have none of these yet.[29]

L: But by that same argument, you wouldn't be depriving an infant of her future because they aren't capable of self-representation. Or even some adults. What if someone is mentally disabled such that she is unable to formulate any future goals or dreams? Would it be permissible to kill her? Or what about a person who can formulate future goals or dreams but just doesn't because he couldn't care less about his future? Would it be permissible to kill him?[30]

C: It's still different. Fetuses don't have a personal future in the same way these individuals have a personal future. In these cases we have human beings who are sufficiently psychologically connected with their future selves.

L: What does that mean, "psychologically connected"?

C: It means that we are mentally connected with our future and past selves. That we, for example, make a goal and then enjoy the fruits of achieving that goal. That we have an intention at one time, and then follow through with that intention. Another example is that we have character traits that continue over time. Or that we experience something and then have a memory of that thing.[31] It's our day-to-day mental connections.

L: Ok, but that, like other things we've talked about, seems to assume rather robust mental capacities. A baby doesn't have psychological connections that are like that.

C: Babies are sentient and conscious beings, though. They are psychologically connected to their future in at least a rudimentary way. They may have undeveloped minds, but they have minds nevertheless. They have desires, and feelings, and perceptions.

L: They do.

C: It is true that the older you get, the more sophisticated or robust your psychological connections become. And the more robust your psychological connections are the more your future is properly *your* future.[32] But a fetus, who lacks any psychological complexity at all, is just not at all mentally connected to a person so as to properly denote that person's life as part of the fetus's future. In order to get to a point where the fetus is sufficiently psychologically connected to their future, a lot of things have to go right. Specifically, they have to be successfully gestated in the body of another human being. A baby, at least, has begun her psychological connection with a future person. A pre-conscious fetus has not begun that journey.[33]

L: I don't see why having a mental life is important for determining whether fetuses have futures of value. A fetus may not be able to formulate goals, desires and so forth, but I don't see how it takes away from their future being *their* future, regardless of whether they have mental connections to their future.

(h) Is the fetus the same being that will later enjoy a future?

C: I think that we're having a different conversation now. It seems that now we're thinking about what philosophers call personal identity: *is* the fetus the same being who will later come to enjoy that future?

L: I am not sure I follow.

C: Remember last time we talked you said that sperm and ova were the ingredients to make a future person, but were not themselves a future person. You then said that if we followed your life in reverse, from adulthood back to childhood and infancy, you would pin-point the beginning of yourself as being when the embryo first came into existence. You were making a claim about personal identity here: you said that the embryo or fetus is the same individual as you are now. You even explicitly said that there was an "identity relation between an embryo and the person the embryo becomes." If that's true, then your life now (which is undoubtedly valuable) was the embryo's or fetus's future of value.

L: You're right, I did make that claim. But I fail to see how such a claim is controversial. It seems clear to me that I was an embryo, and then a fetus, and then a baby, child, and adult. It's all one continuous line.

C: But I want to press you on that, because it is not at all clear to me that this line is as continuous as you say. Let me begin with a distinction. Philosophers make a distinction between accidental properties and essential properties in a person. An accidental property is a property that you may possess, or cease possessing, and it would pose no change to your identity. For example, your hair color is an accidental property. You can change it a million times and you would still be you. But an essential property is one that you must possess in order to retain your identity. Without that property, you cease being who you are.

L: Ok, I am following that distinction.

C: Philosophers have long debated whether there are any essential properties and, if so, what they are. Can you think of an essential property?

L: Well my immediate thought is that it is our soul that makes us who we are. My soul is my essential property.

C: I thought you'd say something like that. But if you want to go down that road, you'd need to explain what a soul is, and give an argument, or evidence, that we even have one. Even if you did all that successfully, you'd then have to argue that a fetus has a soul, and that it acquired that soul at conception, or very shortly thereafter. That's a lot.

L: That *is* a lot. Ok fine. I will leave it out for now. How about our DNA? That seems like a good candidate for an essential property.

C: It is true that your DNA is what makes you a unique individual, but that's not enough for claiming it is an essential property that makes you you. Identical twins have the same DNA, but they are still two distinct human beings, right? They aren't the same person.[34]

L: That is clearly true.

C: There was even a study done on identical twins, one who lived for a year in space, and it was noted that there were changes to his DNA after all that time.[35] So your DNA can change, and you would still be you.

L: Ok, so what's left? Is there anything that is an essential property?

C: Let me propose a possible essential property: you are an *individual* human being. There is only one of you, and you cannot fission off into another human being.

L: Ok, that seems obvious.

(i) A fertilized egg is not an individual human being.

C: Ok, but some philosophers argue that a newly fertilized egg is not yet an individual human being because all newly fertilized eggs can potentially form multiples; twins, or triplets, for example.

L: But most embryos do not form multiples.

C: Right. Most do not, but that's not relevant. The point is that every newly fertilized egg has the *capacity* to form multiples. In a lab you can divide newly fertilized eggs to create twin embryos artificially. This shows that fertilized eggs are malleable. They are not yet a single individual human being.[36]

L: Ok, so when does the fertilized egg become a single individual human being?

C: About two weeks after fertilization, the "primitive streak" begins to form, which is the precursor to the formation of the nervous system. It's the beginning of the human animal – an individual functioning human organism.[37]

L: Well then this is a moot point for abortion because by the time a woman realizes she is pregnant two weeks have surely passed. The embryo has implanted and the individual has started to grow.

C: Right, but it throws a wrench into the whole "life begins at conception" mantra. At conception we still have the "ingredients" for an individual, just like sperm and ova, but not yet an individual. It also has implications for embryo research. As long as the research is done before the embryo is two weeks old, the research is not yet destroying a human individual.

L: Ok, fine, I can concede your point. It is still irrelevant for abortions, since the time for possible twinning has passed by the time you find out you are pregnant.

(j) Personal identity consists in the persistence of a human organism.

C: Ok, but then that leads us to another question about the creation of identity. You want to say that you began to exist when your functioning organism began to exist, right? That the embryonic organism and the fetal organism was you, and that, therefore, your life now was their future back then.

L: Right.

C: So, if true, that means that we have found another essential trait: we are essentially human animals. We come into existence when the human animal does, we persist so long as our animal organism persists, and we die when our animal organism dies.[38]

L: Ok, I'm following.

C: The "future-like ours" account seems to tacitly assume this view of identity as well. It has to. In order for a certain future to properly "belong" to an embryo or fetus, we have to assume that the embryo or fetus is the same individual who will later come to enjoy that future.

L: I don't have a problem with that at all.

C: But what if I challenge the view that our identity consists in the creation and persistence of our animal organism. What if it is something else?

L: What else can it be?

(k) Personal identity consists in the continuation of mental contents.

C: You remember all those movies when you were a kid where the grown-up and the kid switched bodies for a while? In those movies, you go where your mind goes, right? That's what made those movies funny – the idea that a kid is walking around in a grown person's body and vice-versa. We know, of course, that such a scenario is impossible. Our mind is the product of our brain functioning in a certain way, and in these movies there is no brain transplant.

L: Still, movies like that test our intuition about personal identity. In these movies, the person goes wherever their mind goes.

C: Right, but let's imagine a different scenario. Say that it *were* possible to perform a whole brain transplant, so that your brain can reside in a different body. What do you think happens to you in those circumstances?

L: I would think that I now have a new body – that I went along with my brain.

C: Right, and that's the case because you have a continuation of consciousness with that brain. All your mental contents – your likes, dislikes, desires, goals, memories – all of them are preserved in your new body. You didn't go with your body, you went where your mind, your functioning brain, went.

L: Right.

C: But notice that this contradicts the view that we are essentially human animals and organisms. This view of personal identity means that I exist, not if my organism persists, but so long as my mental contents persists. That is, as long as my memories, beliefs character traits, goals, dreams, etc. persist.[39]

L: Ok. I get what you're saying.

C: Well then that means that you didn't really begin to exist when your organism began to exist. Rather, you began to exist when you started forming those beliefs, desires, memories, and goals. And that you persist in existence only as long as those mental contents persist as well.

L: I can see the attraction of this view because of the view that we go where our brains go. But there is still a couple of problems with this view. First, as we have talked about before, having the mental capacity to form goals, beliefs, desires and memories doesn't happen in fetushood, but it doesn't happen in infancy either. Do you mean to say that I was never an infant? Because that seems absurd to me. Also, what about if I am in the advanced stages of dementia? Most of our memories, goals, beliefs, desires, and even character traits are gone by then. Do we say that's not me either? Did I already die and this organism, a sick one, isn't really me anymore?

(I) Personal identity consists in the continuation of a conscious mind.

C: I can see why that would be problematic, yes. Let me push back a bit. If someone has an accident, and is in a coma for 10 years before their organism finally died, when would you say the actual individual died: at the time their organism died, or at the time they went into the coma?

L: Well, legally we aren't dead until all our brain has stopped functioning. When there is no brain activity that can be detected. That's when we consider our organisms no longer functional.

C: That's the legal definition of death, true enough. But notice that if we went with that definition, this entails that very early abortions are not problematic because there is a lack of brain activity in the first few weeks after conception.[40] But I want to get away from the legal definition of death for a minute. Let's look at it another way. Are you familiar with the Terri Schiavo case in 2005?

L: I remember reading about that. This was the case where the husband and her family were fighting over who should get to decide her fate. She was in a vegetative state for many years and the husband wanted her feeding tube removed so she can die and her parents disagreed.

C: Right, that's the one. Well her tombstone, that her husband designed, has two "death dates" on it. It has the date she physically died in 2005 and the date she went into a vegetative state in 1990. Specifically, it is written that she "departed" in 1990 and was "at peace" in 2005.

L: That's an interesting distinction.

C: Think about what that distinction illustrates. That her mind, the individual she was, died when she went into her vegetative state, and her organism died later. This makes a distinction between the organism and the mind too; that the mind can go out of existence, if our brains no longer have cortical function, while the organism is still functioning. If we believe that Terri died when her mind died, when she went into the persistent vegetative state, then we are saying that we are not organisms after all because our organism can still function even when the mind has ceased to exist. Again, I go where my mind goes; or, put another way, I go where my cortical-functioning brain goes.

L: How is this point different than the one we just said was problematic?

C: What if personal identity is not about retaining *mental contents*, so to speak, like memories, goals, and desires, but, instead just retaining the *capacity for consciousness* in some way? Even if it's just a rudimentary consciousness, even if it's just sentience. As long as your brain continuous to function in a manner that allows the capacity for basic consciousness, you retain your personal identity.[41]

L: What are the consequences of such a view?

C: Well, in the previous theory we considered, that personal identity had to do with the retention of mental contents, it would mean that you had no identity relationship between the infant you developed from, or someone in the advanced stages of dementia. I agreed with you that this was problematic. According to this view, however, you would indeed share an identity relationship with your infant self, or your self in the advanced stages of dementia, because in these cases your brain retains the capacity for consciousness. It also can account for the intuition that you go where your brain goes, since what is needed for the preservation of consciousness is the brain functioning in a certain way.

L: I see where this is going. Just like the individual who was Terri Schiavo "died" when her consciousness ceased to exist in 1990, this means that we do not begin to exist until our brain is able to generate the capacity for consciousness. So personal identity is symmetrical between the end of life and the beginning of life. So we're back to the importance of consciousness again.

C: Right. Consciousness is important for two reasons. As we talked about last time, consciousness is needed before we can be said to have interests. And, as we are talking about today, consciousness is needed in order for someone's personal identity to commence.

L: What are the implications of this view for abortion?

C: Well, according to this view, we are a mind with an organism, but we are not the organism itself. This means that you were mistaken when you said we can trace your existence to the embryonic stage. According to this view, we were never embryos or early fetuses. My organism existed during the embryonic and early fetal stage of development, but *I*, my mind, had not yet come into existence. I came into existence when my brain developed the capacity for consciousness – around mid to late gestation, as we talked about last time. Or, put another way, an embryo and an early fetus is a some*thing*, but not yet a some*one*.[42]

L: I see where you're going with this. Relating this back to the "future like ours" view, this means that embryos and early fetuses have no futures yet because who you are – your conscious mind – has not yet come into existence. Fetuses gain a valuable future when their respective mind begins to exist – at the onset of consciousness.

C: Right. Under this view, early abortion *prevents* the existence of an individual with a conscious mind. Before the capacity for consciousness commences, no one exists yet with a valuable future.

L: But shouldn't we let the fetus grow into a being who has the capacity for consciousness and, therefore, a valuable future?

C: But you said earlier, when discussing contraception, that we are under no moral obligation to create new individuals, just to take care of individuals who already exist.

L: You're right, I did say that.

C: Well, apply that same logic here. If aborting a pre con scious fetus is just the prevention of someone with a valuable future, and we are under no moral obligation to create new individuals, then we are under no moral obligation to allow pre-conscious fetuses to attain the capacity for consciousness. Early abortions are more like contraception in this way – they both prevent the existence of an individual with a valuable future.[43] Later abortions are different in that they do kill an existing someone with a valuable future, unless the fetus is so sick that it precludes a valuable future, like Ronan.

L: But let's say we go back to the view that personal identity is not about having the capacity for consciousness but having the same functioning organism over time, so that we began to exist in the embryonic stage, when our organisms first came into existence. Would you then grant me that we can indeed say that fetuses have valuable futures that abortion terminates?

C: Here is where I could agree with you. *If* we assume this view of personal identity, then the embryo and fetus do share an identity relation with a future person, so that that person's life is the embryo's future. But I don't accept that view of personal identity. I am more inclined toward the belief that I began to exist when my brain became capable of cortical function and therefore when I gained the capacity for consciousness.

L: Ha! I got some pro-life view out of you! If we assume that we are organisms, in any case.

(m) Does death harm a fetus to the same degree as it harms a person?

C: Don't celebrate just yet. Even if I agreed that embryos and fetuses have valuable futures, I still don't think that depriving the embryo and fetus of that future is as harmful as killing a child or an adult or any other person. Some kinds of deaths are worse than others.

L: I don't understand how that would be possible. Death is death, and it's all equally bad.

C: It's not. Let's go back to the Terri Schiavo example. Let's say that we agreed that she finally died when her organism did. Still, she had not a single moment of conscious awareness between the time she was diagnosed in a persistent vegetative state and the time she finally died. So an earlier death would not have harmed her, since she had no prospects to ever get back her conscious life. Continued life did not benefit her in any way. And the death of her organism did not harm her in any way. This is not the case for someone who is in a temporary coma. Death *would* harm her, because she had a conscious life to look forward to.

L: Ok, but the embryo and fetus has a conscious life to look forward to as well. So in that sense, they are like persons in a temporary coma.

C: But a person in a temporary coma will *continue* their already established conscious mind. Once she regains consciousness, it would be a *continuation* of her mind, not a creation of a new mind. That is, there would still be psychological connections between the person pre-coma and post-coma. Embryos and fetuses don't have any psychological connections with their future self – no goals, no memories, no beliefs, no desires. I can grant you, for the sake of argument, that it may be their future, but for all intents and purposes, it may just as well be someone else's future.

L: But didn't we agree that mental contents or psychological connections isn't necessary for personal identity to subsist?

C: Even if strong psychological connections may not be necessary for personal identity, I still think it's relevant for how much death harms the person in question. The less psychologically connected you are to your future, the less harm you sustain by not being allowed to attain that future. And the reverse is also true: the more psychologically connected you are to your future, the more death harms you.[44]

L: I am not convinced that there is a relationship between psychological connectedness and how harmful death is.

C: Well fair enough, but how about this. Even if I grant you that fetuses have valuable futures, even if I grant you that psychological connections are irrelevant, and even if I grant you that death does harm an embryo and fetus to some degree, I *still* don't think that abortions are morally wrong, because I am not convinced that the fetus's moral right to life, if it even has a moral right to life at all, entails that they need to be given whatever they need for survival. Say that what you really need for survival is a blood transfusion, and I am a perfect match. I still don't think you have a right to my blood, even if not giving it to you would harm you.

L: So now we're getting into bodily autonomy arguments. That seems like a discussion for another day. We've covered a lot of ground today. But I have to say that this conversation has been tricky. I am starting to see how abortion is a much more complex and nuanced issue than I thought it was.

C: There's one thing I think is really important to note here. Many of our differences here are not moral differences. We both agree that killing innocent persons is morally wrong – we just disagree on what "personhood" means. We may both agree that killing someone with a valuable future is morally wrong, but we can disagree on when the individual comes into existence.

L: I think it's helpful to keep that in mind. They may be less vitriol surrounding this debate if people took the time to really dialogue like we have. I've really enjoyed our conversation.

C: I really enjoyed it too, and I admire that you tried to defend abortion in ways that were not directly related to religion, even though you are religious.

L: Well I think that this is part of living in a religiously pluralistic society, as you said. If you're going to talk about important issues with people from all walks of life, then you have to do it in a way that speaks to them. I can't expect a non-Christian to agree with me that abortion is wrong if I only offer Christian reasons why I believe that.[45]

C: Well how about we come back tomorrow. I think it's my turn to do homework so I can better defend my pro-choice view.

L: Will do. Same time and same place tomorrow.

Notes

1 John Paul II. *The Gospel of Life: Evangelium Vitae*. (1995). United States Conference of Catholic Bishops, p. 107.

2 John Paul II, 1995, p. 5

3 John Paul II, 1995, pp. 99–100.

4 Plato. *The Republic* (1990). Oxford University Press. In reference to euthanasia, Plato writes: "Then you will establish in your state physicians and judges which as we have described. They will look after those citizens whose bodies and souls are constitutionally sound. The physically unsound they will leave to die ..." (p. 100). In reference to infanticide, Plato writes: "... a man shall not take his daughter or daughter's daughter or mother or mother's mother, nor a woman her son or father or her son's son or father's father, and all this only after we have exhorted to see that no child, if any be conceived, shall be brought to light, or, if they cannot prevent its birth, to dispose of it on the understanding that no such child can be reared" (p. 161).

5 Aristotle. *The Politics* (1996). Cambridge University Press. Aristotle writes: "as to the exposure and rearing of children, let there be a law that no deformed child shall live ... if couples have children in excess, let abortion be procured before sense and life have begun" (p. 192).

6 Aristotle writes: "for that some should rule and others be ruled is a thing not only necessary, but expedient; from the hour of their birth, some are marked out for subjection, others for rule... it is clear, then, that some men are by nature free, and others slaves, and that for these latter slavery is both expedient and right" (pp. 16–17).

7 See: BBC News. "Hillsborough Stories: Anthony David Bland." (2014). https://www.bbc.com/news/uk-england-27224172

8 See: The Brittany Maynard Fund (2022) – http://thebrittanyfund.org/about/

9 John Paul II, 1995, p. 27.

10 Emily Rapp. "Rick Santorum, Meet My Son." (2012). https://slate.com/human-interest/2012/02/rick-santorum-and-prenatal-testing-i-would-have-saved-my-son-from-his-suffering.html

11 For an extensive view of the *mizuko kuyo* ritual, see: Jeff Wilson. *Mourning the Unborn Dead: A Buddhist Ritual Comes to America* (2009). Oxford University Press.

12 For example: "Life does not begin at conception under Jewish law. Sources in the Talmud note that the fetus is 'mere water' before 40 days of gestation. Following this period, the fetus is considered a physical part of the pregnant individual's body, not yet having life of its own or independent rights. The fetus is not viewed as separate from the parent's body until birth begins and the first breath of oxygen into the lungs allows the soul to enter the body" (National Council of Jewish Women. "Judaism and Abortion." (2019) https://www.ncjw.org/wp-content/uploads/2019/05/Judaism-and-Abortion-FINAL.pdf).

13 Lindsay Schnell. "Jews, Outraged by Restrictive Abortion Laws, are Invoking the Hebrew Bible in the Debate." (2019). https://www.usatoday.com/story/news/nation/2019/07/24/abortion-laws-jewish-faith-teaches-life-does-not-start-conception/1808776001/

14 Schnell, 2019.

15 Don Marquis. "Why Abortion is Immoral." (1989). *Journal of Philosophy*, 86.4: 183–202. He writes: "It might be said that what makes killing us wrong is the great loss others would experience due to our absence. Although such hubris is understandable, such an explanation does not account for the wrongness of killing hermits, or those whose lives are relatively independent and whose friends find it easy to make new friends" (p. 189).

16 Marquis, 1989: "It might be said that what makes killing us wrong is that a killing brutalizes the one who kills. But the brutalization consists of being inured to the performance of an act that is hideously immoral; hence, the brutalization does not explain the immorality" (p. 189).

17 Marquis, 1989: "The effect of the loss of my biological life is the loss to me of all those activities, projects, experiences, and enjoyments which would otherwise have constituted my future personal life. These activities, projects, experiences, and enjoyments are either valuable for their own sakes or are means to something else that is valuable for its own sake. Some parts of my future are not valued by me now, but will come to be valued by me as I grow older and as my values and capacities change. When I am killed, I am deprived both of what I now value which would have been part of my future personal life, but also what I would come to value. Therefore, when I die, I am deprived of all of the value of my future. Inflicting this loss on me is ultimately what makes killing me wrong" (pp. 189–190).

18 Marquis, 1989, p. 190.

19 Marquis, 1989: "The future of a standard fetus includes a set of experiences, projects, activities, and such which are identical with the futures of adult human beings and are identical with the futures of young children. Since the reason that is sufficient to explain why it is wrong to kill human beings after the time of birth is a reason that also applies to fetuses, it follows that abortion is prima facie seriously morally wrong" (p. 192).

20 Marquis, 1989: "the claim that the loss of one's future is the wrong-making feature of one's being killed does not entail, as sanctity of human life theories do, that active euthanasia is wrong. Persons who are severely and incurably ill, who face a future of pain and despair, and who wish to die will not have suffered a loss if they are killed. It is, strictly speaking, the value of a human's future which makes killing wrong in this theory. This being so, killing does not necessarily wrong some persons who are sick and dying" (p. 191).

21 Marquis, 1989: "At the time of contraception, there are hundreds of millions of sperm, one (released) ovum and millions of possible combinations of all of these. There is no actual combination at all. Is the subject of the loss to be a merely possible combination? Which one? This alternative does not yield an actual subject

of harm either. Accordingly, the immorality of contraception is not entailed by the loss of a future-like-ours argument simply because there is no nonarbitrarily identifiable subject of the loss in the case of contraception" (pp. 201–202).

22 Marquis, 1989: "Of course, embryos can be victims: when their lives are deliberately terminated, they are deprived of their futures of value, their prospects. This makes them victims, for it directly wrongs them" (p. 200).

23 Marquis, 1989: Marquis calls this the "desire account" of the wrongness of killing: "Another rival account is based upon the obvious fact that people strongly desire to continue to live. This suggests that what makes killing us so wrong is that it interferes with the fulfillment of a strong and fundamental desire, the fulfillment of which is necessary for the fulfillment of any other desires we might have. Let us call this the desire account" (p. 195).

24 Marquis, 1989: "One problem with the desire account is that we do regard it as seriously wrong to kill persons who have little desire to live or who have no desire to live or, indeed, have a desire not to live. We believe it is seriously wrong to kill the unconscious, the sleeping, those who are tired of life, and those who are suicidal. The value-of-a-human- future account renders standard morality intelligible in these cases; these cases appear to be incompatible with the desire account" (p. 196).

25 Marquis, 1989: "The desire account is subject to a deeper difficulty. We desire life, because we value the goods of this life. The goodness of life is not secondary to our desire for it. If this were not so, the pain of one's own premature death could be done away with merely by an appropriate alteration in the configuration of one's desires. This is absurd. Hence, it would seem that it is the loss of the goods of one's future, not the interference with the fulfillment of a strong desire to live, which accounts ultimately for the wrongness of killing" (p. 196).

26 Marquis, 1989: Marquis calls this the "discontinuation account" of killing: "… people value the experience of living and wish for that valuable experience to continue. Therefore, it might be said, what makes killing wrong is the discontinuation of that experience for the victim" (p. 195).

27 Marquis, 1989: "If the patient's future is a future of value, we want our account to make it wrong to kill the patient. If the patient's future is intolerable, whatever his or her immediate past, we want our account to allow killing the patient. Obviously, then, it is the value of that patient's future which is doing the work in rendering the morality of killing the patient intelligible. This being the case, it seems clear that whether one has immediate past experiences or not does no work in the explanation of what makes killing wrong. The addition the discontinuation account makes to the value of a human future account is otiose. Its addition to the value-of-a-future account plays no role at all in rendering intelligible the wrongness of killing. Therefore, it can be discarded with the discontinuation account of which it is a part" (p. 197).

28 For example, the Children's Defense Fund Action Council releases a nonpartisan Legislative Report Card, which looks at each member of Congress legislative voting record on policies and programs meant to benefit children, particularly poor and disadvantaged children. Consistently, most Congresspersons who receive a low grade for their voting records are self-proclaimed pro-life advocates. For the latest account of these scores, see: https://cdfactioncouncil.org/reportcard.

29 Mark T. Brown. "The Morality of Abortions and the Deprivation of Futures" (2000). *Journal of Medical Ethics,* 26: 103–107. Brown refers to this kind of future as a "self-represented future of value", and he explains it thusly: "Persons care about their self-represented futures and their memories, their self-represented past, because this self-conception defines who they are and confers meaning and significance upon what they think and do … Killing a person deprives her of this future:

her hopes and dreams are dashed, her goals unfulfilled, her sins unforgiven, longed for reunions and reconciliations never occur. All of this happens in the present, to a person able to unite in a moment of self-consciousness a personal past, present and future" (p. 105).

30 Don Marquis. "Deprivations, Futures, and the Wrongness of Killing." (2001). *Journal of Medical Ethics*, 27: 363–369. "Suppose that Alice, due to severe bipolar disease, is now unable to represent to herself any remotely desirable future of value. Is it permissible to kill Alice because she lacks a self-represented future of value? Surely not. Why not? After Alice is treated for her mental illness, Alice's life will be actually valuable to her ... Consider Charles who lives only for the present and believes that thinking about one's future is a waste of time. 'Eat, drink, and be merry, for tomorrow we may die' he says. Consider the adolescent who has no concept of the value of the life of anyone so old as to be over twenty-five. Surely killing both Charles and the adolescent is wrong, not only because it deprives them of the quite limited life they envisage, but because it also deprives them of the considerable span of life they (probably) will come to value" (p. 367).

31 Jeff McMahan. *The Ethics of Killing: Problems at the Margins of Life* (2002). Oxford University Press. McMahan offers the following examples of "direct psychological connections": "the relation between an experience and a memory of it, the relation between the formation of a desire and the experience of the satisfaction or frustration of that desire, and the relation of an earlier and later manifestation of a belief, value, intention, or character trait." (p. 39).

32 Peter K. McInerney. "Does a Fetus Already Have a Future-Like-Ours" (1990). *The Journal of Philosophy* 87.5: 264–268: "A fetus at an early stage of development has neither a mental life of feelings, beliefs, and desires nor a developed brain and nervous system. There are none of the main relations with a personal future which exist in persons. Although there is some biological continuity between them so that there is a sense in which the later person stages 'are the future' of the fetus, the fetus is so little connected to the later personal life that it cannot be deprived of that personal life. At its time the fetus does not already 'possess' that future personal life in the way that a normal adult human already 'possesses' his future personal life" (p. 267).

33 McInerney, 1990: "A fetus is separated from a personal future by many 'layers' of possibility. The possibilities that are available to a person or even to a young infant are not now available to the fetus. Only if the fetus develops in the right ways (favorable possibilities become present) will it acquire the capacities that make available the infant's possibilities. A great deal of favorable development would be necessary before the fetus could control its future in the way that persons do. The fetus does not now have a personal future" (p. 267).

34 Norman M. Ford. *When Did I Begin? Conception of the Human Individual in History, Philosophy, and Science*. (1991). Cambridge University Press. Ford distinguishes between genetic individuality and ontological individuality, where "ontological individuality" is defined as the "continuous existence of the same body" (p. 91). Ford writes "the existence of identical twins shows that genetic and ontological identity or individuality are not equivalent. The genetic code in the zygote does not suffice to constitute or define a human individual in an ontological sense. Identical twins have the same genetic code but they are distinct ontological individuals" (p. 117).

35 See: Francine E. Garrett-Bakelman, Manjula A. Darshi *et al.* "The NASA Twins Study: A Multidimensional Analysis of a Year-Long Human Spaceflight." (2019) *Science*, 364.6436. https://science.sciencemag.org/content/364/6436/eaau8650

36 Ford, 1991: "The continuity of the same ontological individual ceases when the zygote forms twins. The zygote is not the same ontological individual as either one of the eventual twins that result from its development ... this line of reasoning

does not only apply to those zygotes that actually do give rise to identical twins. It applies across the board to all zygotes, insofar as they all have the natural active potential to form identical twins that may develop into adults, given suitable conditions (pp. 119–120).

37 Ford, 1991: "The appearance of the primitive streak is an important landmark. Indicating the position of the embryo proper with the main features of the new individual's body plan ... the appearance of one primitive streak signals that only one embryo proper and human individual has been formed and begun to exist. Prior to this stage it would be pointless to speak about the presence of a true human being in an ontological sense. A human individual could scarcely exist before a definitive human body is formed" (p. 172).

38 McMahan, 2002: McMahan describes this view of personal identity thusly: "... there remains only one view that seems compatible with the idea that we begin to exist at conception. This is the view that we are essentially human organisms, or, to be more precise, that each of us is numerically identical with a particular human organism or human animal ... the view that each of us is numerically identical with a particular human organism entails that one's history is the history of an organism. The beginning of one's existence necessarily coincides with the coming into existence of an organism and one will cease to exist when that organism does" (pp. 24 and 29).

39 McMahan, 2002: McMahan calls this the "Psychological Account of Personal Identity": "According to the Psychological Account, psychological continuity is the criterion of personal identity. Thus a person P1 at time T1 and a person P2 at T2 are one of the same person only if P2 is psychologically continuous with P1" (p. 40). Psychological continuity is defined by having "strong psychological connectedness" which means that the "number of direct psychological connections from day to day is at least half the number that hold over each day in the life of a normal person" (p. 43).

40 McMahan, 2002: "... if the beginning and end of life must be symmetrical, the idea that an organism dies when brain death occurs implies that [the embryo] begins to be alive (and therefore begins to exist) when brain life occurs – that is, with the onset of significant brain function. But given that there does not appear to be any capacity for significant brain function until at least eight weeks after fertilization, it follows that the human embryo from two to eight weeks after fertilization ... cannot be an individual at all, but is instead a mere bundle or physically contiguous but otherwise isolated tissue and organs" (p. 437).

41 McMahan, 2002: McMahan calls this view the "Embodied Mind Account of Personal Identity": "I suggest that the corresponding criterion of personal identity is the continued existence and functioning ... of enough of the same brain to be capable of generating consciousness or mental activity. This criterion stresses the survival of one's basic psychological capacities, in particular to capacity for consciousness. It does not require continuity of any particular content of one's mental life" (p. 68).

42 McMahan, 2002: "We do not begin to exist until our organisms develop the capacity to generate consciousness. Only then is there *someone* present rather than merely *something*" (p. 267).

43 McMahan, 2002: "If the Embodied Mind Account is right, there is no one to be affected for the better or worse by an early abortion other than the pregnant women, her partner, and anyone else who might care about her or her possible progeny. An early abortion does not kill anyone; it merely prevents someone from coming into existence. In this respect, it is relevantly like contraception and wholly unlike the killing of a person. For there is, again, no one there to be killed" (p. 267).

44 McMahan, 2002: McMahan calls this the "Time Relativist Interest Account" of the harm of death: "The strength of an individual's time-relative interest in continuing to live is itself a function of two factors: first, the amount of future good that the individual may rationally anticipate in an egoistic way, and, second, the degree to which the prudential unity relations would hold between the individual now and itself in the future when the goods it may egoistically anticipate would occur ["prudential unity relations" is defined as "psychological connectedness and psychological continuity" (p. 42)]. In the case of a developed fetus, the amount of good that lies in prospect is normally very great. But the prudential unity relations would hold only very weakly between the fetus and itself in the future. The developed fetus … has no psychological architecture – no beliefs, desires, or dispositions of character – to carry forward into the future. It is, in short, psychologically cut off or severed or isolated from itself in the future. Its future is, figuratively speaking, relevantly like someone else's future" (pp. 275–276).

45 Bertha Alvarez Manninen and Jack Mulder Jr. *A Civil Dialogue on Abortion* (2018), Routledge: "Another pitfall I want to suggest for the pro-life position is to avoid the error of couching its rhetoric too heavily in religious language when speaking in a public forum … while I have no problem with turning to sacred texts for guidance in one's own religious and moral life, when one lives in a religiously pluralistic society, I think one needs to be able to articulate one's convictions about just laws on such important matters as the nature and limits of human life in ways that do not draw all their force from scared texts one cannot expect the rest of the population to revere" (written by Mulder, p. 68).

4

DAY 4

The Bodily Autonomy Argument

Day 4 – Scene: Next day, L and C have come back together at the university coffee shop to discuss some pro-choice arguments

C: Welcome back!

L: Good to be back. What's on the agenda today?

(a) Abortion and the security persons.

C: Last time we talked and dissected some pro-life arguments. So it looks like today is my turn. I want to discuss a famous version of the bodily of autonomy argument. It's such an often-used argument, it merits some discussion. I also want to point out that, like we talked about our first day, I want to argue that women have a *moral* right to an abortion. Abortion is already legal in the United States, so women already have a legal right to an abortion (and hopefully it stays that way). So my arguments here are moral ones.

L: Ok then. Let's begin.

C: Bodily autonomy arguments are affirmed in other countries where abortion is legal. For example, Canada. Did you know that abortion is legal in Canada throughout all stages of pregnancy? Their laws are much more liberal than ours when it comes to abortion.

L: I did not know that.

C: Well, their abortion case was fought much later than ours, in 1988 in a case known as *R. vs. Morgentaler.* The Canadian Supreme Court decided that criminalizing abortion was unconstitutional because it violated women's rights under

DOI: 10.4324/9781003109457-4

Canada's Charter of Rights. Specifically that restrictions on abortion violated a women's "security of person."

L: What is meant by "security of person"?

C: Well, I brought the text of the case so we can read it together. It reads: "State interference with bodily integrity and serious state-imposed psychological stress, at least in the criminal law context, constitutes a breach of security of the person. Section 251 clearly interferes with a woman's physical and bodily integrity. Forcing a woman, by threat of criminal sanction, to carry a foetus to term unless she meets certain criteria unrelated to her own priorities and aspirations, is a profound interference with a woman's body and thus an infringement of security of the person"[1] So it appears that "security of person" refers to a violation of a person's bodily autonomy or integrity.

L: So I'll say right now what I have always thought of these kinds of arguments: bodily autonomy is all well and good when you are solely discussing *your* bodily autonomy. I don't disagree that we have a right to decide what happens with our bodies. But once you're pregnant, you're also talking about the bodily integrity of another human being. Doesn't the baby's bodily autonomy matter?

C: Well, let's talk about that. We've spent an awful lot of time discussing whether fetuses are persons, or whether they have valuable futures. For all the reasons I have stated, I think there are good reasons for concluding that they aren't persons and that they don't have futures in the same sense that you and I have futures. But let's forget that for a moment. Let's say I grant you that fetuses are persons and that killing them deprives them of a future. Let's say that they do have a moral right to life. Still, I want to show you that even granting all this, it still does not follow that women have a moral obligation to gestate them, especially against their will.

L: Ok, let's hear the argument.

(b) Is the right to life a positive right?

C: Well let's begin by asking what the right to life is a right to. That is, what is entailed by having a right to life? There are two kinds of rights: positive rights and negative rights.

L: Positive rights like good rights, and negative rights like bad rights?

C: No it has nothing to do with the goodness or badness of a right.

L: Then explain it to me please.

C: Negative rights are rights of non-interference; that is, the right to be left alone. They create in others a duty to not interfere in whatever is the subject of that right. So, for example, our right to freedom of religion is a negative right. We have the right to worship as see we see fit and the government cannot interfere in that free worship. Freedom of speech is also a negative right, in that the government cannot interfere or punish me for the content of my speech (within limits of course. I still cannot falsely yell "fire" in a crowded theatre).

L: Ok I'm following.

C: Then there are positive rights, which is a right to be provided with, or given, something. It creates in others an obligation to provide you with some goods or service. So if the right to religious freedom were a positive right, that means that I must be provided with the means to facilitate free worship, say continual access to a chapel or church.

L: Are there any examples of positive rights in the law? I'm having a hard time thinking of any. Seems like our more important rights are all negative ones.

C: Well, one example of a positive right is our right to legal counsel and an impartial jury in the event we are charged with a crime. If we cannot acquire legal counsel ourselves, the state is required to provide us with one, and they are required to provide us with a jury of our peers. This is guaranteed to us by the sixth amendment of the Constitution.

L: Ok, I understand the difference now.

C: Ok, so the pivotal question here is what kind of right is the right to life? Is it a right of non-interference – that is, just a right to not be killed – or is it a positive right – a right to be given whatever one needs for survival?

L: At the very least it's a negative right. Our right to life means a right to not be killed, at least not unjustly. We talked last time about the extent of which violence should be allowed, and I stated that self-defense may be one of the few times that killing is permissible. If I killed in self-defense, I have not violated anyone's right to life.

C: What about the right to life as a positive right – the right to be given what is needed for continued survival?

L: I can be convinced that the right to life can be a positive right too.

C: It doesn't appear that, given certain practices, we consider the right to life a positive right. There are many humans who die every day from lack of things like clean water, or immunizations, medical care, or food, or shelter – all of the basic things needed for continued life. If the right to life is a positive right, then by not providing these goods and services to those without, these individuals' right to life is being violated. Indeed, every time someone dies because they were lacking something needed for continued life, then their right to life was violated.

L: I mean, strictly speaking, their right to life isn't being violated. By which I mean that it is not illegal to not provide what people need for survival.

C: Right, so at least in practice, it appears that the right to life is only a negative one. It's only illegal to kill, it's not illegal to fail to give someone what they need for survival.

L: Ok, that's true legally. But morally it may be another question altogether. Maybe not giving others the bare minimum of what they need for survival is immoral. Maybe we *should* make access to clean water, immunizations, food, medical care, and shelter part of having a right to life.

C: I don't disagree with you. I am all in favor of universal healthcare, as I mentioned before, and would have no problems providing for the poor the basic needs for continue sustenance.

L: So you think the right to life is a positive right?

C: It's definitely a negative right, and in some cases it is a positive right as well. But, there are limits. I don't think people are entitled to *anything* needed for survival.

L: What limits do you foresee?

C: Every semester we see blood donation trucks on campus asking people for donations. They try to entice us with a shirt, or a coupon for some goods or services. The people have to *volunteer* for a donation; they can't be forced to donate, no matter how dire the need for blood is.

L: Right.

C: What if one of the things you needed was access to someone else's body. Say I needed a blood transfusion and you were a match. Can I force you to give me blood? I mean, it's what I needed for continued life.

L: No, I don't think I am comfortable with that.

C: Neither am I. I am not denying that people have a right to life. I am just asking, for now, what having a right to life entails. I am challenging the idea that having a right to life automatically means that I have a right to *anything* at all I need for survival – even if this means intruding on someone else's bodily autonomy.

L: Bring this back to abortion, although I think I see where you're going with this.

C: Ok, how about this. I will grant you that the fetus is a person from conception onwards, and that it has the same moral rights as you and me. Even so, according to the article I brought with me today, this concession does not entail that the fetus has a right to use the woman's body for continued survival.

L: Let's take a look at that argument.

(c) The violinist example.

C: Ok, let me start by reading you a quote. This is called "the violinist example." Here's what it says *(reads from essay)*: "You wake up in the morning and find yourself back to back in bed with an unconscious violinist. A famous unconscious violinist. He has been found to have a fatal kidney ailment, and the Society of Music Lovers has canvassed all the available medical records and found that you alone have the right blood type to help. They have therefore kidnapped you, and last night the violinist's circulatory system was plugged into yours, so that your kidneys can be used to extract poisons from his blood as well as your own. The director of the hospital now tells you, 'Look, we're sorry the Society of Music Lovers did this to you-we would never have permitted it if we had known. But still, they did it, and the violinist now is plugged into you. To unplug you would be to kill him. But never mind, it's only for nine months. By then he will have recovered from his ailment, and can safely be unplugged from you.' Is it morally incumbent on you to accede to this situation? No doubt it would be very nice of you if you did, a great kindness. But do you have to accede to it?"[2]

L: In other words, do have I have a moral obligation to stay hooked up? I mean, it would be a good thing if I did.

C: It would be a "great kindness" if you did, no doubt, but do you *have* to do it? Would you be doing something morally wrong if you didn't do it? And should you be *forced*? That is, is it morally right to *compel* you into staying hooked up to the violinist?

L: I am torn because I want to say it would be a good thing if you agreed, but I don't want to say that it would be morally permissible to force you to do it.

C: We need to separate two questions here. One is whether it would be a nice or kind thing if you allowed the violinist to stay hooked up to you. And no one is denying that it would be. But that is a different question than asking whether the violinist has a *right* to use your kidneys for continued survival. And whether you should be forced to use your body to sustain his life were it the case that you didn't volunteer to do so.

(d) Is the violinist example too weird?

L: I guess I'll say that you cannot be forced to stay hooked up to the violinist. But is this example supposed to be analogous to pregnancy? Because this is a really weird example. I am not sure it has any real world applications. This would never happen in real life. Pregnancy is not this weird, unnatural phenomenon. Pregnancy is the opposite of weird. It's the most natural thing in the world.[3]

C: Two things. First, this is a thought-experiment. It's not meant to be a real case. What we are debating here is: when the moral right to bodily autonomy and the moral right to life conflict, which one wins out? It may actually be an advantage that this example is so fantastical, since that way you can divorce any preconceptions and feelings you may have and just focus on the example.

L: So its weirdness is a good thing?

C: Well, it may not even be as weird as you may think. There are real world cases that mirror the violinist example in relevant and important ways.

L: No one has ever been connected to musician without their consent in order to save his life.

C: No, but there *have* been cases where one person is in need of someone else's body for continued survival.

L: Like what?

C: Well consider organ donation. There is always an organ shortage. People die waiting for an available organ. Still, we do not take organs from dead bodies without consent of the individual before she died, or without the family's consent. Surely the sick people have a right to life, but that right does not entitle them to an organ without consent. So, in this way, we respect the wishes and bodily autonomy of a dead person even if it costs others their lives.

C: Are there other examples?

C: Have you ever heard of the concept of savior siblings? These are babies who are deliberately conceived with the hopes that they will be suitable matches for a sick sibling, either for blood or bone marrow, or sometimes even an organ. So for example, say that a child is suffering from a certain kind of cancer and needs a bone marrow transplant. Siblings are a good bet here for a genetic match because they share genes. Some families will fertilize several eggs outside the womb, have them tested for genetic matches, and only implant the embryos that can serve as a suitable match for their sick child.

L: And the rest get discarded? That makes me super uneasy.

C: Yes we talked about that. But here's my question. Let's say that the child is born as a savior sibling and, after years of serving as a donor for their sick brother or sister, decides that they don't want to do it anymore. Should the child be forced to serve as a donor for her sibling? What if what the sick child needs is an organ – say a kidney. You can live with one kidney. So can the healthy child be forced to donate her kidney?

L: No I really can't say that I am comfortable with that at all.

C: Good! I agree with you. Here's yet another example. This was a real case. In 1978, in Pennsylvania, there was a man named Robert McFall who was suffering from a condition known as aplastic anemia and needed a bone marrow transplant. His cousin, David Shimp, was a suitable donor, but he refused to undergo the donation. So McFall took his cousin to court with the hopes that the judges would force Shimp to undergo the procedure. What do you think happened?

L: I think Shimp should have voluntarily given him the donation.

C: Well maybe so. But that's not the question here. The question is whether Shimp could be compelled – whether his bodily autonomy was stronger or weaker than McFall's right to life, and whether McFall had a right to access Shimp's body.

L: Well given that you are using the example, I suppose he was not forced.

C: That's right. Here's what the court said in their response: *(reads from smartphone)* "The common law has consistently held to a rule which provides that one human being is under no legal compulsion to give aid or to take action to save another human being or to rescue ... Introspection, however, will demonstrate that the rule is founded upon the very essence of our free society ... Our society, contrary to many others, has as its first principle, the respect for the individual, and that society and government exist to protect the individual from being invaded and hurt by another ... In this case, the chancellor is being asked to force one member of society to undergo a medical procedure which would provide that part of that individual's body would be removed from him and given to another so that the other could live. Morally, this decision rests with defendant, and, in the view of the court, the refusal of defendant is morally indefensible. For our law to *compel* defendant to submit to an intrusion of his body would change every concept and principle upon which our society is founded. To do so would defeat the sanctity of the individual, and would impose a rule which would know no limits, and one could not imagine where the line would be drawn ... for a society which respects the rights of *one* individual, to sink its teeth into the jugular vein or neck of one of its members and suck from it sustenance for *another* member, is revolting to our hard-wrought concepts of jurisprudence."[4]

L: But notice that the court said that Shimp's decision was morally indefensible.

C: But they also still held that the decision rests solely with him, and that to force him to use his body in a way he does not want in order to save his cousin (who died two weeks later) contradicted "the respect for the individual" and "every concept and principle upon which our society is founded."

L: So how is this relevant here?

C: Well, these seem to be close to real life violinist cases. In both cases, *McFall v. Shimp,* and reluctant savior siblings, you have someone in need of someone else's body for survival, and someone who does not want to use their body in this way. So the question becomes whether you should force someone to do it against their will. You agree you shouldn't force a savior sibling to use their body in a way she doesn't want to. The courts ruled that Shimp could not be forced to give his bone marrow to McFall and, similarly, the person attached to the violinist cannot be forced to stay attached.

(e) The violinist example's relevance to abortion.

L: Ok, but bring this back to abortion – I feel like we have strayed too far.

C: Well, the typical anti-abortion argument relies on the fetus's personhood and their purported right to life to make its case. All persons have a moral right to life. The fetus is a person. So the fetus has a moral right to life. Because the fetus has a moral right to life, abortion is morally wrong (and should be illegal). I'll grant you the argument that fetuses are persons. But because a fetus is a person with a right to life, it is automatically assumed that their right trumps a woman's right to her body. Pro-life arguments assume that, in the event the right to life is in conflict with the right to bodily autonomy, the right to life always wins. But these examples show why that's not always the case. We have three examples – the violinist example, savior siblings, and *McFall v. Shimp* – where the right to bodily autonomy wins out over the right to life when the two conflict.

L: And you want to say, I assume, that abortion is justified using similar logic – that the woman's right to her body trumps the fetus's right to life.

C: Exactly right. Moreover, these examples point towards a limitation on the right to life, if it's a positive right. A case can be made that you have the moral right to food, water, medical care, shelter, etc. But the positive right to life has limits. These examples help us delineate those limits. Maybe you have the rights to *some* of what you need for survival, so in that sense maybe the right to life is both a negative right and a positive right to *some* degree, but you don't have an unlimited right to *whatever* you need for survival.

L: So how can we draw the line? Let's say the right to life is positive in nature and that you have the right to *some* of what you need for survival. How do we determine what you do or don't have a right to?

C: That's a fantastic question. I don't have an answer for every case. But I do think, as the examples have shown, I can argue that access to other people's bodies is not something you have a moral right to.

L: Ok, let's hear your argument then. Why doesn't McFall have a moral right to Shimp's blood marrow? Why doesn't a sick sibling have a moral right to her brother or sister's bodily fluids (especially since that's what they've been created for)?

C: Well let's go back to the "security of persons" statement. Canada isn't the only place where it comes up. Article 3 of the United Nation's Universal Declaration of Human Rights reads that "everyone has the right to life, liberty and security of person."[5]

L: And we said that "security of person" had to do with a person's bodily integrity.

C: Right. To violate a person's body integrity is a violation of her security of person because it means you are violating *her*. People don't own their bodies the way that they own a car or a house. They don't just live in their bodies. Whatever your view is on the issue of personal identity as we discussed last time, humans either *are* their bodies or are so intimately related to their bodies that whatever happens to their bodies also affects their mind and their cognition. A violation someone's body is a violation of the self. This is one of the reasons crimes like rape are so horrible. When you rape someone you are not just stealing their property, you are violating *the person*.[6]

L: So "security of person" means that the person has a right to not be violated, and you're arguing that violating bodily autonomy is an example of that.

C: That's right. Now let me appeal to something I know you're against: forced abortions. During China's one-child policy, many women experienced forced abortions by the state.[7]

L: How horrible.

C: It sure was. But it was horrible for several reasons. Not just that fetuses were being killed against the desires of parents who really wanted them, but also that women were being pinned down and forced to undergo a bodily procedure that they did not want. This is another example of a violation of the "security of person."

L: I can totally see that. But I can't see pregnancy as being equivalent to forced abortions. In a forced abortion, your very wanted baby is being ripped from your womb. In pregnancy, nothing like this is occurring. The fetus only needs your body for a few months and then you can both go on your way when it's over if you cannot raise the child.

C: You aren't taking pregnancy as seriously as you should. Being pregnant isn't like renting a room to a tenant for nine months, where he can just live in your house and then be on his merry way when he no longer needs your house.

L: I didn't mean to suggest otherwise.

C: But when you say things like "the fetus *only* needs a woman's body for nine months" it downplays the effects of pregnancy. Pregnancy and labor can take a tremendous toll on the body. A woman can experience severe morning sickness, gestational diabetes, preeclampsia (where her blood pressure gets so high that it can cause damage to her organs or a stroke), deep vein thrombosis (blood clots forming in a vein that is deep in your body), and can have traumatic births where she may excessively bleed, or may require major abdominal surgery, or can cause tearing in your vagina.

L: You're focusing on the worst cases.

C: That's not the point. A particular pregnancy and delivery may be easy, but that doesn't change the fact that at any time it could have taken a turn. Pregnancy is a very

precarious state of affairs. So pregnancy isn't just like renting out an extra room in your house for a few months.
You are sharing your self with another being – a sharing
that can have dangerous and lasting repercussions on your
body and your health.

L: I can't deny that these things happen with pregnancy, but
I don't think killing the fetus is the proper response to
these dangers. These are the kinds of things you think
about before you have sex and make a baby.

C: We're going to talk more about that line of reasoning,
don't worry. For now, let me ask you. Have you ever
heard of the philosopher Immanuel Kant?

L: I haven't.

C: He wrote a lot of famous philosophical works. He is what
philosophers and ethicists call a deontologist – which
means he thought that morality is based on fulfilling
moral duties or moral obligations. One of his most famous
works is a book called the *Groundwork for the Metaphysics of
Morals*, where he wrote about his view on morality.

**(f) Kant's
principle of
humanity and
its relation
to pregnancy
and abortion.**

L: OK, what did he write that is relevant to our conversation?

C: Well, one of the things he wrote about was that human
persons have intrinsic value because of their capacity
for reason and autonomy, and because they can follow
what he called the "moral law." This is opposed to animals, who can do no such thing. Animals don't have
free will, they aren't autonomous, and they cannot follow the laws of morality because they don't understand
what morality is.

L: So what separates humans from animals, what makes
us valuable beings, is our ability to reason and follow
morality.

C: Yes. Now, in order to decipher what our moral duties
are, which acts are morally permissible and impermissible, Kant came up with what he called categorical imperatives. These are a kind of test, if you will. If you are
having trouble deciding whether something you want to
do is morally permissible or not, you have to pass them
through these categorical imperatives, and if they fail the
test, you have a moral obligation to *not* act in that way.

L: How many categorical imperatives are there?

C: There are at least three, but only one is important for our
purposes. Keeping in mind how highly he holds persons,
one thing Kant says is that it is absolutely impermissible
to treat persons as mere instruments, or as mere means to

an end. This is called the principle of humanity version of the categorical imperative. Kant writes: "Act in such a way that you treat humanity, whether in your own person or in the person of any other, never merely as a means to an end, but always at the same time as an end."[8]

L: That's a mouthful. What does that mean?

C: It means a few things. It means that we cannot treat other people in ways that they would not consent to. Humans treat each other as means all the time. For example, if I take an Uber to the airport then I have used the driver a means of getting to my destination, and she, in turn, used me as a means of attaining her salary. But in this case, we have each consented to the transaction, so we aren't treating each other as a *mere* means.

L: But what does it mean to treat someone as a *mere* means?

C: We must treat every person with respect given their rational nature. We must never treat a person in a way they would not consent to. Nor can we manipulate, instrumentalize, or coerce them in order to attain our own ends and goals. Persons aren't things or objects that we can use to achieve our own ends. One example Kant focused on a lot was lying or deception. When you lie to someone in order to attain something from them, you are treating them as an instrument for your personal desires, as a mere means, and you are certainly doing it in a way they would never consent to (since people aren't typically ok with being lied to).

L: What about the other part? What does it mean to treat someone "as an end"?

C: Well, it means that you don't treat someone as a mere tool or instrument to get what you want out of them, but also that you recognize that persons, given their autonomy and rational nature, have goals and desires of their own, their own ends, and part of respecting the person is respecting those self-formed ends.

L: You said that this was relevant to our conversation?

C: Yes, this is going back to the question of how we can know the limits of our positive right to life. We may have a right to some of what we need for survival, but we never have a right over a person's body without their consent because this violates the principle of humanity – it treats the person as a mere means, a mere instrument, to our own desires and goals.

L: What if the goal or end is a good thing, like saving someone's life?

C: It doesn't matter if the ends are laudable or not; you still cannot manipulate someone or treat a person as a mere instrument to get what you want out of them.

L: Give one real world example of treating someone as a mere means.

C: Well, this is why it would have been immoral to forcibly extract Shimp's bone marrow, or force a savior sibling to serve as a means for bodily fluids or even organs. In these cases, you are treating them in ways that they clearly do not consent to in order to attain an end.

L: So relating this to abortion ...

C: To force a woman to gestate a fetus against her will is clearly treating her in a way she does not consent to. It is to treat her as an incubator for someone else against her wishes and her desires for her life and her body. It violates the principle of humanity as much as it would have been to force Shimp to donate his bone marrow or to force savior siblings to continue giving their services.[9]

L: I see where you're going with this. But I have one question. Doesn't aborting the fetus violate the principle too? Aren't you killing a person in order to attain something that you want that pregnancy and childbearing interferes with? Whether that's to continue your education, or a job, or just because any extra mouth to feed would be too much to handle, it looks like you're treating the fetus as a mere means to your ends too. Certainly the fetus wouldn't consent to their own abortion, so you're treating the fetus in a way they would not consent to.

C: Well, Kant was clear his categorical imperatives apply only to persons, since it is only persons who are rational, autonomous, and could follow the moral law. So if the principle of humanity applies to fetuses, that assumes that fetuses are persons. And it seems odd to say that fetuses could not consent to their own abortion when fetuses aren't capable of consenting to anything.

L: But we're not debating fetal personhood, right? You granted me from the get-go today that fetuses are persons.

C: Fair enough. In this case it seems that no matter what we do, whether we force a woman to gestate or allow her to get an abortion, some person will be getting used as a mere means to an end.

L: So we're stuck. Either way, we are violating Kant's principle of humanity.

C: Well, we have some guidance here. It seems like we should appeal to some sort of precedent, no? In cases where someone needs the body of another in order to survive, the choice is ultimately left in the hands of the person whose aid is needed. It was only Shimp who could decide how to use his own body, and his decision not to donate his bone marrow cost McFall, a person, his life. A savior sibling always has to continually decide whether she wants to continue serving her sick sibling, and the decision always rests with her. Similarly, the woman is the one who gets to decide whether she wants to use her body to sustain the fetus, even if the fetus is a person.[10]

L: I can see how you're drawing this conclusion. But I am still not convinced. Let's go back to the violinist example again. I want to point out ways that pregnancy and abortion are different than the violinist example.

C: Ok, let's do that.

(g) The violinist example as analogous to rape.

L: Well, one important difference is the circumstances that brought each person to their state of unwanted bodily intrusion. In the violinist example, you were forced into a state of interdependence against your will. And you didn't *do* anything to get yourself into that mess. This is the opposite of what happens in pregnancy. Unless you are raped, if you choose to have sexual intercourse voluntarily, then you are choosing to take a chance in creating a being who is dependent on your body.[11]

C: But didn't you say a couple of days ago that you were against abortion, even in the cases of rape? Like you said, whether you have a right to life doesn't stand or fall on how you were created, or what circumstances led to your creation.[12]

L: And I still believe that. But what I was doing is pointing out a relevant dissimilarity here between pregnancy and the violinist example. Many pro-life persons do grant an exception for rape and incest. If so, this may be a reason why. In the violinist example, you aren't morally responsible for being in the state that you are in. If you had voluntary sexual intercourse, then you are responsible.

(h) The responsibility objection.

C: What exactly are you responsible *for*?

L: You are responsible for the existence of the fetus and their need for your body. Had you not had sex, or had you been more careful and used contraception, the fetus wouldn't exist and need your body for continued sustenance.

C: Well, first off, contraception can fail, so we shouldn't assume that a woman who becomes pregnant does so because she was "careless" with contraception. But let me challenge you a bit. Essentially what you're telling a woman in this case is that she shouldn't have done an action that led to the creation of a fetus. But she did, so now she has to care for them. And I am assuming you say this because you think abortion harms the fetus.

L: Like we discussed last time, I think it is obvious that abortion harms the fetus.

C: But in this case, you're saying that she shouldn't have created the fetus in the first place. When you harm someone, you are making them worse off than they otherwise would have been. So what harm befalls a fetus who is aborted, if the alternative to the abortion was not having existed in the first place, either because your potential parents abstained from intercourse or used effective birth control?[13]

L: Because once they come into existence, two choices can be made on behalf of the fetus: either continued life or being killed, and clearly the latter makes the fetus worse off than he otherwise would be when the "otherwise" is continued existence.

C: But that's the point I am trying to make. The alternative to the fetus being aborted is not having existed in the first place. There is no alternative where the fetus could have existed without the need for your body, and that there was something that you did to make him dependent on you when he otherwise would not have been. It's hard to see how aborting a fetus who otherwise wouldn't be created harms them in any significant way.

L: Ok, let me put it another way. Suppose that you were in a car accident that you caused and that resulted in someone getting run over. Say he lost a lot of blood and needs a transfusion, that you can provide. Don't you have at least *some* responsibility to the person you harmed, exactly because you caused him to be in a state of dependence given your negligence?

C: But this case is not analogous to pregnancy. In the case of the negligent driver you have a person who already existed and was living a life independent of any need and was made dependent on another because of some negligent action that they did.

L: Right, just as the fetus is made dependent because of some negligent action the woman (and her partner) did.

C: But in the fetus's case, the alternative for not doing the "negligent action", not having sex, is not existing in the first place. For our negligent driver example, his victim's alternative state of affairs is to continue living healthily without being dependent on anyone else. For the fetus it's never having been created at all. It's hard to see how abortion harms a fetus when the alternative for that fetus – according to you – is not having existed if sex wouldn't have happened.

L: Ok, I can see what you're saying here.

C: Moreover, in this case we already agree that the person in question has a right to not get run over. We already agree that being run over as a result of negligence results in an unjust harm. But that is precisely the question being debated here: *is* abortion an unjust harm? I know that you think it is, but the point is that this is the conclusion that needs to be argued for, not assumed. You're begging the question again.[14]

L: So you're saying that a woman is not at all responsible for the pregnancy when she took actions that knowingly led to the creation of the fetus?

C: I am not convinced that she is, no. But how about this. Let's assume that you're right that a woman bears some responsibility in the creation of a fetus from voluntary sexual intercourse. Why think that whatever responsibility she does incur is *so strong* that it entails the unwilling sacrifice of her bodily autonomy? There are limits to what kind of rights we sacrifice, even if we are being negligent. For example, say that I leave my windows wide open because the house is stuffy knowing that there is a burglar on the loose in my neighborhood. Say the burglar comes into my home, as I knew may be the case. Am I now so responsible for this "negligence" that I must let the burglar invade my home?[15]

L: But the fetus isn't a burglar. It's not trying to harm you or violate your rights. The burglar is.

C: It's not the fetus that is violating a woman's right to her body, it's the government that compels her to remain pregnant against her will by taking away abortion access. If an innocent person stumbles into my house via my open window, and the government now tells me I must let him stay, since I opened my window in the first place, it's the government that is harming me, not the innocent person. But you're missing the point of my response. It doesn't matter if the person in question is a burglar or an innocent person, the point is that neither are allowed in my house without my consent. Even if I was "careless" in leaving my window open, that doesn't mean I forfeit the right to my property. There are some rights you don't give up, even if you are being careless. My right to my body is certainly one of them, especially when we are talking about pregnancy and all the risks it can have to my health and livelihood.[16]

(i) The tacit consent objection.

L: How about if we word the objection a little differently. You argue that a fetus cannot be allowed to use the body of a woman without her consent. But what if we hold that by consenting to voluntary sexual intercourse, she tacitly consents to allowing the fetus use of her body, because she knows that pregnancy is a possible consequence of having sex? Because she knows this, consenting to sex implicitly means you consent to gestation.

C: So you're saying that if you voluntarily perform an action x that foreseeably results in outcome y, you have directly consented to x and implicitly consented to y as well.

L: That's right.

C: I don't think that follows at all. What if I voluntarily go for a walk in a neighborhood known for sexual violence? I am voluntarily performing an action that I know may lead to a certain outcome, but clearly you wouldn't say I have tacitly consented to being assaulted.

L: I think you should have been more careful.

C: Maybe so. But that's not the issue. The question is whether you want to say that I tacitly consented to the assault because I voluntarily performed an action that foreseeably resulted in getting sexually assaulted.

L: But in the assault case another party is knowingly harming you and violating your rights. We can assume that you don't consent to being assaulted because you don't consent to your rights being violated. But, as I said above, there is no party harming you in the case of an unwanted pregnancy. The fetus is not a rapist or a violent actor.

C: Again, the person harming someone in these cases is not the fetus, but a government that forces a woman to stay pregnant against her will. But what if I give you another example. Say that you check into a hospital for a cosmetic treatment, knowing that there may be a computer glitch that may result in you being plugged into the violinist instead. Say you wake up and notice that's exactly what has happened – a computer glitch has resulted in you not having received cosmetic surgery and, instead, you are plugged into the violinist. In this case, there is no one who exists who has deliberately harmed you, since plugging you in was an accident, and something happened that you knew could have possibly happened. In other words, you consented to an action that had a foreseeable consequence. But surely you wouldn't say in this example that you tacitly consented to being plugged in.[17]

L: You're right, I don't think that constitutes consent.

C: Plus let's go back to the *McFall v. Shimp* example again. Say that Shimp had consented to the bone marrow transplant, knowing that McFall may need more than one round of bone marrow. After the first round, though, he finds the experience too painful and decides not to undergo any more. Surely you don't think he can be forced into more transplants because he consented to the first one, even though he knew that additional transplants may be needed.[18]

L: You're right. Shimp has to consent to each extraction and transplant as he goes along, and consenting to one does not mean consenting to the others.

C: Or, take a more commonplace example. Whenever I give blood, I am read a series of warnings about the potential side-effects of donation, light-headedness being one of those. Say I began the donation procedure knowing the possible risks. I have consented to the beginning of the donation, but then I do indeed start to feel light-headed. Surely I am allowed to rescind my consent and stop the donation right? I can't imagine the medics would say: "well you consented to the donation knowing you may get light-headed, so you have also consented to suffering through the light-headedness and you have to finish the donation."

L: You do seem to be right about that. I have been light-headed in the past too and they always continually ask me if I want to stop the donation.

C: They ask me that too. What does that show you though? To me, it shows two things. One, it is not the case that, because you consent to something with a foreseeable consequence, you also consent to that consequence. Me having consented to donating blood knowing I could get light-headed does not mean I consent to suffering through light-headedness. Second, it shows me that, when it comes to using your body to help another human being, you are in control one hundred percent of the time. Only you can decide if you will use your body to help another and how far you are willing to go in using your body. Moreover, you are allowed to rescind that decision whenever you want, even if that means the person in need of your body has to go without.

(j) The special
relationship
objection.

L: Alright fine. Let's leave this one aside for now. There are other objections I can think of. How about this one. In the case of the violinist, you are being asked to sustain a total stranger. But when it comes to an unwanted pregnancy, you are not sustaining a stranger, you are sustaining *your child*. Clearly we have moral obligations to our children that we don't have for total strangers, don't we?[19]

C: Well I would caution you before you go that route because if the argument is that abortion is impermissible because women have obligations to her children that she doesn't have to total strangers, what would happen in cases of surrogate pregnancies, where the fetus is not related to the pregnant woman?

L: But in those cases she clearly consented to allow the embryo to be implanted in her womb.

C: Ok, how about a scenario where a woman goes into the hospital for one treatment and, by mistake, has an unrelated embryo implanted in her. Can she now abort the embryo because they are not her child?[20]

L: You're right, I cannot agree to that.

C: Plus let's push back here on the assumption that the fetus is related to the woman in a morally significant way. What grounds our moral obligations to our family members? Is it our shared genetic relationship, or something else?

L: I would think it's our shared genetic relationship no?

C: Is it? Would a sperm donor have any moral obligations to resulting children because of their biological relationship? And don't adoptive parents have special obligations to their adoptive children even though they share no genetic relationship?

L: Yes that seems right too.

C: So what's doing the moral work here isn't just a genetic relationship, but something else – an interpersonal relationship built upon years of trust and care. Imagine if all in the same day I find out my 12 year old child is not my child biologically and, also, that I had a long lost genetically related brother. Wouldn't it be odd if I were able to transfer all my feelings of love and care to my new brother while treating my daughter like a stranger?[21]

L: You're right, that would be weird.

C: Our familial relationships are cultivated by years of love, care, and intimacy, not just genetics. Adoptive siblings love each other as much as genetically related siblings do.

L: I don't have any adoptive siblings, but I do know them and you're right – they appear to love each other as much as genetically related siblings do.

C: I would feel more morally obligated to donate bone marrow to my adopted sibling or adopted child than I would be for a genetic brother who I just met. I mean, I may still do it, but not because I have a moral obligation to do it. But I do think I may have some moral obligation to donate to the adopted child I have loved and raised for years. Similarly, I think I have a moral obligation to care for my frail and elderly mother not because we are biologically related, but because of all the years of love and care that we shared, and because she took care of me when I needed it. In fact, I would say that I had much more of an obligation to my adoptive mother than a biological mother who I never met and who never took care of me.

L: I can see this being the case, yes.

C: Well, if that's the case, then, it does not really matter that the embryo or fetus is biologically related to the pregnant woman. The interpersonal experiences that ground moral obligations to our family members are simply absent during pregnancy, unless the woman chooses to commence such a relationship. And many women do feel like their journey to parenthood begins during pregnancy. But many women do not. That seems like it is something that is up to the pregnant woman to initiate.

L: Ok, I can see why just sharing genetics may not be sufficient for establishing moral obligations.

C: Ok, but let me grant you for a second that having a genetic relationship is sufficient for establishing *some* moral obligations. Would one of those be the obligation to use your body against your will and desires? That's quite an obligation no? Can you be *forced* to do it?

L: I'll admit that using your body to save someone else can be onerous.

C: It would mean that Shimp could have been forced to donate after all, since he was biologically related to McFall. It would mean that savior siblings could be forced to use their bodies continually to serve their sick sibling as much as needed. After all, that's what they were created for anyways.

L: You're right – that does sound difficult to swallow.

C: And in many of these cases, the imposition being asked of one human being for another person is much less burdensome than nine months of pregnancy and childbirth. If we cannot compel one human being to donate blood to another person, regardless of whether it is a stranger or a family member, then it's much harder to justify forcing a woman to undergo an extremely burdensome bodily state, one that can have dangerous and lasting effects on her body and health, for the sake of another human being, even if that human being is a person with full moral rights.[22] In essence, pro-life advocates aren't saying that fetuses should be granted the same rights as all other persons, you're advocating that they'd be granted *additional* rights that no other human being possesses. No human being has the moral right (or legal right) to use another person's body in an extremely burdensome and potentially dangerous way in order to survive. So even if we grant the fetus the same rights as all other persons, that doesn't mean they can be granted a right to use someone else's body for sustenance.

L: Ok, I can see why these counter arguments don't work. I have one more.

C: Ok, let's hear it.

(k) The killing vs. letting die distinction.

L: In the violinist example, you are disconnecting yourself from the violinist and allowing him to die. In abortion, you are actively killing another human being. Clearly directly killing a human being is much worse than just allowing a human being to die. Plus, there is a difference in how death is achieved in both cases. In the violinist case, you are disconnecting yourself from a human being, which I will assume is relatively painless. In abortion you are tearing apart the embryo's or fetus's body and limbs in particularly gruesome ways.[23]

C: You're already stacking the deck in your favor with that last bit.

L: How so? Do you deny that abortions destroy fetuses in this way?

C: I deny that ways of doing abortions are gruesome in the same way tearing a person limb from limb is gruesome. What is troubling about doing it to a person is the immense amount of pain and suffering that comes with being killed in this way. But abortions, at least early to mid- term abortions, don't hurt fetuses in any which way because fetuses that young are not capable of feeling pain or suffering, as we discussed the other day. Whatever way abortions destroys the embryo or fetus produces no more pain than pulling a weed from a lawn.

L: Ok, but it is still an instance of direct killing. In the violinist example, you're unplugging yourself and letting the kidney ailment run its course. The cause of death is the kidney ailment, not your actions. But in abortion you are directly causing the death of the fetus. That's a significant moral difference between the two cases.

C: So, I have two things to say about that. First, I have a question for you. If we somehow derived a way to obtain an abortion in a way that was more like letting die than killing, would you be ok with that?

L: What do you mean? Can you be more specific?

C: Well there's one way a destruction of a fetus could happen that wouldn't be directly killing it. What if, instead of a traditional abortion, a woman were to obtain a hysterotomy. Do you know what that is?

L: I don't. What is it?

C: It's typically performed during a c-section, but it's the process of removing a fetus through an incision in the abdomen. If we were using it for abortion, we would remove the fetus and then just allow them to die.[24] Would that method of abortion be permissible in your eyes, since in that case you are just letting the fetus die, rather than actively killing it?

L: You're right that I would have a hard time accepting that.

C: Plus the killing versus letting die distinction is not as clear as you think. Take this example. Suppose there were two men, Jones and Smith, and they were both guardians of a little boy who was left with a lot of money after his parents died. If the boy dies, they each get to inherent his money. Both devise a plan to kill the boy as he is bathing. Smith does just that; he pushes the kid's head underwater and waits until he is done thrashing around. Jones was ready to do the same, but as he was creeping up on the boy, the little guy slips, hits his head on the tub, and lands face down. Jones stands there, waiting in case the boy pops his head up. But he doesn't and the boy dies. Now in this case, Smith actively killed the boy, while Jones just watched him die. Is Jones absolved from the killing while Smith is not? Did Jones behave any better than Smith?[25]

L: No, I feel like both acted equally bad.

C: Agreed, but in one case Jones just let him die, whereas Smith killed him. Doesn't that mean that the method of death is irrelevant?

L: But in this case both Jones and Smith had murderous intentions.

C: Right, but what this shows, I think, is that what matters is whether the death is justified or not. In this case, because the death of the child was not justified, both methods are equally morally wrong. If there is a death that is justified, however, then the way that the death is brought about is irrelevant, unless one method causes much more pain and suffering than the other.

L: But when it comes to abortion, I think almost all instances are morally unacceptable.

C: I know you do. That's why you'd still have a problem with abortion even if it were done via a hysterotomy. But if you think abortions can be justified instances of killing, like I do, then, again, the method of killing is unimportant, especially a method that produces no pain and suffering to any being, as is the case with early to mid-term abortions. What matters for determining the morality of any case of killing is only whether the killing was justified, not the method of death that took place, unless, again one method causes more pain and suffering than another method. In the case that there is pain and suffering associated with one kind of killing, that's reason against using that kind of killing. But, again, that's not relevant when fetuses can feel no pain in early to mid-gestation.

L: What if I change my mind and say that disconnecting yourself from the violinist is an instance of actively killing, as is all cases of abortion? Let's dissolve the distinction altogether.

C: So are you saying now that it would actually be immoral to unplug yourself from the violinist? Should you be forced to stay plugged in?

L: No I guess I don't want to say that. I don't want to say you can be *forced*, but that doesn't mean that maybe you shouldn't volunteer, out of the goodness of your heart, you keep yourself plugged into the violinist.

C: I can see why you may have that intuition, but for me it's a matter of choice. Maybe there are good reasons why I should choose to stay hooked up to the violinist, maybe there are good reasons Shimp should have chosen to help his cousin, but in the end it has to remain a choice. Same with abortion.

(I) Restricting abortion after viability.

L: How far does this choice go, in your eyes? You said our first day that there may be *some* restrictions on later abortion that may be justified, but you didn't say much more. So let's talk about that here. Should a woman be able to

terminate a pregnancy at any point? Would you be ok
with a woman terminating a pregnancy when she is, say,
35 weeks along? Seeing premature babies shows us that
by 35 weeks a fetus is pretty much a fully formed baby.

C: That's a great question. There is something towards
the end of the essay I read for today that may give us an
answer *(reads from essay)*: "I have argued that you are not
morally required to spend nine months in bed sustaining
the life of the violinist; but to say this is by no means to
say that if, when you unplug yourself, there is a miracle
and he survives, you then have a right to turn around and
slit his throat. You may detach yourself even if this costs
him his life; you have no right to be guaranteed his death,
by some other means, if unplugging yourself does not kill
him … I agree that the desire for the child's death is not
one which anybody may gratify, should it turn out to be
possible to detach the child alive."[26]

L: Ok, how does this relate to abortion exactly?

C: When I mentioned restricting abortion after viability,
you said that you didn't see why viability would be significant. Well, here is one reason why: once the fetus is able
to survive on its own, without the use of the woman's
body, it would be morally wrong to kill them if they can
be "detached" alive. So this means that if a fetus survives
an abortion attempt, they should be given life sustaining
measures just like you would give any other newborn
baby. If the fetus survives, you don't have the additional
right to demand their death.

L: I am not clear what you mean. You are saying that a
woman has a right to terminate the pregnancy, but she
doesn't have a right to demand the fetus's death? So are
you saying that, after viability, the method of termination
used should be one that preserves the fetus's life?

C: Right. A woman does not have the right to demand
the death of the baby were it possible to "detach" the
child alive.

L: That presents some complications, though, if you still
want to maintain she has the right to terminate the pregnancy. Terminating a pregnancy in a way that leads to a
premature birth has many complications, especially for
the baby. They can go on to suffer from an array of lifetime disabilities, physically and cognitively. It seems like
deliberately terminating a pregnancy by delivering the
baby prematurely is very damaging to the child. This a
morally, legally, and medically problematic.

C: Hmmm … Yes that's a good point. A very good point. I don't want to commit myself to saying that it would be morally permissible to deliberately cause a premature birth, for the reasons you have listed. But I also agree that the right to an abortion does not involve the right to kill the fetus were it possible that the fetus could survive on its own. Like I said the first day, I may be open to saying that *some* restrictions on abortion after viability may be morally permissible. But I say this with a caveat that there should be exceptions to any restrictions that are implemented. Some instances of later abortions, after viability, may still be permissible; for example, if you find out that the fetus is suffering from a debilitating condition or disability.

L: We can talk about that tomorrow. So you do agree that there may be some instances where abortion may be restricted?

C: Yes, in some instances, I do believe *some* restrictions on later abortions may be permissible. It should not be permissible to kill a fetus if it can survive without the woman's body and can therefore be "detached" alive. But delivering a live fetus prematurely can cause medical problems we should not deliberately cause. But, again, I say this with the caveat that there ought to be exceptions to these restrictions.

(m) Can we compel using someone's body to save another?

L: I consider that a victory! But let me shake things up a little bit here. I take back what I said earlier — let's say that maybe there is a case to be made that you *should* stay hooked up to the violinist after all. Maybe we *should* be taking organs from dead people without prior consent. Maybe the courts *should* have required that Shimp donate his bone marrow to McFall. After all, it is not a horribly painful procedure, and perhaps he could be compensated for his time and effort. Some countries mandate military service, so why not other life-protecting services?

C: I think it largely goes back to Kant. In all these cases, you are still using a person as a mere means to an end, and it is especially egregious that you are doing so explicitly against their consent. I cannot say that I would like to live in a society where person's wishes about matters pertaining to themselves and their bodies are ignored and contradicted.

L: But some societies already do this with compelled military service. Is such a society violating Kant's imperative?

C: I would be tempted to say so, but there are still important differences. Compelled military service exists for the public good, and it is not the same as violating your bodily autonomy to save an individual. A society that requires military service is requiring that soldiers risk their lives for the common good, but that same society does *not* require that individuals risk their life to save someone else's. For example, if someone jumped off a bridge in order to commit suicide, the government can't legally mandate that you jump after them to save them. So requiring that someone risk their life for the common good when it comes to military service is not the same thing as requiring that someone risk their life to save an individual.

(n) The compensation objection

L: But what if we compensate someone for using their body to sustain other? Could life-protecting services be mandated if the person who is doing the sacrificial act is properly compensated?

C: Well, I've never heard a pro-life advocate argue that pregnant women should be compensated for carrying an unwanted pregnancy to term. It would be interesting to see how much compensation such a woman would be given. But nevertheless, let's say we can agree on a monetary amount. I still think carrying the pregnancy should be a choice, regardless of whether there is compensation. The objection assumes that the woman would be doing something morally wrong if she rejects the compensation and aborts the pregnancy anyway. Let's say that society compensates someone who risks their life to save a suicidal person. According to you, it would be morally wrong for the person to not accept the offer and refuse to jump in after the suicidal person. After all, you would be compensated for it! But it seems clear to me that you still have a right to decide for yourself if you wanted to jump in after the person, even if you stand to be handsomely compensated. Same goes for a pregnant woman. Even if she is compensated for carrying the pregnancy to term, it must remain a choice as to whether she wants to continue that pregnancy.[27]

L: Well, once again, we have covered a lot of ground.

C: We have, but I really hope you can see now why I am pro-choice, and why conceding that the fetus is a person does not get you as far as you think it does. This is another reason why I am against Personhood Amendments, as we talked about the other day. Granting fetuses personhood does not get you to the conclusion that abortions should be prohibited, but it can bring about other unwanted states of affairs, as we discussed our first day.

L: I have to admit that you've given me quite a lot of food for thought. Anything else we can talk about?

C: I feel like we should still have a conversation on "hard cases." There has to be cases that challenges both of our perspectives. I can't imagine that you're totally comfortable with the idea of forcing a 15-year-old rape victim to gestate her rapist's fetus.

L: And I can't imagine you'd be ok with a woman choosing to abort for problematic reasons, for example, for sex-selection.

C: There can be individual cases of abortion that I think may be problematic, but I still wouldn't take the woman's choice away. I think we can discuss the morality of individual abortion choices while still maintaining it's a choice that needs to remain in a woman's hands alone.

L: Let's call it quits here and take this up next time – that sounds like it's worthy of an entire conversation of its own!

Notes

1 Supreme Court of Canada. *R. vs. Morgentaler* (1988). https://scc-csc.lexum.com/scc-csc/scc-csc/en/item/1053/index.do

2 Judith Jarvis Thomson. "A Defense of Abortion" (1971). *Philosophy and Public Affairs*, 1.1: 47–66, at pp. 48–49.

3 John Wilcox. "Nature as Demonic in Thomson's Defense of Abortion" in *The Ethics of Abortion*, edited by Robert Baird and Stuart Rosenbaum. (2001). Prometheus Books: 257–271. Wilcox writes: "… the violinist example is *weird*. No one in the history of mankind has ever been kidnapped for the purpose Thomson explains. It is not clear, medically, that anyone could be in the situation described – such that only that person's kidneys could save the violinist. But pregnancy is the opposite of weird … we all, every man Jack of us, and every woman Jill, too, begin in our mother's body. If there is a key to human life, surely it is pregnancy. So in Thomson's essay we have something as universal and necessary as pregnancy compared to something so rare it has never happened and perhaps never could happen" (p. 260).

4 Common Pleas Court of Allegheny County, Pennsylvania. *McFall v. Shimp* (1978). https://www.leagle.com/decision/197810010padampc3d90189

5 United Nations. *Universal Declaration of Human Rights*. (1948). https://www.un.org/en/universal-declaration-human-rights/

6 See: Bertha Alvarez Manninen. *Pro-Life, Pro-Choice: Shared Values in the Abortion Debate*. (2014). Vanderbilt University Press: "'Security of person' can best be understood as the right of the individual to live in safety; to not have to constantly worry about such things as murder, rape, or assault. Violating another's person, then, means violating the individual herself. Because of the intimate relationship between the person and her body, preservation of bodily autonomy is a key aspect of respecting the 'security of person.' Violating my body is not equivalent to violating my house or violating my car; a violation of my body is a violation of *me*" (p. 24).

7 Here is one such case: "Liang Yage and his wife Wei Linrong had one child and believed that – like many other couples – they could pay a fine and keep their second baby. Wei was 7 months pregnant when 10 family planning officials visited her at home on April 16. Liang describes how they told her that she would have to have an abortion, 'You don't have any more room for maneuver', he says they told her. 'If you don't go [to the hospital], we'll carry you.' The couple was then driven to Youjiang district maternity hospital in Baise city. 'I was scared', Wei told NPR. 'The hospital was full of women who'd been brought in forcibly. There wasn't a single spare bed. The family planning people said forced abortions and forced sterilizations were both being carried out. We saw women being pulled in one by one.' The couple was given a consent agreement to sign. When Liang refused, family planning officials signed it for him. He and his wife are devout Christians – he is a pastor – and they don't agree with abortion. The officials gave Wei three injections in the lower abdomen. Contractions started the next afternoon, and continued for almost 16 hours. Her child was stillborn." (Louisa Lim. "Cases of Forced Abortions Surface in China" (2007) *National Public Radio Website*. http://www.npr.org/templates/story/story. php?storyId=9766870)

8 Immanuel Kant. *Grounding for the Metaphysics of Morals*. (1981). Hackett Publishing Company, p. 36.

9 Donald H. Regan. "Rewriting Roe v. Wade" (1979) *Michigan Law Review*, 77.7: 1569–1646. Regan writes: "Pregnancy is painful. It involves a significant risk of death. It represents an intrusion into the most intimate parts of the woman's body ... the woman who is compelled to carry a fetus she does not want is in effect being used as an incubator. She is being used as a physical object ... laws forbidding abortion involve the requisitioning of the woman's body by the state ... [it] relegate[s] [women] to the status of a broodmare (for this is how the pregnant woman may well view the matter) by society at large" (pp. 1616–1617).

10 Regan, 1979: Regan writes: "When I suggest that the woman should not be compelled to subordinate her interests to those of the fetus, I sometimes meet with the response: 'But if she is allowed to have an abortion, the fetus is subordinated. It is just a question of who shall be subordinated to whom.' In a sense, of course, this is correct. There is a conflict of interest between the woman and the fetus, and someone is going to lose. But that is true in every samaritan situation. There is a conflict between the distressed party's need for aid and the potential rescuer's desire not to give it. The point is that our law generally resolves this conflict in favor of the potential samaritan. When a woman is pregnant, it is the fetus that needs aid and the woman who is in a position to give it. If the conflict between the woman and the fetus is to be resolved consistently with the resolutions of the most closely analogous cases, the woman must prevail" (p. 1610).

11 Wilcox, 2001: "In the violinist scenario, you do nothing to get yourself into the mess; you wake up one morning and simply 'find yourself' hooked up to the violinist. Worse, you are in the predicament only because you were kidnapped – which means your rights have been violated, you have been done an injustice. So we have injustice and a total lack of voluntariness ... But in the normal case of pregnancy, one has voluntarily engaged in the sexual relations which led to conception; and therefore in the normal case one is not pregnant only through some injustice, some violation of one's rights. So it is not at all clear that one's obligations in the violinist case really parallel a woman's obligations in a normal pregnancy – that is, a pregnancy not due to rape" (p. 261).

12 Thomson, 1971: Thomson notes this as well. She writes: "in this case, of course, you were kidnapped; you didn't volunteer for the operation that plugged the violinist into your kidneys. Can those who oppose abortion on the grounds I

mentioned make an exception for a pregnancy due to rape? Certainly. They can say that persons have a right to life only if they didn't come into existence because of rape; or they can say that all persons have a right to life, but that some have less of a right to life than others, in particular, that those who came into existence because of rape have less. But these statements have a rather unpleasant sound. Surely the question of whether you have a right to life at all, or how much of it you have, shouldn't turn on the question of whether or not you are the product of a rape" (p. 49).

13 See: David Boonin. *A Defense of Abortion.* (2003). Cambridge University Press, pp. 176–178.

14 Boonin, 2003: "… in the case of drunk or negligent driving, we already agree that people have a right not to be run over by cars and then determine that a person who risks running over someone with a car can be held culpable if he has an accident that results in a violation of this right … in the case of unintended pregnancy, on the other hand, the question of whether the fetus has a right not to be deliberately deprived of the needed support the pregnant women is providing for it is precisely the question at issue. So it is difficult to see how an argument from an analogy with such cases can avoid begging the question" (p. 168).

15 Thomson, 1971: "If the room is stuffy, and I therefore open a window to air it, and a burglar climbs in, it would be absurd to say, 'Ah, now he can stay, she's given him a right to the use of her house – for she is partially responsible for his presence there, having voluntarily done what enabled him to get in, in full knowledge that there are such things as burglars, and that burglars burgle'" (pp. 59–59).

16 Manninen, 2014: "No matter what voluntary actions are undertaken by an individual, *some* rights are not forfeited simply because a person places herself in a compromising situation. The key question, therefore, is whether one's prima facie right to bodily security is a right one loses in cases of unplanned pregnancy when one knowingly engages in sexual intercourse. Again, because of the extraordinary physical and mental enmeshment that comes with pregnancy and giving birth, because there always exists a risk to a woman's health and life while pregnant, and because of our society's consistent refusal to violate one person's bodily integrity even if this entails the death of another person, the onus seems to fall on anti-choice advocates to argue that pregnancy is an exception to what seems to be a well-accepted rule. Even if we grant that a woman who engages in voluntarily sexual intercourse is responsible for the fetus's dependence to some degree, this alone is not sufficient to render abortion impermissible. It must be *further* illustrated that the woman is *so* responsible that she can be forced to use her body to sustain the fetus when such bodily sacrifice is not required by any other nonpregnant person" (p. 55).

17 This entire exchange is taken from Boonin, 2003, pp. 162–163.

18 Boonin, 2003: "Suppose that because of your unique compatibility, the violinist will die unless you undergo a series of nine painful bone marrow extractions over the next nine months, and with a clear understanding of the nature of the procedure and its potential risks, you freely volunteer to undergo the first extraction. After the second round of extraction, however, you find that the burden is considerably more than you are willing to bear on his behalf. Do you really believe that it would now be morally impermissible for you to discontinue providing aid to the violinist merely because you began providing aid voluntarily?" (p. 165).

19 Wilcox, 2001: "A second difference between pregnancy and the violinist scenario is that the woman and her fetus are of one flesh and blood, the child is *her* child; she is its mother; but that violinist is a total stranger." (p. 260).

20 Boonin, 2003, pp. 231–232.

21 Manninen, 2014, pp. 48–49.

22 Regan, 1979: If abortions were not permitted, then "women who want abortions are required to give aid in circumstances where closely analogous potential samaritans are not. And they are required to give aid of a kind and an extent that is required of no other potential samaritan" (p. 1622).

23 Christopher Kaczor. *The Ethics of Abortion: Women's Rights, Human Life, and the Question of Justice.* (2011). Routledge Press: "Imagine for instance that you are to separate yourself from the violinist by poisoning him or by taking an axe to his body or tearing him limb from limb or by putting him through an incredibly powerful suction machine ... we are not simply separating ourselves or cutting a cord that links us to the violinist. Rather, we are doing something to the body of the violinist who, if he is a person, has as much right to boldly integrity as we do" (p. 152).

24 Boonin, 2003, p. 193.

25 This example appears in: James Rachels. "Active and Passive Euthanasia" (1975). *New England Journal of Medicine*, 292.2: 78–80.

26 Thomson, 1971, p. 66.

27 Boonin, 2003: "... the compensation objection must still be rejected. The objection turns on the claim that if the pregnant woman is offered fair compensation, then it would be morally impermissible for her to decline to accept the offer. And while this claim may be superficially appealing, it is ultimately unacceptable. For suppose that we decide on the dollar amount that would fairly compensate you if you were the one who lost an arm in the factory accident. Let's say $10 million would do the trick. The claim needed in order to sustain the compensation objection would then entail that so long as someone is willing to pay you $10 million, it would be morally impermissible for you to refuse to save someone's life if doing so would cost you an arm. And that is very difficult to accept. The fact that we would fulfill all our duties to you by giving you $10 million if you lost your arm in an accident does not entail that you would have a duty to sacrifice your arm in order to save someone's life if you knew ahead of time that we would compensate you for doing so with $10 million" (pp. 273–274).

5

DAY 5

Abortion in Hard Cases

Day 5 – Scene: Next day, L and C have come back together at the university coffee shop one last time before they finally start outlining their presentation for class.

L: We've been here so much people are going to start knowing us by name.

C: The barista already knew what I wanted to order!

L: We need to finish up soon so we can start putting together the presentation. I thought that today we can talk about some examples of abortion in hard cases, like later abortions, or abortions due to disability or sex-selection. How could a pro-choice advocate defend these hard cases?

C: If we do that, then I think you equally have to defend why you want to prohibit abortions even in cases of rape, or incest, or severe fetal abnormalities that are incompatible with life. Pro-life advocates have their share of hard cases too.

L: That's fine. It's only fair that we both get asked the hard questions. But I thought, for the presentation, it would be nice to end on a positive note and highlight any points of agreement or areas of convergence. I don't want people to think that pro-choice advocates and pro-life advocates have to be at each other's throats all the time.

C: I agree that's a good way to end the conversation.

L: Ok, so let's begin for today. Let me start by asking you – you said the very first day we met that one of the reasons you are pro-choice is that you identify as a feminist.

DOI: 10.4324/9781003109457-5

(a) Pro-choice and feminism.

C: That's right. I think anyone who calls themselves a feminist must agree that women have a right to control their fertility, and when and where, and even if, they want to have children. Abortion rights is one of the pivotal ways women are given control over their reproductive lives.

L: So in your view, feminism goes hand in hand with being pro-choice?

C: Yes. *Planned Parenthood vs. Casey* put it best when the Justices wrote: "the ability of women to participate equally in the economic and social life of the nation has been facilitated by their ability to control their reproductive lives."[1]

L: Well, I don't think pro-choice advocates have the market cornered on feminism. I did some research last night and came across a whole bunch of information on the pro-life feminist movement. Pro-life feminists also believe that women should have control over their reproductive lives, they just also think abortion is an illegitimate method of exercising this right.

C: I have never heard of pro-life feminism. I doubt whether the two can go together, but I am open to hearing about it from you.

(b) Early feminism and pro-life advocacy.

L: Well let me begin by asking you: I am assuming you are aware of figures like Susan B. Anthony, Mary Wollstonecraft, and Elizabeth Cady Stanton.

C: Of course. Wollstonecraft is famous for her essay "A Vindication of the Rights of Women." Anthony and Stanton were pivotal in women attaining voting rights.

L: Right. You would never deny their commitment to feminism, would you?

C: Of course not. We wouldn't have feminism today were it not for their work.

L: Ok, well, did you know that all three were openly pro-life?

C: I have to admit that I did not know that.

L: For example, I wrote it down in my notes, Elizabeth Cady Stanton maintained that abortion was "the masculine element everywhere overpowering the feminine" and that abortion leads to the "suffering and murder of helpless children." Susan B. Anthony said that abortion is "violence against both mother and child, caused by male control over female lives."[2]

C: Can you tell me more about why they thought that the right to an abortion was regarded as exhibiting male control?

(c) Does abortion allow for the sexual exploitation of women?

L: Well there are two pro-life feminist groups that warrant mention. There is the organization Feminist for Life of America. (FFL). This group was founded in 1973 by two women: Patricia Goltz and Catherine Callahan. Both agree that abortion access means that men can use women sexually in whatever way they wish without facing the consequences of sex. It facilitates, in other words, the sexual exploitation of women.[3]

C: So because abortion is legal, that means that men can continue to exploit women by getting "rid" of the consequence of sexual intercourse instead of standing up and caring for those children?

L: That's right.

C: But men abandoning women and their children still happens with or without abortion being legal. It's not like, in pre-*Roe* days, men were equal caregivers with women when it comes to their babies. There was still plenty of sexual exploitation of women going on before abortion was made legal.

L: You brought up the notion of women as caregivers. How do you feel about that?

C: Well, women have always been, and mostly still are, the default caregivers in their families – and not just for infants, for ailing family members as well. At times, women have had to do both: caring for a child and caring for other family members.

L: But do you think that's a detriment?

C: I don't see a problem with being a caregiver for anyone who needs care. What I have a problem with is the assumption that women are the default caregivers and that they have to sacrifice other aspects of their life, their work or their education, for example, in order to fulfill the obligations of caregiving.

(d) Abortion and pro-family support policies.

L: That was another point that the FFL brought up. Instead of challenging and arguing against the stereotype of women as caretakers, FFL embraced the role of women as caretakers and argued, instead, that abortion rights lead to the minimizing of caretakers' rights, and it also allows the state to get away with not doing much to support women who want to both have a career and be a caretaker of children. In other words, by getting rid of the child, you are getting rid of any need to change society that favors more rights and more resources for women and their babies.[4]

C: Again, it doesn't seem to follow that it is the existence of abortion rights that leads to a dismissive attitude against women and children. What was life like before *Roe*? It certainly wasn't this paradise of care and support for women-as-caretakers. We didn't live in such a society before *Roe*, and we don't live in one now. If it was easier to balance childbearing and societal roles for women before *Roe*, it wasn't because we, as a society, cared more for mothers and children, it was because fewer women worked outside the home, and motherhood and wifehood were taken to be a woman's natural, and default, state.

L: But the point is that having access to abortion contributes to the view that children are burdens, rather than blessings, and it allows society to continue to make laws and policies antithetical to balancing parenting and work, or education.[5] If we, as a society, welcomed children in our lives, and regarded parenting as something of the utmost importance, we would have more policies that allow women to balance parenthood with other aspects of their lives.

C: So I agree with you that, generally, the United States has awful "pro-family" policies. Our maternity leave policies are a joke compared to other countries. The Family and Medical Leave Act just requires employers to provide 12 weeks of *unpaid* leave. Many people cannot afford to take the time off once their baby is born. In Canada, for example, a woman can take up to 15 weeks of *paid* leave. In other countries in Europe, that number is much higher.

(e) Areas where pro-choice and pro-life feminists agree.

L: So that's one point of agreement – we both agree that we need better laws and policies that allow women (and men) to better balance family and work expectations.

C: Absolutely. But I also think looking at these other countries shows that the reason we have poor parental leave policies has nothing to do with legalized abortion. There are many countries with paid maternity leave for women that also have legal abortions – Canada being one of them, for example. Sweden allows up to 16 *months* of paid parental leave (which men can take as well as women), and they have legalized abortion. So the problem seems to be that the United States doesn't take the welfare of babies and new parents sufficiently seriously. It has nothing to do with abortion laws.

L: Well here's another point that both pro-life and pro-choice feminists can agree on. Both sides think that women should be in charge of their reproductive lives.

The second pro-life feminist group I want to bring up is called American Citizens Concerned for Life (ACCL). They thought it was important to find commonalities with pro-choice feminists and work with them on certain issues. The ACCL, for example, agreed that women need access to affordable and effective contraception. During the 1970s the ACCL, along with pro-choice feminists, supported the Pregnancy Discrimination Act of 1978, which prohibits any kind of discrimination against pregnant women in the workforce. They also supported federal laws funding contraception.[6]

C: What else does pro-life feminism have in common with pro-choice feminism?

L: Well, Alice Paul was a FFL member, and she also played a big part in the women's suffrage movement. She also wrote the original Equal Rights Amendment, which stated that men and women were equal in every respect under the law in the United States. She also thought that abortion was "the ultimate exploitation of women."[7] Both pro-life and pro-choice feminists agreed that if abortions are to be reduced, we needed to attend to the underlying reasons women seek abortions. Both kinds of feminists fought for better healthcare for mother and child, for programs aimed at allowing pregnant teenagers to remain in school, and they fought for better and affordable childcare.[8] And they did it together, despite their differing views on abortion.

C: All of these are worthwhile goals, I agree. These are fights that we're still having in this country.

L: I would think that, for pro-choice advocates, it would be important to you that a woman's choice for abortion would be completely autonomous – that she wasn't being compelled by anyone or any set of circumstances.

C: Yes, I agree with that. True freedom of choice implies that women, if they choose abortion, that they do so because this is what they truly want to do. This means that they should not be coerced; not by someone else, and not by any societal obstacles, such as lack of money. If financial limitations are the primary reason a woman chooses abortion, when she otherwise would have chosen to have the baby, then she is being coerced by her financial situation. Same thing if she is coerced by a society that makes her choose between her education or career and parenthood.

L: Agreed. This is something else that pro-life feminism and pro-choice feminism have in common. The ACCL were just as concerned with reproductive choice as pro-choice feminists, but they disagreed on how to best attain free-dom of choice. Both agreed, however, that certain soci-etal policies can coerce women to seek abortions.[9]

C: I can totally see that.

L: The concern, also, is that a lot of women turn to abor-tion to resolve "crisis pregnancies", many of whom have been abandoned by their partners and face a world where there is lack of economic and social support of pregnant women and mothers.[10]

C: Addressing these issues is definitely something to praise. Like I said, to be pro-choice, one must agree that a choice to abort should be an autonomous choice that reflects a woman's real desires. So fighting hard for a society that cares more for pregnant women and infants is certainly a worthwhile goal that both pro-choice and pro-life advo-cates can work towards together.

L: I am happy that you feel that way. I do as well. This adds to some areas of convergence between us.

C: So what happened to these groups? How come we don't hear as much anymore from them?

L: Some of them are still around. Feminist For Life are, for example. The very first thing you see on their webpage is the claim that "abortion is a reflection that we have not met the needs of women,"[11] but their influence on the abortion debate in this country is more minimal than it used to be. This is primarily because the pro-life move-ment was taken over more and more by the religious right, who also opposed things like the Equal Rights Amendment, which pro-life feminists supported. At the same time, feminist groups like the National Abortion Rights League (NARAL) and Planned Parenthood began arguing that the pro-life movement was synony-mous with anti-feminist movements. Social conservatism began to identify as pro-life and feminism began to iden-tify as pro-choice. Pro-life feminists found themselves increasingly alienated by people on both sides of the abor-tion debate, so they gradually started losing influence.[12]

C: I have to admit that's a shame. I think there's a lot to be said for finding some common ground on issues affect-ing women.

(f) Abortion due to sex-selection.

L: Agreed, but let's move on from this. I have another question for you. One of the things pro-life femi-nists really were against is abortion for the purposes of sex-selection, especially in order to get rid of female fetuses. This was deemed by many as one of the worse kinds of violence against women. Sex-selection abortion against girl fetuses was really prevalent in some Asian countries, for example India and China.[13] As a feminist, how can you not be opposed to sex-selection abortion? Isn't it indicative of a horrible prejudice and discrimination against women?

C: So I have to admit that this is a tough question, and it is one on which I have had difficulties forming a position. On the one hand, I agree that abortion for the purposes of getting rid of a female fetus reinforces gender bias against women. In India, for example, daughters are often considered a burden because parents have to supply a dowry upon marriage Sons are also the ones who support parents in old age, whereas daughters often live with and provide care for the husband's family. While I do think these kinds of abortions are morally problematic, I don't think that the answer is to enact laws that prohibit abortions for these reasons.

L: Why on earth not? If there is ever a reason to stop abortions, I would think this would be the one, from a feminist prospective.

C: Because my concern is that such laws will snowball and lead to other reasons to restrict abortion choice. It leaves the door open for prying into women's lives and the choices that they make over their own bodies and their reproductive lives. Second-guessing women's autonomous decisions isn't the way to resolve abortion for sex-selection.

L: So what is the way to "resolve" it?

C: Well, to be honest I am not sure, but that leads to my second concern. Not only do I think a ban on such abortions leaves the door open for more restrictive bans, I also think that that banning abortions because of sex-selection doesn't do much to rectify discrimination against women. Because there is such a high ratios of males to females in countries like China and India, laws have been enacted to combat abortions for the purposes of sex-selection, but studies show that these prohibitions, like most abortion restrictions, are ineffective − they don't stop sex-selection abortions.[14] What we need to do, instead, is identify why there is such a strong preference for male fetuses and work to challenge those preferences.

L: How can we do that?

C: I mean, this is a big problem right? You're asking me how to rectify centuries of sexist attitudes against women.

There is no overnight solution. One thing that can be done is that the societies in question can have better social policies to support parents in their old age instead of relying so much on their children, their sons in particular. This may reduce the tendency towards son-preference. We have also seen that targeting sexist attitudes towards women is a promising way for stopping abortion due to sex-selection. For example, in southern India, where women are held in higher regard, the birth ratios between males and females is more equitable; abortions aren't being used for sex-selection as much.[15] So the solution is to tackle discrimination against women on a societal level, rather than just attempt to prohibit one particular kind of abortion.

L: So are you or are you not in favor of abortion for sex-selection purposes?

C: I am not in favor of such abortions, but that doesn't mean I approve of prohibiting abortions for this reason. The prohibition doesn't do any good and it seems like the first step to trying to prohibit abortions overall. But I am completely in favor of addressing the underlying social issues that leads to abortion due to sex-selection.

L: But, as a pro-choice person, you seem to be agreeing that some uses of abortions are morally wrong, no? You say that you're not in favor of sex-selection abortions, so you must think that these kinds of abortions are morally wrong? And just yesterday you said you'd be open to the position that some post-viability abortions are morally problematic and that some of these abortions may warrant restriction.

C: Yes, I suppose I do mean that.

L: Ok, then you're admitting that some abortions are wrong. Doesn't that put your pro-choice position in jeopardy? If some abortions are wrong, doesn't that clear the pathway to all abortions, or most abortions, being wrong?

(g) Virtue theory and abortion.

C: No I don't think it does. I think we need to make a distinction between abortion being something women have a right to do and whether all exercises of that right are good ones.

L: I don't understand what you mean.

C: I read an article once where the author said that there are two questions that must be asked when it comes to abortion (and to most of our rights actually). First, do we actually have a moral right to x, and second, whether every exercise of that right is a good, or what she called a "virtuous", one. By which she means, indicative of a good moral character. This is in contrast of things done for "vicious" reasons, which reflect a dubious moral character.[16]

L: I am not sure I can see the distinction.

C: Ok, well how about this example. We both agree that we have a right to freedom of speech, no? We have a legal right to it given the First Amendment of the Constitution, and some would argue that we also have a moral right to freedom of speech.

L: Right.

C: Ok, so we agree that we have a right to freedom of speech, both moral and legal; does that mean that every exercise of that right is morally good or bad in other ways? What if I use my freedom of speech to stand on a corner across the street and yell racist and sexist things to the passersby? Doesn't that reflect a bad character?

L: It absolutely does. It would be wrong to do that.

C: But still within my rights, no?

L: Yes, I suppose so.

C: Another example: I have the right to do whatever I want with the money I have earned, but it would be just downright immoral to go up to a homeless person with my money and taunt him with it.

L: Yes, that would be a horrible thing to do as well. Definitely not indicative of a good moral character.

C: But still within my rights?

L: Yes, still within your rights.

C: All these examples illustrate that there are two questions that we need to untangle from each other. First, is whether I have a moral (or legal) right to something. Second, is what is the most morally virtuous way of exercising those rights. The first is a question about the nature of our rights. The second question is about the best ways of using those rights.

L: Ok, I can see that distinction now.

C: Some exercises of a right is a good, or virtuous, one. Choosing to use my freedom of speech to spread warmth and cheer is virtuous. Or delivering an inspirational speech is virtuous. Using my money to help a homeless person buy food is virtuous. All these examples reveal something good about my character as a human being. But not every exercise of a right is a good, or virtuous one, as the examples we just talked about show.[17]

L: Ok, but let's bring this back to abortion.

C: Sure. I have spent most of my time with you talking about whether women have a moral right to an abortion. Yes, I do think women have such a right, for the many reasons we've already talked about. But that doesn't end the conversation. There are other layers to morality that we should discuss. Do I think every exercise of that right is a virtuous one? No, there may indeed be instances of abortion choice that would not be good, or virtuous. Abortion for sex-selection may qualify as one of those reasons.

L: *May* qualify?

C: I say "may" because I think it is important to take into account the kind of society a woman who makes this decision lives in. If she lives in a society where having a daughter results in financial hardships for her and for her family, I can't just say that she is expressing a vicious character if she seeks an abortion as a way of having to navigate and survive within that society. The viciousness in this example is not expressed by her, but by the society she lives in.

L: In other words, it's society's fault more than the woman's fault?

C: I do think it says a lot about how vicious the society itself is, and no doubt that a society that discriminates against women, or discriminates against anyone, to the point that their deaths are thought of as preferable to their life, has some morally vicious tendencies that need addressing. But, again, I think that's different than blaming someone who has to make choices in accordance with having to live in such a society. Aborting a female fetus in that society may be about preserving the financial health of her existing family, or at least not making it worse than it already is.[18]

L: So you think that some cases of abortion due to sex-selection may be "vicious" as you put it, and that some reflect the "viciousness" of the society the woman lives in, but you still don't think such abortions should be prohibited or regulated?

C: It's just not effective. Restricting abortion because of sex-selection does not stop abortions due to sex-selection.

L: But you still think that there are some reasons for aborting that are bad, or "vicious" reasons?

C: I am open to this possibility.

L: Can you give me an example of an abortion that you think is "vicious"?

C: Well, let's say you become pregnant and, seven months into the pregnancy, you want to get an abortion so that you can travel abroad. I would think that this is a vicious, or indecent, reason for getting an abortion.[19]

L: Are there non-vicious reasons for getting an abortion?

C: In general, I think most of the reasons for which women choose abortion are not vicious. I trust women to make the best decisions about their reproductive lives. Getting an abortion because one has already too many mouths to feed is not vicious. Getting an abortion because parenthood interferes with their career or education is not vicious. Getting an abortion so that you are not tied down to an abusive partner is not vicious. No abortions for these reasons reflect a bad moral character, and I do think that the majority of abortions are of this kind.

L: You mention that you think it would be immoral to abort late in pregnancy just so that you can take a trip abroad. What about other reasons for late abortions?

C: Like what reasons?

(h) Later abortions.

L: You said earlier that at some point, later abortions, abortions happening after fetal viability, may be more morally problematic than early abortions. And you even agreed that some restrictions on post-viability abortions may be justified.

C: I did say that. But I also added a caveat that I don't want to condemn all later abortions outright. I think the reasons for aborting a later fetus, especially a viable fetus, need to be more compelling than the reasons for aborting an early fetus. I may also be ok with *some* restrictions on later abortions. But I also think that there are some cases of later abortions that are morally justified and that should be permitted.

L: Like what? What reasons could exist for killing a fetus that is pretty much every bit a fully formed baby.

C: Well, first, let's talk about the scope of abortions that you're worried about here. Remember the stat I told you on our first day; according to the Centers for Disease Control, 91% of abortions occur before 13 weeks gestation. Only 1.3% of abortions take place within the third trimester. This is hardly an epidemic.[20]

L: That's still like thousands of abortions; thousands of almost fully term babies who are being killed.

C: But out of that 1.3%, most of these cases are due to some kind of fetal abnormality – some which are so bad that they are incompatible with life. These are illnesses or defects such that the fetus will not survive once they are born, if it even survives birth at all. This is a hard case for you as a pro-life advocate. Can you still be against abortion for fetuses who are so sick that they will suffer and die shortly after birth?

L: Can you maybe give an example of the situations you're concerned with here?

(i) Abortion for non-viable pregnancies.

C: Sure. I have a case in mind that I have read about. (*Looks up case on smartphone*). Here is a story about a woman named Erika Christensen. She had an abortion at 32 weeks gestation when she discovered that her fetus had an affliction that would result in the baby being unable to breathe once he was born. The baby would, essentially, suffocate to death. Christensen and her husband chose late abortion because, as she puts it, "it was the most humane possible conclusion to this pregnancy."[21] At the time, later abortions were illegal in New York. So she and her husband had to travel to Colorado and pay $10,000 to obtain the procedure.

L: That's a horribly sad story.

C: Yes it is. This baby was clearly very wanted. This was not an abortion because the woman did not think she was ready for parenthood, or because she was afraid she couldn't balance her work and single parenthood. This abortion was *for the sake of the baby*, who would have died an excruciating death had he been born. Instead, he died in the comfort of her womb, pain-free.

L: What a horrible decision she had to make. I feel for them.

C: As do I. There are many cases similar to this one. None of the traditional arguments against abortion apply in cases like the Christensens. These fetuses have no potential to become persons. They have no future of value of which they are being deprived. I think that these are difficult, heart-wrenching cases, and that late abortions must remain legal, at the very least when pregnancies are not viable, so that the family can make the best decision for themselves and their baby. The government should have no role in deciding these cases.

L: I am not convinced that these abortions are ethical because they still involve the process of directly killing a human being. Maybe the best thing to do is to allow these babies to be born and have them go straight into hospice care, where they are made as comfortable as possible before they die.

C: I am not convinced that hospice can totally alleviate the infants' suffering in these kinds of cases. I suppose that, for me, cases like the Christensens illustrate that there are some situations where killing a human being is the most humane route to take.

L: I have to admit that these are really difficult cases. I still want to say that abortion is wrong, but I can understand what motivates these parents.

C: I wouldn't even call these cases instances of abortion. These are much more like instances of euthanasia. None of these can be classified as "abortions of convenience" as many pro-lifers generally refer to abortion. In each and every one of these cases, the abortion is considered *for the good of the child*. Death is deemed to be in the child's best interest. Now, of course, you can disagree that euthanasia is ever permissible.

L: I do disagree with it. I think it's one thing to allow someone to die because of an underlying disease, but it is quite another to actively kill a human being, even with the best of intentions. I understand why the Christensens did what they did, but it's still killing. It's still wrong.

C: We can probably do a whole presentation in itself about the ethics of euthanasia. That's too tangential, of course. What I want to emphasize is that, once again, late abortions are very, very rare, and in the rare cases they do happen, they are typically because some defect is found in the fetus that either results in their death shortly after birth, or a life, typically also shortened, full of immense pain and suffering.

L: The Christensens' case, and others like it, are heartbreaking no doubt. But let me bring up another hard case. Certainly not all instances of late abortions are because the fetus is terminal. What do you say about abortions late in gestation for reasons not related to fetal health?

C: Well you just admitted that you can understand abortion in these cases, and I can give a little too. I admit that late abortions for reasons unrelated to fetal health are much more morally problematic. I think what's important is to look at the reasons *why* women choose later abortions instead of earlier ones and do our best to meet those needs so that they don't have to make that choice. I've read that one primary reason women wait are logistical delays. They have trouble finding a provider, or being able to afford it.[22] So I'd say that, if we really want to avoid late abortions, we should work towards a society where early abortions are a lot more accessible and affordable.

(j) Abortion due to fetal disabilities.

L: Ok, what about another kind of case of later selective abortion? One in which the fetus is not terminal, but instead has some kind of a disability; one that is perfectly compatible with continued life, and not necessarily a life that is full of pain or sufferings. I am thinking of, for example, Down Syndrome. People with Down Syndrome can go on to lead perfectly wonderful lives. Yet the vast majority of Down Syndrome pregnancies are terminated, many later in pregnancy, if the disability is not discovered early. I read a story that Down Syndrome has been all but eradicated in Iceland because almost 100% of women who test positive for Down Syndrome end up aborting the fetus.[23]

C: I would say that is a private decision in the hands of the parents alone.

L: But should it be though? Think about the message behind these kinds of abortion: that people with disabilities should not exist; that they are defective in some way, that they should have been eradicated before coming into the world. These kind of abortions are not for the sake of the baby, but for the sake of parents, and society, who do not want to deal with the added weight of a disabled child.

C: Can you blame them, however? The statistics for raising a child with a disability can be overwhelming. The cost alone is daunting for many families.[24]

L: But that's not the child's fault. If anything that's the fault of a society that does not do enough to integrate persons with disabilities. This goes back to your saying that abortions due to sex-selection reflect a vicious society. Doesn't abortions due to fetal disability also reflect a vicious society that does not do enough to care for and embrace people with disabilities?

C: That may be true, but that doesn't change the fact that families with disabled children have to deal with much additional costs. I can't blame them for not wanting to deal with it. And, anyways, often the life of a child with a disability has additional pain and suffering that wouldn't be the case for a non-disabled child. Take Down Syndrome again – there is a reduction of cognitive capacities there that reduces positive life aspects and prospects. Some may argue that we have a moral duty to abort in those cases in exchange for creating a child without a disability and, therefore, one with greater life experiences and life prospects.

(k) Is there a duty to have the "best" child?

L: Whoa there now! That's a much stronger statement than what we've discussing. There's a big jump from abortions being morally permissible to abortions being morally *required* in some cases. Are you seriously saying that there are times where the morally right decision is to abort?

C: I think it's appropriate to be a utilitarian in this case, where morality requires us to act in ways that maximizes happiness and minimizes pain for everyone affected by our ethical choices. Let's go back to the IVF examples we've talked about. Say you have two embryos, A and B, and only wanted to implant one. Embryo A is genetically healthy, but embryo B has a genetic predisposition for some kind of defect. Doesn't it seem clear that you should implant the embryo without the genetic defect?[25]

L: No, that doesn't seem clear to me at all. Tell me why it's clear to you.

C: Because, like I said, we should, as much as possible, strive to reduce pain and increase happiness. Embryo A would have a happier, better, and more beneficial life than embryo B. Like it or not, having a disability reduces individual well-being.

(l) Subjective stories of families with disabled children.

L: That's a really controversial statement. On what grounds are you basing this on? You're arguing from your own perspective as a non-disabled person and concluding that because *you* wouldn't want to be disabled that disability is intrinsically worse than non-disability.

C: I suppose I am taking this perspective from my own point of view.

L: Well, that point of view may be biased. There have been plenty of studies about disabled persons and their perceived quality of life. Their subjective self-report illustrates that they are not any less happy with the quality of their lives than non-disabled persons. In terms of familial happiness, studies show it is no more stressful to raise a child with a disability that it is to raise one without a disability. There are different *kinds* of stress associated with each one, but there's not a significant difference in terms of amount.[26]

C: Even if that's true, I still think people should have a choice concerning what kinds of stress they're willing to undergo. No one but the family who is experiencing the prospect of that stress is fit to determine whether or not they should raise a child with significant impairments, even if the impairment is not lethal.

L: But women who are pregnant with a child with Down Syndrome are often pushed into getting an abortion, and sometimes even belittled if they have chosen to bring the pregnancy to term and raise the child. This is by people in the medical community, who have a lot of influence over people's medical decisions because they are regarded as experts.[27]

C: Well, being pro-choice, I certainly don't agree that women should be coerced at all in her reproductive choices. She should make the decision based on the best data available.

L: But that's part of my point; women rely on medical experts to gain that data. But many medical experts are already biased against birthing children with disabilities. They ignore all the research that shows that people with disabilities report that they are generally happy with their lives, and families with disabled children often fare well. It's not really an informed decision when only the negative data is made available to these women and all the positive data is left out.

C: That's a fair point.

(m) The expressivist argument against selective abortion.

L: Plus, have you ever thought about what message selective abortion, aborting fetuses because of their disability, conveys about the value of disabled persons? It conveys a negative and discriminatory attitude against them. It's not unlike racism in important ways. With racism, one takes a single property of a person, their skin color, and uses it to represent the whole person. When choosing abortion due to disability, you're doing the same thing. You are forgoing the opportunity to get to know the whole of your child, and you're letting that one trait, the disability, stand in place of the whole person.[28]

C: I certainly don't mean to endorse such a perspective, but I think there is a difference between disparaging persons with disabilities and wanting to avoid having a child with certain impairments. Disability can often lead to pain and suffering, and even if not, it impairs some important life prospects. It limits educational and job opportunities, and independence. If abortion is permissible, as I think it is, it is certainly permissible for avoiding these states of affairs.[29]

L: But the abortions are performed for different reasons. When a woman obtains an abortion because she doesn't want to, or can't, become a parent for whatever reason, she would abort *any* fetus that she becomes pregnant with. When a woman selectively aborts due to disability she is aborting a fetus who was originally very wanted, but it now discarded due to that disability. The fetus goes from wanted to disposable because of a disability. How can this not convey a negative and prejudicial attitude against that disability – when you're willing to kill an otherwise wanted baby to avoid the disability?[30]

C: Yes, I can see that distinction and why it may be problematic.

(n) The parental attitude argument against selective abortion.

L: Another concern is that such kinds of selective abortion betray a flawed conception of parenthood – one that thinks that parents should be able to guarantee perfection from their children. Also, to allow that one fact about your child to stand in for the whole child; to think that disability precludes joy in parenting. Parenting is about accepting and loving the child you receive, not picking out the ideal child, or lamenting the child you wish you would have had.[31]

C: But in the cases of selective abortion, it's not that one is shooting for perfection. No one is expecting a perfect child, or a perfect parenting experience. No one goes into parenting with that perspective. We all know parenthood is hard and challenging. Parenting children with disabilities makes it especially hard for the reasons I have listed, and it seems perfectly reasonable to want to avoid those difficulties.

L: I don't deny that parenting a child with disabilities brings with it its own unique set of difficulties. But are those difficulties intrinsic to the child, or a byproduct of a society that has failed to sufficiently value, and thus integrate, persons with disabilities?

C: That's a very fair question. Like you said, this may display some viciousness in society, just like the anti-women societies that lead to sex-selection abortion.

L: Right. The correct response is not to get rid of the disabled child, but to work towards a more just and virtuous society that welcomes and integrates persons with disabilities. The solution to the very real concern that a child with disabilities would not be sufficiently cared for after the death of the parents is not to get rid of the child, or to prevent their existence, but to work towards a society in which caring for such persons is wanted and welcome; where such persons are treated with dignity and care. We don't attain that by getting rid of "the problem" through selective abortion.[32]

C: I have to admit that you've given me a lot of think about. There are many more hard cases than I thought there were.

L: Thank you for being willing to listen. I have just one more hard case I want to talk about.

C: Shoot.

(o) Fathers and abortion.

L: What about men and abortion?

C: What about it? This is a non-issue. You don't have a uterus, you don't get to decide what women do with theirs.

L: I figured you would say something like that, but I think the issue is more complex than you're willing to grant it. There are two "horns" to this dilemma. There are men who want to keep the baby, but whose partner obtains an abortion against their consent. Then there are men who want the abortion and the woman wants to keep the baby. Why should they be "on the hook" to care for that child when they didn't want it?

C: The chance to think about those things was before they chose to have sex. Once the woman is pregnant, it's out of his hands.

L: But is that fair? If women get a "second chance" to decide on whether they want to be a parent after conception occurs, isn't it unfair that men can't do the same? Even if they don't choose abortion, women can still give up their babies without question. Consider Safe Haven laws in many states across the U.S., which allows women to give up their newborn infants, typically within a few days after birth, at hospitals, police stations, or fire stations without facing criminal charges. Men don't get to decide the same.

C: I don't see what's unfair about it. If the man doesn't want the baby, but the woman does, then he doesn't need to avail himself of any Safe Haven law, or they both can avail themselves of this law if neither want the baby.

L: But what I am saying is that there seems to be a difference here between what avenues a woman has and what avenues a man has. If a woman can give up her baby no questions asked using Safe Haven laws, why can't men do so as well without being on the hook for 18 years of child support?

C: That's a good point. I hadn't thought of that.

L: Ok, let's consider the reasons women choose abortion. Oftentimes it's to avoid certain kinds of responsibilities.

They can't afford the child, or having a child would interfere with some life prospects that are important to her, like her education or her career.

C: Right.

L: And according to you she should be allowed to make that choice and abortion is a legitimate means of exercising that choice.

C: Correct.

L: But what about the prospective father? Isn't he also facing future responsibilities he may not want? What if he can't afford the child, or what if having a child potentially interferes with his education or his career. Why are these reasons sufficient for granting women a "second chance" after having sex to decide whether she wants to be a mother but men have no such "second chances" after having sex to decide whether he wants to be a father?

C: Well what are you suggesting – that men should also be given the right to an abortion? That's a bit – er – impossible no?

(p) The right of refusal.

L: Of course men can't be granted abortion rights, since they can't get pregnant. I also don't think men should be able to force a woman to get an abortion if she doesn't want to (or at all, really, since I am pro-life). But some philosophers I read in preparation for today's discussion argue that there should be what is called a "right of refusal." That is, if we believe that men and women should have equal moral rights (I am assuming this is true without controversy), then during the time a woman can abort a pregnancy, men can have a correlative right – a right to refuse any future responsibility for the child, should she choose to have it against his will. He can do this without consulting the mother, just like she can have an abortion without consulting him. He can unilaterally decide he wants to avoid all the responsibilities (and rights) that come with fatherhood, just like a woman has the mechanism to avoid future responsibilities (and rights) to the child via abortion.[33]

C: You can't really believe this, do you?

L: Oh no of course I don't believe it. I do believe men have a moral duty to provide for their children regardless of whether they want the baby or not, or, at least, to put the child up for adoption so someone else can care for the baby. But I also don't think women have a right to avoid the rights and responsibilities of parenthood through abortion. But for someone like you, who does believe women have a right to an abortion, it seems that, if you also believe that there should be equal rights between men and women, men should have some parallel right to avoid future parenthood like women have a right to avoid future parenthood.

C: This is a tough one. You're right that I do think men and women should have equal rights, and I also believe that women have a right to an abortion. It seems like the woman has a right that a man lacks. Giving him the right of refusal goes some ways to enacting a parity of rights here, but creates the unwanted consequences of concluding that men should be able to get out of caring for their children. That means, for example, he can't be forced to give child support.

L: Right. If you believe men don't have a right of refusal because they have an obligation to care for their child, then either you have to conclude that men and women should not have equal rights (since the woman has a right that the man lacks) or that women shouldn't have a right to abortion (since, like the man, she can be compelled to care for a child she doesn't want).

C: Man you really got me on this one.

L: Yes, victory!

C: Well hold on a minute. I think there may be a way out of this dilemma. If you believe in the right of refusal, then that means you interpret the right to an abortion as a right to avoid the future duties of parenthood. Since women have such a right, men should too right? That's the crux of the argument?

L: Essentially, yes.

C: Ok, but let's go back to our conversation from last time. I argued in favor of a moral right to an abortion on the grounds that women have a right to decide whether or not they want to use their body to sustain the life of another human being. In other words, the right to an abortion is a subset of the wider right to bodily autonomy. This is a right that *all* persons possess, both men and women. Men are not required to use their body to sustain the life of a person either, as was clearly shown in the *McFall v. Shimp* case. Women also have this right in the case of pregnancy because that is a kind of bodily intrusion that only women can experience. But that's just a fact about biology. If men had to use their bodies to sustain another life, then the same rights would apply to them – they too would have a right to decide if that's the kind of way they want to use their body.

L: But you can't deny that women use their abortion right as a mechanism to get out of the future responsibilities of parenthood.

C: They may *use* it that way, but that's different than saying that this is what the right to an abortion *is*. Say Shimp really hated his cousin McFall, so much so that he wanted him dead. The fact that McFall is in need of his bone marrow in order to live gives Shimp an opportunity to fulfill his wish to see him dead. Still, you wouldn't say that Shimp has a right to kill McFall, even though he is using his right to bodily autonomy as a way to ensure McFall's death. What he has a right to is his own body. Similarly, maybe women use the right to an abortion to prevent the responsibilities of parenthood, but that doesn't mean that women have a right that men lack. Both men and women have a right to decide whether they want to use their body to save someone's life. Both men and women can refuse to do so, even if it costs an innocent person their life. There is no right here that women have that men lack.[34]

L: That seems like a tricky sleight of hand.

C: No sleight, no sleight. I have always defended the moral right to an abortion using considerations of bodily autonomy.

L: But go back to our conversation about *Roe v. Wade* on our first day. The reasons the court decided to give women the right to abort is because of all the social problems that would arise for the woman if she were forced to have a baby she did not want. Women have reproductive autonomy – motherhood is not something that can be compulsory. Shouldn't men also have reproductive autonomy – shouldn't fatherhood also be something that cannot be compulsory?

C: We haven't really talked much about this understanding of reproductive rights. *Roe v. Wade* may have argued in favor of abortion rights using considerations of reproductive autonomy – that motherhood cannot be compulsory – but that does not mean that this is the best way to argue for abortion rights. Maybe I can grant you that, using *Roe v. Wade*'s logic, women are given a right that men lack. But throughout this entire conversation I have always defended abortion using considerations of bodily autonomy. Given that both men and women have bodily autonomy, there is no disparity in rights when abortion rights is understood this way.

L: Ok, I'll let you get away with it. But what about the second horn. What about cases where men really want to keep the baby but the woman aborts nevertheless?

C: What about those cases?

(q) Men and grief over abortion.

L: Well, I mean, don't you feel bad for those men? They're suffering the loss of their potential child. Abortion can have emotional and psychological repercussions for them as well. In some sense, it may even be worse for them, since our society provides no socially sanctioned way for them to express their grief. Since women are the ones who decide on the abortion, only their perspective and their feelings are taken seriously. But men can, and sometimes do, suffer as a result of his partner's abortion.[35]

C: I don't want to appear callous here and ignore any resulting grief men may have after an abortion. I mean, if some women feel grief afterwards, I can certainly imagine that men can feel grief too. However, there's nothing that can be done about that other than offering men counseling of some sort, if they wish to take it.

(r) Can a man force a woman to gestate?

L: You don't think a man should be able to stop his partner from getting an abortion? At the very least shouldn't the woman seek his approval?

C: Again, this is a woman's choice to make. Should a woman tell her partner if she wants to get an abortion? She should, unless she has a good reason not to. What if her partner is violent? What if she has reason to believe he will try to coerce her into not getting an abortion? I think women should be trusted to make the best decisions for themselves. If she trusts her partner enough, she will likely tell him, maybe even involve him in the decision making process.

L: And if she decides against his will to get the abortion anyway?

C: Then that is her choice to make alone.

L: Even if it causes him grief? There is nothing he can do to save his child?

C: What is the alternative? Allowing men to force women to gestate against their will? Do you really think men should have such control over women's bodies? I sure don't. If I don't think a woman should be forced to use her body to save and sustain someone's *life*, I certainly won't agree that she can be forced to use her body to satisfy a, comparatively weaker, desire to be a father. If people can't be

forced to donate lifesaving bodily fluids, like bone marrow, to save someone's life, certainly the desire to be a
father is not a sufficient reason to force a woman to use her
body in a way to which she does not consent.[36]

L: I just can't agree that a man has no say here. If he cares
enough about the fetus to care whether they are aborted,
certainly he sees the fetus has his child already. I can't
imagine the pain of standing by and seeing someone kill a
being you consider to be your child.

C: I'll give you this – I can agree that what you're describing
would be a very painful experience. If a woman is with
a man who deeply values the fetus as his child, then I
agree she should take that under consideration and not be
callous about how the abortion would affect him. Maybe
I can agree that in certain circumstances it would be virtuous for her to *choose* to carry the child for the sake of
the father. By which I mean, it would display a virtuous
or good character for her to agree to gestate a fetus she
doesn't want for the sake of the father. *But* it must always
remain *a choice*. There can be no mechanism that allows a
man to force a woman to gestate a fetus. Giving men such
control over women's bodies is certainly a bad idea.[37]

L: I can see why you think that. I just think it's sad that a
man would have to go through that.

C: I don't disagree that it would be sad. These are the kinds
of things that make it so important to have conversations
like this before couples start having sex. People don't talk
enough about the important things.

L: I can definitely agree with that.

C: Ok, my turn. You've been giving me a lot of hard cases
to think about today. My turn to give you another one.
We already talked about abortion in cases where the fetus
has an affliction incompatible with life, and even still you
disagree that abortion should be an option then.

L: Yes. While I can sympathize with the parents who choose
abortion in these cases, I can't agree that killing the fetus
is the best way to deal with this problem. Some sort of
hospice care for the baby is preferable than killing him.

(s) Abortion in cases of rape.

C: You have already said when we first met that you were
against abortion even in the case of rape, right? I want to
explore that more.

L: I figured we come back to this eventually.

C: We have to talk more about it because I really can't
believe that you think that abortions are wrong, even

then. How about this case. I read about a girl in Paraguay who was 10-years-old and pregnant after her stepfather raped her. In Paraguay, abortions are only legal when necessary to save the mother's life – which is the only concession you gave as well. The girl's mother submitted a request to the government to allow for abortion in this case. Pregnancy and birth for a child as young as 10 is very dangerous, since her body is not prepared for such an ordeal. What should have been done? Should the child, a little 10-year-old girl, be forced to undergo pregnancy and childbirth, which could kill her, when she was already victimized once?[38]

L: If the pregnancy is such that it puts her life at risk, then that would be the one time I would think that abortion is acceptable, which I've already conceded to. Otherwise, I can't justify killing an innocent child. The mother is an unwilling innocent victim when she is raped, but the resulting child is also just as innocent. Why is it ok to make the baby pay for the sins of his father?

C: Because it's not *about* making the baby "pay" for anything. It's about the deep psychological harm that comes to women are who forced to carry and give birth to their rapist's baby. I brought a book with me about the issue that I wanted to read from. You have to have an appreciation for what being a rape victim *does* to a woman's identity. Let me read this part to you: "… the mother of a child conceived in rape has her own, separate primary damage to negotiate. Her identity as a mother proceeds from her identity as a rape victim. Her child embodies the violence done against her and gives manifest permanence to what she may ache to forget."[39] Can you imagine the trauma not just of being raped, but then having to live with a reminder of that rape, day in and day out, for every second she's pregnant.

L: Rape is trauma, agreed. But she will have to, sadly, live with it every day regardless of whether she is pregnant. There's no way to get away from that memory, even if you do abort the child.

C: Have you thought of the consequences to the woman and the child after the baby is born? There are cases in this book of women who could never bring themselves to fully love or accept a child that resulted from rape. There's one example of a woman whose mother refused to let her call her "mom", and who was always treated in a cold and uncaring manner by her, especially when compared to her sister, who was a wanted child.[40] There is another case in the book where the mom says that "the laughter of my little boy often reminded me of the hideous laughter of this guy as he had raped me. I took it out on my son."[41] And yet another case, where a woman pleads to the author of the book as he is interviewing her to "fix" her because "why can't I hug my daughter? I love her, but when she touches me, it feels like a hundred razor blades scraping across my skin, like I'm going to die."[42]

L: I can't imagine how devastating it would be to have to live that way, for both the woman and the baby.

C: There are cases in the book about the systematic rape of women during periods of war and genocide. During the Rwandan genocide, babies who were born as a result of rape were called *enfants de mauvais souvenir,* or "the children of bad memories."[43] Women who were victims of rape during the genocide often "self-induced abortion, attempted suicide, or committed infanticide. Some women left rape babies on church steps; the country is peppered with orphanages."[44] In what was one of the more disturbing parts to read, there is a story of a woman who was the victim of a rape in Kosovo. When the baby was born the woman "cradled him to her chest, she looked into her boy's eyes, she stroked his face and she snapped his neck ... in her psychiatric detention cell ... she has been weeping ever since."[45]

L: These are just horrendous stories.

C: They are. In our first meeting you were worried that it was abortion that led to emotional and psychological issues for women. We saw that even a pro-life Surgeon General would not agree that this was the case. However, it seems that we have evidence that it is forcing a woman to carry and give birth to a baby conceived from rape that is more damaging to her psyche.

L: Are they all like this? Are there any stories of women who gave birth in these circumstances and were happy about having kept the child?

C: Admittedly yes, there are a few cases like that. There was one woman who says that she thanks "God every day that I have my child. But I can't ignore the fact that it's a very painful thing, why she's here."[46] There's another woman who says that she is the lucky one, instead of her rapists, because "all I know is that I have something that these people will never know. Never know that they have a beautiful daughter. Never know that they have beautiful grandchildren. They'll never know. But I do. And so, as it turns out, I'm the lucky one."[47]

L: Well, see, there you go.

C: See what?

L: It's not all gruesome and disturbing stories. Some women can find meaning and joy in their children even after rape.

C: That's not what I think we should be taking from these stories. All these women are traumatized. Some of this trauma is exacerbated by giving birth to the child, or having to parent the child.

L: But for some of the women, the child is a way to heal.

C: Yes, but that's the point. For *some* of the women it's trauma and for *some* of the women it's a method of healing. The point is that *no one is entitled to make that decision except for the woman herself.* Remember being pro-choice isn't about pushing abortion, it's about offering women a genuine choice over their bodies and reproductive decisions on the basis that she is capable of doing so and that no one else is entitled to make that decision. If she wants to choose abortion as a way of lessening her trauma, she should be allowed to. If she wants to keep and raise the baby as a way of lessening her trauma, she should be allowed to. If we're really interested in women's health, both physically and psychologically, then being pro-choice is the best way to go, rather than forcing or compelling pregnancy.

L: I don't, ultimately, agree with you, but I can't deny that it would be traumatic for some women who were raped to be forced to carry the baby to term. But I still can't shake the belief that the baby's life matters as well.

C: And I can't shake the belief that choice, in the end, is the best way to go when dealing with any kind of unplanned pregnancy.

(t) Final thoughts.

L: So where does this lead us? We're right back where we started. Has this whole conversation been useless?

C: I don't think it has. We did agree on some things right? For example, we agree that access to sex education and affordable and effective contraception was one way to combat unwanted pregnancies. We both agree that minimizing abortion is a laudable goal, and we agree on some ways of achieving that. We agree that our society needs to implement more family centered policies, like paid maternity leave. We also agree that being pro-life is also about supporting or helping that life once it is born, and not just when it is in utero.

L: So we did agree to some things. We should end the presentation highlighting these areas of agreement.

C: I think that would be an excellent way to end.

L: I also think it's important that we mention how our conversation these last five days has changed us or our position on abortion. I have to admit that one of the best things I have gotten from this whole conversation is a respect for the pro-choice position, as well as people who espouse it. I used to think that you were doing nothing but supporting infanticide. I don't think that anymore. I think you're genuinely concerned over the plight of women, and that you think abortion rights are an integral part of that.

C: Well, you've taught me that not all pro-life persons are just religious fanatics trying to impose their religious views on the rest of us. You have also taught me that women being barefoot and pregnant is not your final goal. We disagree on whether the fetus is morally equivalent to a baby, but if someone truly believes they are, I can see why they would find abortions unacceptable. You've helped me see it from a new perspective. It's not a perspective I agree with, but I can now respect it.

L: Same here. We started a dialogue, successfully completed it, and, despite these differences, became friends. On a topic that constantly has our society at each other's throats. I think we've come a long way, and that we have a lot to offer for our presentation.

C: Agreed. I just hope it's enough for an A!

Notes

1 United States Supreme Court. *Planned Parenthood v. Casey* (1992). https://www.law.cornell.edu/supremecourt/text/505/833

2 Quoted in: Linda B. McClain. "Equality, Oppression, and Abortion: Women Who Oppose Abortion Rights in the Name of Feminism" in *Feminist Nightmares: Women at Odds: Feminism and the Problems of Sisterhood*, edited by Susan Ostrov Weisser and Jennifer Fleischner. (1994). New York University Press: 100–116, at p. 103.

3 Mary Ziegler. "Women's Rights on the Right: The History and Stakes of Modern Pro-life Feminism." (2013) *Berkeley Journal of Gender, Law, and Justice*, 232: "FFL set out one view of pro-life feminism: progressive feminists, the argument went, could logically support sex equality while opposing abortion as a degradation of women and as an excuse for men seeking to exploit them … abortion allowed men to use women sexually without suffering any consequences …" (p. 238).

4 Ziegler, 2013, p. 238.

5 Laury Oaks. "What are Pro-Life Feminists Doing on Campus?" (2009). *National Women's Studies Association Journal*, 21.1: 178–203: "[According to pro-life feminism] the legal option of abortion supports anti-motherhood social attitudes and policies and limits respect for women's citizenship; women come to see pregnancy and parenting as obstacles to full participation in education and the workplace" (pp. 179–180).

6 Ziegler, 2013, pp. 241-242: "[ACCL's former director, named Warren Schaller] articulated the organization's position that 'women should be able to control their own reproductive functions and couples should be able to determine the size of their family'... women could avoid abortion only if they could effectively avoid unwanted pregnancies."

7 Oaks, 2009, p. 185.

8 Ziegler, 2013, p. 242.

9 Ziegler, 2013: "Representatives of the two groups agreed, however, on a funda-mental point: true reproductive choice required government protection against sex discrimination, particularly for women who did not want to have to sacrifice their careers ... ACCL members, like feminists who supported abortion rights, endorsed state-sponsored family planning services and argued that women should have welfare rights and freedom from sex discrimination – both of which would make reproductive decisions truly voluntarily and meaningful" (pp. 243–245).

10 McClain, 1994, p. 103

11 Feminist for Life of America. https://www.feministsforlife.org/

12 Ziegler, 2013, pp 246–248.

13 Therese Hesketh, Li Lu, and Zhu Wei Xing. "The Consequences of Son Preference and Sex-Selective Abortion in China and Other Asian Countries." (2011). *Canadian Medical Association Journal*, 183.12: 1374–1477.

14 Sneha Barot. "A Problem and Solution Mismatch: Son Preference and Sex-Selective Abortion Bans." (2012) *Guttmacher Policy Review*, 15.2. https://www.guttmacher.org/gpr/2012/05/problem-and-solution-mismatch-son-preference-and-sex-selective-abortion-bans

15 Barot, 2012: "As in China, India has considerable fluctuations across differ-ent regions and localities. For example, the northern Indian states of Haryana and Punjab are notorious for their exceedingly disparate ratios, at 830 and 846, respectively, with some districts dipping into the 770s. In contrast, south India has normal sex ratios. In this regard, it is worth noting that the status of women in parts of south India is higher than in the rest of the subcontinent; gender discrimination – and thereby son preference – apparently is not motivating women and their families to use the same accessible technology for sex-selection purposes in these regions."

16 Rosalind Hursthouse. "Virtue Theory and Abortion." (1991). *Philosophy & Public Affairs*, 20.3: 223–246.

17 Hursthouse, 1991: "But, putting all questions about the justice or injustice of laws to one side, and supposing only that women have such a moral right, nothing follows from this supposition about the morality of abortion, according to virtue theory, once it is noted (quite generally, not with particular reference to abortion) that in exercising a moral right I can do something cruel, or callous, or selfish, light-minded, self-righteous, stupid, inconsiderate, disloyal, dishonest – that is, act viciously. Love and friendship do not survive their parties' constantly insisting on their rights, nor do people live well when they think that getting what they have a right to is of preeminent importance; they harm others, and they harm themselves. So whether women have a moral right to terminate their pregnancies is irrelevant within virtue theory, for it is irrelevant to the question 'In having an abortion in these circumstances, would the agent be acting virtuously or viciously or neither?'" (pp. 234–235).

18 Hursthouse, 1991: Hursthouse says something similar when talking about the societal realities and hardships that cause some women to seek abortions. She argues that the "viciousness" comes not from the woman in these cases, but by the society in which the woman must survive: "To go through with a pregnancy when one is utterly exhausted, or when one's job consists of crawling along

tunnels hauling coal, as many women in the nineteenth century were obliged to do, is perhaps heroic, but people who do not achieve heroism are not necessarily vicious. That they can view the pregnancy only as eight months of misery, followed by hours if not days of agony and exhaustion, and abortion only as the blessed escape from this prospect, is entirely understandable and does not manifest any lack of serious respect for human life or a shallow attitude to motherhood. What it does show is that something is terribly amiss in the conditions of their lives, which make it so hard to recognize pregnancy and childbearing as the good that they can be" (pp. 239–240).

19 Judith Jarvis Thomson. "A Defense of Abortion" (1971). *Philosophy and Public Affairs*, 1.1: 47–66. Thomson calls these instances of abortion "indecent": "It would be indecent in the woman to request an abortion and indecent in a doctor to perform it, if she is in her seventh month, and wants the abortion just to avoid the nuisance of postponing a trip abroad" (pp. 65–66).

20 Centers for Disease Control and Prevention. "Data and Statistics on Reproductive Health." (2016). https://www.cdc.gov/reproductivehealth/data_stats/index.htm

21 Erika Christensen. "New York Forces Women Like Me to Carry Nonviable Pregnancies to Term." (2017) https://rewire.news/article/2017/05/23/new-york-forces-women-like-carry-nonviable-pregnancies-term/

22 According to a study from the Guttmacher Institute: "women seeking later abortions typically experience more logistical delays – including difficulties finding a provider, raising funds for the procedure and travel, finding a facility and securing insurance coverage – than women who receive a first-trimester abortion … [over half of the women surveyed] "wish[ed] that they could have obtained their abortion earlier." (Guttmacher Institute. "Later Abortions." (2019). https://www.guttmacher.org/evidence-you-can-use/later-abortion).

23 Julian Quinones and Arijeta Lajka. "'What Kind of Society Do You Want to Live In'? Inside the Country where Down Syndrome is Disappearing." (2017). https://www.cbsnews.com/news/down-syndrome-iceland/

24 Tom Shimabukuro, Scott Grosse, and Catherine Rice. "Medical Expenditures for Children with an Autism Spectrum Disorder in a Privately Insured Population." (2008). *Journal of Autism and Developmental Disorder*, 38.3: 546–552. As an example of the added expenses of raising a disabled child, this study noted that, when it comes to children diagnosed with autism spectrum disorder (ASD), "medical expenditures for individuals with ASD were 4.1 – 6.2 times greater than those without an ASD. Differences in median expenditures ranged from $2,240 to $3,360 per year with median expenditures 8.4–9.5 times greater. These findings add to a growing body of evidence that children and adolescents with medical diagnoses of an ASD incur elevated medical utilization costs" (p. 546).

25 Julian Savulescu. "Procreative Beneficence: Why We Should Select the Best Children." (2001). *Bioethics*, 15.5/6: 413–426. Savulescu calls this "procreative beneficence": "couples (or single reproducers) should select the child, of the possible children they could have, who is expected to have the best life, or at least as good of a life as the others, based on the relevant available information" (p. 415).

26 Erik Parens and Adrienne Asche. "The Disability Rights Critique of Prenatal Genetic Testing: Reflections and Recommendations in *Prenatal Testing and Disability Rights*, edited by Erk Parens and Adrienne Asch. (2007). Georgetown University Press: 3–43. Parens and Asche write: "… families that include disabled children fare on average no better or worse than families in general … while disability critics of prenatal diagnosis acknowledge that disability is likely to entail some amount of physical, psychological, social, and economic hardship, they hold that when viewed alongside any other life, on balance, life is no worse for people who have disabilities than it is for people who do not … there is no more stress in raising a child with a disability

than in raising any other child, even if at some times there is more stress, or different stress. In that sense, the disability community claims that disability is on balance neutral" (pp. 20 & 26).

27   Parens and Asche, 2007: "A recent study designed to understand the experience of mothers who received a prenatal diagnosis of Down Syndrome and chose to continue the pregnancy found problematic attitudes toward people with disabilities, evidenced in the way that medical professionals spoke to those prospective mothers ... some genetic counselors reacted negatively to women who intended to bear and raise children with Down Syndrome. A woman who was told that the fetus she was carrying would have Down Syndrome reported the following: '[The genetic counselor] treated me as though I couldn't accept this news, although I told her I could. She asked, 'What are you going to say to people when they ask you how you could bring a child like this into the world'? To say nothing of this counselor's failure to discuss the woman's decision without judging it, her words suggest that she has not thought deeply about what disabilities mean for individuals who live with them and for their families" (pp. 6–7).

28   Parens and Asche, 2007: Parens and Asche call this the expressivist argument against selective abortion: "Prenatal testing seems to be more of the discriminatory same: a single trait stands in for the whole (potential) person. Knowledge of that single trait is enough to warrant the abortion of an otherwise wanted fetus...the test sends the hurtful message that people are reducible to a single, perceived-to-be undesirable trait" (p. 14).

29   Bonnie Steinbock. "Disability, Prenatal Testing, and Selective Abortion in *Prenatal Testing and Disability Rights*, edited by Erik Parens and Adrienne Asch. (2007). Georgetown University Press: 108–123. Steinbock writes, in defense of selective abortion, "it is reasonable for parents to wish to avoid having a child with a serious disability, like spina bifida or Down Syndrome or cystic fibrosis, because these conditions may involve undesirable events, such as pain, repeated hospitalizations and operations, paralysis, a shorted life span, limited educational and job opportunities, limited independence and so forth ... if abortion is permissible at all, it is permissible to avoid such outcomes, or the risk of such outcomes" (p. 119).

30   Parens and Asche, 2007: Parens and Asche call this the "any/particular" distinction: "... most abortions reflect a decision not to bring any fetus to term at this time; selective abortions involve a decision not to bring this particular fetus to term because of its traits" (p. 15).

31   Parens and Asche, 2007: "According to the parental attitude argument, prospective parents should keep in mind that the disabling trait is only one of a fetus's characteristics. The activity of appreciating and nurturing the particular child one has is what the critics of selection view as the essence of good parenting. Loving and nurturing a child entails appreciating, enjoying, and developing as best one can the characteristics of the child one has, not turning the child into something she is not or lamenting what she is not" (pp. 17–18).

32   Parens and Asche, 2007: "According to the disability rights critique of prenatal testing, if people with disabilities were fully integrated into society, then there would be no need for the testing. In the world they seek to create, if a given health status turned out to be a handicap, that would be because of societal, not personal, deficits; the appropriate response would be to change society so that the person could live a full life with a range of talents, capacities, and difficulties that exist for everyone. In a society that welcomed the disabled as well as the nondisabled, there would be no reason to prevent the births of people with traits now called disabling" (p. 23).

33   Stephen Hales. "Abortion and Fathers' Rights" in *Analyzing Moral Issues*, 3rd edition, edited by Judith Boss. (2005). McGraw Hill Press: 118–125. Hales writes: "The right of refusal is to be designed as a parallel ... of the mother's

right to an abortion. Let us put it this way: A man has the moral right to decide not to become a father (in the social, nonbiological sense) during the time that the woman he has impregnated may permissibly abort. He can make a unilateral decision whether to refuse fatherhood, and is not morally obliged to consult with the mother or any other person before reaching a decision. Moreover, neither the mother nor any other person can veto or override a man's decision about becoming a father. He has the first and last say about what he does with his life in this regard." (p. 120).

34 Bertha Alvarez Manninen. *Pro-Life, Pro-Choice: Shared Values in the Abortion Debate*. (2014). Vanderbilt University Press. Manninen writes: "The right to an abortion is a subset of the broader right to bodily autonomy. On the basis of this interpretation of abortion rights, Hales's argument … fails. There is no unique right women possess that men do not because men also have a right to decide whether to use their bodies to sustain the life of another human being. The right to an abortion provides a mechanism for women to exercise the same right that men have: the right to refuse bodily intrusion" (p. 170).

35 Stacey Kalish. "Hidden Made Grief" (2004). *Psychology Today*. https://www. psychologytoday.com/us/articles/200405/hidden-male-grief
Kalish discusses specific examples of men who felt some degree of grief after their partner obtained an abortion, even though they fully supported the decision. For example: "Years later, Michael, along with many men who've faced an unplanned pregnancy, feels a lingering weight from the experience but has no socially sanctioned means of talking about his emotions. The sharply divided politics of abortion can make it difficult even for staunchly pro-choice men, like Michael, to express sadness. David, a student from Washington state, strongly supports a woman's right to abortion but had feelings of both 'relief and regret' after his girlfriend ended a pregnancy … [the emotional toll of abortion on men] can manifest itself in low self-esteem, substance abuse, failed relationships and sexual dysfunction … Years later, Michael says he still thinks about the experience. He feels it 'seeps into the subconscious and always stays with you.'"

36 Bertha Alvarez Manninen. "Pleading Men and Virtuous Women: Considering the Role of the Father in the Abortion Debate." (2007). *International Journal of Applied Philosophy*, 21.1: 1–24. Manninen writes: "… should a woman be compelled to gestate a fetus for the purpose of securing a man's interest in becoming a father to this specific child? … surely if the interest in continued existence … is not strong enough to force bodily intrusion upon another human being … the interest in becoming a parent cannot be strong enough to warrant such bodily intrusion either" (p. 5).

37 See: Manninen, 2007 for a detailed argument of this sort using considerations of virtue ethics and care ethics.

38 Debbie Sharnak. "Raped, Pregnant, and Denied a Life-Saving Abortion – All at 10-years-old." (2015). *Amnesty International*. https://www.amnestyusa.org/raped-pregnant-and-denied-a-life-saving-abortion-all-at-10-years-old/

39 Andrew Solomon. *Far From the Tree: Parents, Children, and the Search for Identity*. (2012). Scribner Press, p. 478.

40 Solomon, 2012, pp. 503–504.

41 Solomon, 2012, p. 486.

42 Solomon, 2012, p. 511.

43 Solomon, 2012, p. 527.

44 Solomon, 2012, p. 527.

45 Solomon, 2012, pp. 529–530.

46 Solomon, 2012, p. 483.

47 Solomon, 2012, p. 489.

ANNOTATED BIBLIOGRAPHY

Day 1

Battin, Margaret P. "Sex and Consequences: World Population Growth vs. Reproductive Rights." (1997). *Philosophic Exchange*, 27.1: 19–31.

> In this article, Margaret Battin argues in favor of universally distributing reversible contraception for all fertile women (and when the technology exists, all fertile men), so that the contraception would have to be deliberately removed when a couple wants to conceive. Battin argues that this would reduce population growth, abortion, and enhance reproductive freedom.

BBC News. "World's Smallest Surviving Premature Baby Released from U.S. Hospital." (2019). https://www.bbc.com/news/world-us-canada-48458780

> Story of "baby Saybie" who was born at 23 weeks and 3 days, weighing only 8.6 oz. She was released from the hospital after a five-month stay in the neonatal intensive care unit.

Boonin, David. *A Defense of Abortion.* (2003). Cambridge University Press.

> In this book, David Boonin argues in favor of the right to an abortion, mostly by defending Judith Jarvis Thomson's arguments in her seminal essay "A Defense of Abortion." Boonin then goes through many of the objections often posed to Thomson's argument and responds to them. He also considers arguments in favor of allotting the human fetus a right to life and illustrates why the arguments are ultimately unsuccessful. Finally, Boonin considers other arguments against abortion that do not depend on a fetal right to life, and argues that those, also, should be rejected.

Centers for Disease Control and Prevention. "Data and Statistics on Reproductive Health" (2016). https://www.cdc.gov/reproductivehealth/data_stats/index.htm

> This article summarizes relevant data and statistics on issues in reproductive health in the United States. This includes abortion, but also assisted reproductive

technologies, infant health, women's reproductive health, maternal health and pregnancy, teen pregnancy, tobacco use and pregnancy, and unintended pregnancy.

Cohen, Susan. "Abortion and Mental Health: Myths and Realities." (2006). *Guttmacher Policy Review*, 9.13. https://www.guttmacher.org/gpr/2006/08/abortion-and-mental-health-myths-and-realities

> This article combats disinformation concerning the alleged connection between abortion and mental and physical health. The article covers multiple studies conducted by the American Psychological Association that concludes that there is no causal link between abortions and negative mental health problems. Studies noting no negative link between abortions and future fertility are also discussed.

Guttmacher Institute. "Abortion Worldwide 2017: Uneven Progress and Unequal Access" (2018). https://www.guttmacher.org/report/abortion-worldwide-2017

> This article provides current information on abortion incidences around the world. Laws regulating abortions are discussed, as well as the impact of abortion laws on women's health.

Guttmacher Institute. "An Overview of Abortion Laws" (2021). https://www.guttmacher.org/state-policy/explore/overview-abortion-laws

> An overview of the United States' abortion laws, broken down by state, including abortion restrictions.

Guttmacher Institute. "Medicaid Coverage of Abortion" (2021). https://www.guttmacher.org/evidence-you-can-use/medicaid-funding-abortion

> Information on state laws and policies pertaining to Medicaid's funding of abortions.

Guttmacher Institute. "The U.S. Abortion Rate Continues to Drop" (2019). https://www.guttmacher.org/gpr/2019/09/us-abortion-rate-continues-drop-once-again-state-abortion-restrictions-are-not-main

> A study on the decline of abortion rates in the United States. The authors conclude that the decline is more likely the result of a reduction in unplanned pregnancies rather than imposed abortion restrictions.

Kim, James H. and Anthony R. Scialli. "Thalidomide: The Tragedy of Birth Defects and the Effective Treatment of Disease." (2011). *Toxicological Sciences*, 122.2: 1–6.

> An article about the 1960s thalidomide scare, including how the incident changed the United States' toxicity testing protocols.

Kost, Kathryn and Stanley Henshaw. "U.S. Teenage Pregnancies, Births and Abortions, 2010: National and State Trends by Age, Race and Ethnicity." (2014). https://www.guttmacher.org/sites/default/files/report_pdf/ustptrends10.pdf

> A report on the incidences of teenage pregnancies and teenage abortion in the United States, broken down by individual states, and race and ethnicity.

Manninen, Bertha Alvarez. "Beyond Abortion: The Implications of Human Life Amendments." (2012). *Journal of Social Philosophy*, 43.2: 140–160.

> In this essay, Bertha Alvarez Manninen argues that various states' attempts to pass Personhood Amendments, which would grant legal protection to embryos and fetuses from conception, has implications beyond just abortion. Manninen argues that fertility treatments would be affected, women would be more likely to be implicated for miscarriages and stillbirths, and there would be other limits to women's autonomy. Finally, Manninen argues that such amendments would render violence against abortion doctors justified. Because of these negative consequences, Personhood Amendments should, ultimately, be rejected.

Manninen, Bertha Alvarez. *Pro-Life, Pro-Choice: Shared Values in the Abortion Debate.* (2014). Vanderbilt University Press.

> In this book, Bertha Alvarez Manninen defends a pro-choice view on abortion ethics by supplementing Judith Jarvis Thomson's arguments in "A Defense of Abortion." She also tries to dispel many stereotypes that pro-choice advocates face, including the belief that they are "pro-abortion" and that they do not care about children, families, or motherhood. Manninen also writes about what role potential fathers should play when it comes to abortion, and she works to highlight areas of agreement between pro-choice and pro-life advocates, with the hope that such a focus can help pave the way for fruitful dialogue between the two sides.

New York Times. "They Were Jailed for Miscarriages. Now, Campaign Aims to End Abortion Ban." (2018). https://www.nytimes.com/2018/04/09/world/americas/el-salvador-abortion.html

> News story reporting on the incidences of jailing women for miscarriages and stillbirths in El Salvador, a country with one of the most restrictive abortion laws in Latin America.

State of New York. *S. 240 Reproductive Health Act.* (2019). https://legislation.nysenate.gov/pdf/bills/2019/S240

> On January 22, 2019, on the 46th anniversary of *Roe v. Wade*, New York state passed the Reproductive Health Act (RHA). The law removes abortion from the state's criminal code and renders it a public health issue, thereby protecting any medical professional who performs abortions from prosecution. It also reaffirms abortion, as well as contraception, as a "fundamental component of a woman's health, privacy and equality." The RHA specifies three conditions under which an abortion is obtainable in New York:
>
> > A health care practitioner licensed, certified, or authorized under title eight of the education, law, acting within his or her lawful scope of practice, may perform an abortion when, according to the practitioner's reasonable and good faith professional judgement based on the facts of the patient's case: the patient is within twenty-four weeks of pregnancy, or there is an absence of fetal viability, or the abortion is necessary to protect the patient's life or health.

Sedgh, Gilda and Jonathan Bearak *et al.* "Abortion Incidence Between 1990 and 2014: Global, Regional, and Subregional Levels and Trends." (2016) *The Lancet*, 388: 258–267.
http://www.thelancet.com/pdfs/journals/lancet/PIIS0140-6736%2816%2930380-4.pdf

> Large study of the incidences of induced abortions in both the developed and developing world. Among other conclusions, the study found that abortion rates are declining in the developed world, but not in the developing world. The study concludes that access to contraception, sex education, and reproductive healthcare reduces the rates of unplanned pregnancy and abortion.

Tennessee Supreme Court. *Davis v. Davis.* (1992). https://law.justia.com/cases/tennessee/supreme-court/1992/842-s-w-2d-588-2.html

> This case involves a formerly married couple, Mary Sue Davis and Junior Davis, who disagreed as to the fate of their cryogenically preserved embryos. Ms. Davis wanted to, at first, use the embryos herself to try to conceive, and then wanted them donated to a childless couple. Mr. Davis disagreed, stating he did not want to be a genetic parent to these embryos. The court ruled in favor of Mr. Davis stating that, in most cases, the party wishing to refrain from procreation should prevail, though using the embryos should be considered in cases where no other alternative to becoming a parent exists.

United States Supreme Court. *Doe v. Bolton.* (1973). https://www.law.cornell.edu/supremecourt/text/410/179

> This Supreme Court case rendered Georgia's restrictive abortion laws unconstitutional. Mary Doe (a pseudonym) sued Arthur Bolton, the attorney general of Georgia, challenging Georgia's abortion laws making it illegal for her to obtain one unless she was raped, if it were necessary to save her life, or in cases of fetal deformity. The case was decided 7-2 in favor of Doe.

United States Supreme Court. *Eisenstadt v. Baird.* (1972). https://supreme.justia.com/cases/federal/us/405/438/

> The 1972 court case establishing the right of unmarried people to obtain contraception, after *Griswold v. Connecticut* (1965) established the right for married couples. William Baird was charged with distributing contraception to unmarried persons at Boston University. The case was decided 6-1 in favor of Baird and of extending the same rights to contraception to unmarried persons as was given to married persons.

United States Supreme Court. *Planned Parenthood v. Casey.* (1992). https://www.law.cornell.edu/supremecourt/text/505/833

> In Pennsylvania, new laws were enacted restricting abortions, including a 24-hour waiting period, requiring minors seeking an abortion to obtain the consent of at least one parent, and requiring a married woman to notify her husband of her intent to obtain an abortion. Planned Parenthood challenged these laws, and the Supreme Court, in a 5 to 4 split, upheld the new abortions laws except for the spousal notification one because it was deemed to cause an "undue burden" on pregnant women. The court also overturned the trimester framework of *Roe v. Wade*, and allowed states to impose abortion restrictions after the

onset of fetal viability regardless of when in gestation it takes place (mostly in the third trimester, but also during the latter part of the second trimester).

United States Supreme Court. *Roe v. Wade.* (1973). https://www.law.cornell.edu/supremecourt/text/410/113

> The landmark 1973 case that rendered Texas's restrictive abortion laws unconstitutional. Jane Roe (her real name was Norma McCorvey) sued Henry Wade, a district attorney, challenging Texas's abortion laws making it illegal for her to obtain one unless it was necessary to save her life. The case was decided 7-2 in favor of Roe, with the Justices arguing that a woman's right to privacy, guaranteed by the 14th Amendment, includes a right to terminate her pregnancy without limitations during the first trimester. During the second trimester, abortion procedures can be restricted by the state only when deemed harmful to women's health. However, states are able to place abortion restrictions in the third trimester in order to advance the government's interest in protecting human life, after the onset of fetal viability.

University of California San Francisco's Bixby Center for Global and Reproductive Health. "Turnaway Study" (2019). https://www.ansirh.org/sites/default/files/publications/files/turnaway_study_brief_web.pdf

> In this study, over 1000 women who sought abortions in over 30 facilities across the United States were interviewed over a 5-year period, some who had received abortions and some who were turned away because the pregnancy had surpassed the gestational age limit for that state. The researchers concluded that obtaining an abortion does not harm women, finding no correlations between abortion and negative mental health. Moreover, the study found some positive outcomes for women who did receive abortions, noting that 95% of women did not regret their abortions, believing that it was the right decision for them at that time in their lives. On the other hand, there were harmful outcomes associated with women who were denied abortions, including negative financial repercussions and adverse impact on women's health.

Day 2

Beckwith, Francis. *Defending Life: A Moral and Legal Case Against Abortion Choice* (2007). Cambridge University Press

> In this book, Francis Beckwith argues in favor of fetal personhood and of including embryos and fetuses in the moral community. He calls his main argument the "substance view of persons", arguing that fetuses are essentially rational moral agents throughout the entirety of their existence. Beckwith also responds to some common pro-choice arguments, including the argument from bodily autonomy, and argues against the Supreme Court Justices' decision in *Roe v. Wade.*

Burgess, J.A. and S.A. Tawia. "When Did You First Begin to Feel It? – Locating the Beginning of Human Consciousness." (1996). *Bioethics,* 10.1: 1–26.

> In this paper, J.A. Burgess and S.A. Tawia address the issue of when a human fetus first becomes conscious. They look at the electrical activity in the cerebral cortex, which underpins the capacity for consciousness, and argue that there is

no specific moment in gestation where the fetus suddenly become conscious. Instead, consciousness develops in a human being gradually, as "isolated discontinuous puddles." While electrical activity can be found in a fetal brain as early as 10 weeks gestation, this alone is not sufficient for conscious awareness, as there has to be cortical brain activity. They conclude that the earliest time these "puddles" of consciousness can be located is 20 weeks gestation, but that more pronounced sleep/wake cycles, while varying from fetus to fetus, can be found between 30 and 35 weeks gestation.

Feinberg, Joel. *The Moral Limits of the Criminal Law, Volume 1: Harm to Others* (1984). Oxford University Press..

In this book, Joel Feinberg focuses on a utilitarian principle known the "harm principle", which states that a government may curtail its citizens' liberties only when it is necessary to prevent harm to others. Feinberg defines harm as the setting back or defeating of interests, which are defined as things one has a stake in, or things that matter to a person. Feinberg distinguishes between welfare interests, which are more foundational interests, such as life and health, and ulterior interests, which are the goals and desires individuals set for themselves. Feinberg then applies his argument to practical moral issues, detailing what acts a government may legitimately criminalize in order to prevent harm to others.

Kuljis, Rodrigo O. "Development of the Human Brain: The Emergence of the Neural Substrate for Pain Perception and Conscious Experience" in *The Beginning of Human Life*, edited by F.K. Beller and R.F. Weir. (1994). Kluwer Academic Publishers: 49–56.

Rodrigo Kuljis argues that addressing the issue of when the fetus becomes a person with a functioning brain, in addition to other questions in reproductive technology, requires an understanding of what neural structures in the brain are necessary for consciousness and pain perception. This paper provides an accessible explanation of the neural substrate necessary for human consciousness and pain perception, with a focus on the development of the cerebral cortex.

Manninen, Bertha Alvarez and Jack Mulder Jr. *A Civil Dialogue on Abortion* (2018). Routledge.

In this book, Bertha Alvarez Manninen and Jack Mulder Jr. each argue for their respective views on abortion (Manninen is pro-choice and Mulder is pro-life), while also responding to each other's arguments. They also have a jointly written chapter where they highlight their areas of agreement in the hopes that the book will model civil dialogue on a controversial moral issue.

Nobis, Nathan and Kristina Grob. *Thinking Critically About Abortion: Why Most Abortions Aren't Wrong and Why All Abortions Should Be Legal.* (2019). Open Philosophy Press. https://www.abortionarguments.com/p/full-text.html#bad

This accessible book first covers some of the problematic arguments from both the pro-choice and pro-life sides and illustrates why they are flawed. Nathan Nobis and Kristina Grob then offer better arguments from both perspectives, but ultimately support arguments that show that most abortions are not morally problematic.

Noonan, John. "An Almost Absolute Value in History" in *The Morality of Abortion: Legal and Historical Perspectives*, edited by John Noonan. (1970). Harvard University Press: 51–59.

John Noonan defends a genetic account of humanity and personhood, arguing that if you are conceived from human parents, then you are a human being. He argues against alternative accounts of when a fetus "becomes human", rejecting viability, consciousness, and social visibility. He also offers a probability argument in favor of personhood, stating that the chance for a fertilized egg to become a human person is about 80%. This is a sufficient marker for determining if one is human, thereby rendering conception the best account of when a human life has begun to exist.

Science News. "Which Fertilized Eggs Will Become Human Fetuses? Researchers Predict with 93% Accuracy." (2010). https://www.sciencedaily.com/releases/2010/10/101003205930.htm

A brief overview of a study in which researchers can predict with 93% accuracy which fertilized eggs will successfully implant in the womb and go on to become human fetuses.

Singer, Peter. *Practical Ethics*, 2 ed. (1993). Cambridge University Press.

Peter Singer covers many topics in this book, applying the utilitarian moral theory to issues such as abortion, euthanasia, the environment, animal rights, and our moral obligations to the poor. He argues that what makes killing generally morally wrong is that it thwarts the individual's desire, or preference, for continued existence. In order to have these desires, however, it must be possible to conceive of oneself as a distinct entity who exists over time, i.e., one must be robustly self-aware. Individuals with self-awareness are persons, and Singer argues that the term should be separated from the term "human" since not all human beings are self-aware. Fetuses lack self-awareness, and so they have no interest in continued existence and therefore no right to life.

Singer, Peter and Deanne Wells. *The Reproduction Revolution: New Ways of Making Babies*. (1984). Oxford University Press.

An overview, and moral assessment, of new advances in reproductive technologies, such as in vitro fertilization, genetic engineering, and surrogate motherhood, and how they can help shed light on the moral status of nascent human life.

Steinbock, Bonnie. *Life Before Birth: The Moral and Legal Status of Embryos and Fetuses* (1992). Oxford University Press.

In this book, Bonnie Steinbock argues in favor of the interest view of moral status, which states that possessing the capacity for consciousness is both a necessary and sufficient condition for having interests, and therefore moral status. Embryos and early fetuses, lacking the capacity for consciousness, have no interest in continued existence, and therefore abortions during this time in pregnancy are morally permissible. Steinbock also addresses other issues, such as the legal status of fetuses, women's right to privacy, and issues in maternal/fetal conflict.

Stone, Jim. "Why Potentiality Matters." (1987). *Canadian Journal of Philosophy*, 17.4: 815–829.

> Jim Stone argues that the fetal potential for personhood is a morally relevant trait that bestows upon the fetus an interest in continued existence. Stone begins by arguing against various philosophical claims against the relevance of fetal potential, and makes a distinction between weak and strong potentiality. A has the weak potential to become B if A is a causal element in producing B, and that the matter that makes A will help produce the matter that makes B. In addition to these two conditions, A has the strong potential to become B if A will produce B if allowed to continue normally, and also that B was once A; that is, if there is a continuous identity relationship between A and B. Embryos and fetuses have a strong potential to become persons, since there is an identity relationship between the embryo or fetus and the person they will become, and this grounds their interests in continued existence.

Tooley, Michael. "Abortion and Infanticide." (1972). *Philosophy and Public Affairs*, 2.1: 37–65.

> In this essay, Michael Tooley argues that the morality of abortion and infanticide needs to be re-examined, and that both are morally permissible. He writes that the term "person" needs to be separated from the term "human being", and that only persons possess a serious right to life. In order to have a right to life, it must be possible that an individual has the capacity to desire continued existence, and in order to have that desire, the individual must be able to see themselves as a distinct entity who exists over time. In other words, one must be self-aware – a person. Since no fetus or infant possesses such self-awareness, neither should be considered persons and neither have any serious claim to a right to life.

Van Scheltema, P.N.A., S. Bakker, F.P.H.A. Vandenbussche, D. Oepkes. "Fetal Pain." (2008) *Fetal and Maternal Medicine Review*, 19.4: 311–324.

> A study concerning when the human fetus is able to respond to noxious stimuli presented in the womb, implying that fetuses can feel stress and pain around mid-gestation.

Warren, Mary Anne. "On the Moral and Legal Status of Abortion." (1973) *The Monist*, 57.1: 43–61.

> Mary Anne Warren argues that there are two definitions of the term "human being" which are often conflated in pro-life arguments. First, "human being" can be used in a biological sense, referring to members of the species *Homo sapiens*. Second, the term can be used in the moral sense, to denote beings who are part of the moral community and who have rights. Warren argues that the latter kind of human beings are persons, and they possess important cognitive traits (consciousness, self-awareness, reasoning abilities, self-motivated activity, and the capacity to communicate). While it may not be necessary to possess all of these mental traits to be a person, a being who possesses none of them (like embryos and early fetuses) are not persons and not part of the moral community.

Day 3

Aristotle. *The Politics*. (1996). Cambridge University Press.

> In this writing Aristotle explores questions dealing with what constitutes a just city-state (or a "polis"). He also explores questions concerning how to form a virtuous household, with a discussion on the role of marriage and the rearing of children (and in doing so argues that slavery is to be expected and is just), what are intellectual and moral virtues, and what education looks like in an ideal city-state.

BBC News. Hillsborough Stories: Anthony David Bland." (2014). https://www.bbc.com/news/uk-england-27224172

> A news story on Anthony Bland, a 19-year-old man who was crushed during what has come to be known as the Hillsborough disaster, when people rushed into the stadium during a football game. Bland was in a persistent vegetative state for four years, until he became the first English patient to be allowed die by the courts via the withdrawal of life sustaining treatment.

Boonin, David. *A Defense of Abortion*. (2003). Cambridge University Press.

> In this book, David Boonin argues in favor of the right to an abortion, mostly by defending Judith Jarvis Thomson's arguments in her seminal essay "A Defense of Abortion." Boonin then goes through many of the objections often posed to Thomson's argument and responds to them. He also considers arguments in favor of allotting the human fetus a right to life and illustrates why the arguments are ultimately unsuccessful. Finally, Boonin considers other arguments against abortion that do not depend on the fetal right to life, and argues that those, also, should be rejected.

The Brittany Maynard Fund. (2022). http://thebrittanyfund.org/about/

> A website devoted to Brittany Maynard's story about accessing physician assisted suicide services (which is legal in the state of Oregon) after she was diagnosed with terminal brain cancer. At the time Maynard lived in California and physician assisted suicide was illegal there (it became legal in California in June 2016). Maynard was required to set up residence in Oregon to be able to avail herself of their Death With Dignity Act, which allows doctors to prescribe life-ending medication that the patient self-administers at a time of her choosing. Towards the end of her life, Maynard advocated for patients' rights and in favor of the legalization of physician assisted suicide. Maynard died on November 1, 2014, after voluntarily taking the medication, surrounded by her family.

Brown, Mark T. "The Morality of Abortions and the Deprivation of Futures." (2000). *Journal of Medical Ethics*, 26: 103–107.

> In this essay, Mark T. Brown argues against Don Marquis's "future-like-ours" view for the moral impermissibility of abortion, maintaining that Marquis uses the term "future of value" in ambiguous ways. The term could mean "potential future of value" or "self-represented future of value." Neither, however, leads to the conclusion that abortion is immoral. First, if Marquis means the former, having a "potential future of value" does not give people a right to whatever is needed for survival. If Marquis means the latter, he is mistaken that fetuses

possess a future of value, since fetuses are not cognitively able to have a "self-represented future of value" because they are incapable of having desires, hopes, goals, or dreams about their lives and futures.

Children's Defense Fund Action Council. "Children's Defense Scorecard." (2021). https://cdfactioncouncil.org/reportcard.

A legislative "report card" where members of Congress are rated in terms of their support for legislation meant to benefit children and families. Many of the lower graded members of Congress are self-proclaimed pro-life advocates.

Ford, Norman M. *When Did I Begin? Conception of the Human Individual in History, Philosophy, and Science.* (1991). Cambridge University Press.

In this book, Norman Ford looks at embryonic development and argues that newly fertilized eggs are not human individuals. The main reason for this is because early embryos are malleable and have the capacity to divide into identical multiples. This illustrates that embryos are not individual human beings until the primitive streak or embryonic disc first appears, around two weeks after fertilization. Ford then looks at the implication of this view for issues such as the ethics of in vitro fertilization and embryonic experimentation.

Garrett-Bakelman, Francine E and Manjula Darshi *et al.* "The NASA Twins Study: A Multidimensional Analysis of a Year-Long Human Spaceflight." (2019) *Science*, 364.6436. https://science.sciencemag.org/content/364/6436/eaau8650

An article summarizing the case of Scott and Mark Kelly, identical twins who were separated when Scott spent a year in space and experienced notable changes to his DNA. The experiment enhanced our understanding of how space can affect human physiology.

Manninen, Bertha Alvarez and Jack Mulder Jr. *A Civil Dialogue on Abortion* (2018). Routledge.

In this book, Bertha Alvarez Manninen and Jack Mulder Jr. each argue for their respective views on abortion (Manninen is pro-choice and Mulder is pro-life), while also responding to each other's arguments. They also have a jointly written chapter where they highlight their areas of agreement in the hopes that the book will model civil dialogue on a controversial moral issue.

Marquis, Don. "Deprivations, Futures, and the Wrongness of Killing." (2001). *Journal of Medical Ethics*, 27: 363–369.

In this essay, Don Marquis responds to Mark Brown's arguments in Brown's article "The Morality of Abortions and the Deprivation of Futures." Marquis first responds to Brown's argument that having a "potential future of value" does not entail that we have rights to whatever we need for survival (so that a fetus's potential future of value does not entail that it has a right to a woman's body). Marquis writes that his own view leads to no such entailment and that, even if it did, there is a case to be made that we do have rights to some of the things we need for survival. Marquis then argues that it is not necessary to be able to have "self-representations" of a future in order to have a valuable one. Fetuses, therefore, can be said to have futures of value even if they lack the psychological capacities for self-representation of their lives or their futures.

Marquis, Don. "Why Abortion is Immoral." (1989). *The Journal of Philosophy*, 86.4: 183–202.

> In this essay, Don Marquis argues that what makes killing any human being morally wrong is the deprivation of a valuable future. Because the human fetus is a being who possesses a valuable future, killing a fetus is as morally wrong as killing an adult human being. Marquis goes through several reasons why his view offers a better account of the wrongness of killing than other competing views, with the ultimate goal of showing that most abortions are seriously morally wrong.

McInerney, Peter K. "Does a Fetus Already Have a Future-Like-Ours" (1990). *The Journal of Philosophy*, 87.5: 264–268.

> In this essay, Peter McInerney argues that fetuses do not have a personal future of value in the same way that children or adults have personal futures of value. This is because the fetus lacks any psychological connections with its future self – they lack a mental life, and have no feelings, no beliefs, and no desires. For this reason, fetuses have no personal futures of which abortion wrongly deprives them.

McMahan, Jeff. *The Ethics of Killing: Problems at the Margins of Life.* (2002). Oxford University Press.

> In this book, Jeff McMahan considers the issue of personal identity over time, and argues in favor of the embodied mind account of personal identity, which states that we persist as the same individual over time so long as we retain the capacity for consciousness. This, however, is not sufficient for determining whether we have a strong interest in continued existence, and therefore whether death would harm us. What matters here is that we have strong psychological connectedness over time, what McMahan refers to as the time-relative interest account of the wrongness of killing. According to this view, it would not be as wrong to kill a post-conscious fetus (who does share an identity relation with a future person given its continuing capacity for consciousness) as it would be to kill a child or an adult, as the latter two are sufficiently psychologically connected to their future selves in order to have a strong interest in continued existence. McMahan then applies his views to several issues in bioethics, including abortion, euthanasia, and the definition of death.

National Council of Jewish Women. "Judaism and Abortion." (2019). https://www.ncjw.org/wp-content/uploads/2019/05/Judaism-and-Abortion-FINAL.pdf

> Using texts from the Hebrew Bible and the Talmud, this article details a Jewish defense of abortion rights.

Paul, John. *The Gospel of Life: Evangelium Vitae.* (1995). United States Conference of Catholic Bishops.

> Pope John Paul II's writings about the sanctity of human life and how it relates to contemporary moral issues, such as abortion, euthanasia, and the death penalty. The Pope calls on Catholics to help shape society in a way that shows reverence to the sanctity of human life.

Plato. *The Republic*. (1990). Oxford University Press.

> One of Plato's most influential works, here he explores, in dialogue form between Socrates and other interlocutors, many important socio-political philosophical questions, including: the nature of justice, the characteristics of a just city-state, the kind of education necessary in order to foster a virtuous city-state, the tripartite soul, and how to cultivate a just moral character.

Rapp, Emily. "Rick Santorum, Meet My Son." (2012). https://slate.com/human-interest/2012/02/rick-santorum-and-prenatal-testing-i-would-have-saved-my-son-from-his-suffering.html

> Emily Rapp tells the story of her experiences parenting her son Ronan, who was afflicted with Tay-Sachs disease, a degenerative muscle condition. In her story, she admits that had she known Ronan had Tay-Sachs she would have opted for abortion to avoid her son living with debilitating pain and suffering before his inevitable death.

Schnell, Lindsay. "Jews, Outraged by Restrictive Abortion Laws, are Invoking the Hebrew Bible in the Debate." (2019). https://www.usatoday.com/story/news/nation/2019/07/24/abortion-laws-jewish-faith-teaches-life-does-not-start-conception/1808776001/

> This piece highlights the views of some Jewish scholars, politicians, and activists who support abortion rights. These individuals often have a different interpretation of religious texts, particularly some passages of the Hebrew Bible (also known as the Old Testament), than Christians who offer Biblical defenses of abortion restrictions. According to many of the people interviewed in the article, respect for religious freedom means that religion should not be invoked when deciding public policy, given that there is such a wide diversity of religious viewpoints. When it comes to abortion, laws that restrict abortion access violate the religious freedom of many who do not share conservative Christianity's view on abortion.

Wilson, Jeff. *Mourning the Unborn Dead: A Buddhist Ritual Comes to America*. (2009). Oxford University Press.

> In this book, Jeff Wilson explores the Japanese Buddhist ritual of *mizuko kuyo*, a ceremony meant to pay respects to the souls of dead fetuses, either due to miscarriage or abortion. Wilson also examines how the ritual has been adopted by many women in American culture, given that in the United States of America there are limited ways of mourning pregnancy loss. Whereas in Japan, the *mizuko kuyo* ritual largely exists to pacify the souls of fetuses who have died, in America the ritual has evolved to serve as an expression of grief after pregnancy loss.

Day 4

Boonin, David. *A Defense of Abortion*. (2003). Cambridge University Press.

> In this book, David Boonin argues in favor of the right to an abortion, mostly by defending Judith Jarvis Thomson's arguments in her seminal essay "A Defense

of Abortion." Boonin then goes through many of the objections often posed to Thomson's argument and responds to them. He also considers arguments in favor of allotting the human fetus a right to life and illustrates why the arguments are ultimately unsuccessful. Finally, Boonin considers other arguments against abortion that do not depend on the fetal right to life, and argues that those, also, should be rejected.

Common Pleas Court of Allegheny County, Pennsylvania. *McFall v. Shimp* (1978). https://www.leagle.com/decision/197810010padampc3d90189

> In this case, Robert McFall was suffering from a condition known as aplastic anemia, where the body stops producing new blood cells. In need of a bone marrow transplant, McFall looked to his cousin David Shimp, who was found to be a genetic match. Shimp, however, refused to undergo the donation procedure, prompting McFall to take him to court in the hopes Shimp would be compelled. The court ruled against McFall, arguing that it cannot force a human being to undergo an unwilling intrusion to his body, even to save someone's life.

Kaczor, Christopher *The Ethics of Abortion: Women's Rights, Human Life, and the Question of Justice.* (2011). New York: Routledge Press.

> Christopher Kaczor presents a number of secular arguments against the moral permissibility of abortion, and argues that all fetuses, from conception onwards, are rational persons worthy of respect and rights. He responds to a number of pro-choice arguments that deny fetal personhood, and addresses some "hard cases" for both pro-life advocates (such as abortion in cases of rape) and pro-choice advocates (such as abortion for sex-selection). Kaczor ends the book by considering what impact the advent of ectogenesis (artificial wombs) would have on the abortion debate.

Kant, Immanuel. *Grounding for the Metaphysics of Morals.* (1981). Hackett Publishing Company.

> One of the most influential books ever written in the field of ethics and philosophy, in this book Immanuel Kant lays out his view on morality. Being a deontologist, Kant believes that the basis of all ethical decisions are moral duties, rather than foreseeable consequences. In order to discover what one's moral duties are, Kant devises what is known as the categorical imperative. Arguably the most famous version of the categorical imperative is the principle of humanity, which proscribes treating rational persons as mere means, or instruments, to some other end or goal. Rather, every rational person must be treated as an end in themselves – as a being with intrinsic moral value and dignity.

Lim, Louisa. "Cases of Forced Abortion Surface in China." (2007). *National Public Radio.* https://www.npr.org/2007/04/23/9766870/cases-of-forced-abortions-surface-in-china

> A story featured on NPR about incidences of forced abortion in China during the time of the strict "one child" rule. Some women also claimed that they were forced to abort their first child if they were unmarried.

Manninen, Bertha Alvarez. *Pro-Life, Pro-Choice: Shared Values in the Abortion Debate.* (2014). Vanderbilt University Press.

> In this book, Bertha Alvarez Manninen defends a pro-choice view on abortion ethics by supplementing Judith Jarvis Thomson's arguments in "A Defense of Abortion." She also tries to dispel many stereotypes that pro-choice advocates face, including the belief that they are "pro-abortion" and that they do not care about children, families, or motherhood. Manninen also writes about what role potential fathers should play when it comes to abortion, and she works to highlight areas of agreement between pro-choice and pro-life advocates, with the hope that such a focus can help pave the way for fruitful dialogue between the two sides.

Rachels, James. "Active and Passive Euthanasia" (1975). *New England Journal of Medicine*, 292.2: 78–80.

> In this essay, James Rachels argues that the traditional distinction between active and passive euthanasia (where the former is prohibited but not the latter) is morally indefensible. First, he shows that there is no intrinsic moral difference between killing and allowing to die because both arrive at the same consequence: the death of the patient. Then he argues that there are some cases where active euthanasia, intentionally hastening the death of a patient, is morally preferable to passive euthanasia, where the patient is allowed to die from their underlying disease, because sometimes letting a patient die a slow and painful death causes more suffering than directly killing the patient.

Regan, Donald H. "Rewriting Roe v. Wade." (1979). *Michigan Law Review*, 77.7: 1569–1646.

> In this essay, Donald H. Regan sets out to "rewrite" the Supreme Court decision of *Roe v. Wade* by offering what he thinks is a stronger argument in favor of a woman's right to an abortion than the ones offered by the Supreme Court. His argument relies on the premise that pregnancy and child birth fall under the jurisdiction of "good Samaritan" laws, which are laws that articulate when a human being is under a legal obligation to render aid to someone in need. If abortion is prohibited, pregnant women would be the only ones who are required to use their body to sustain the life of another person; that is, pregnant women would be required to be "good Samaritans" in ways not required of men or non-pregnant women. Therefore, laws against abortion violate a pregnant woman's claim to equal protection under the law.

Supreme Court of Canada. *R. vs. Morgentaler.* (1988). https://scc-csc.lexum.com/scc-csc/scc-csc/en/item/1053/index.do

> The 1988 Supreme Court of Canada's decision that decriminalized abortion. Before the decision, Canada's Criminal Code only permitted abortions solely in hospitals for therapeutic reasons (that is, if the pregnancy was deemed dangerous to the woman's health). Three doctors, Henry Morgentaler, Leslie Smoling, and Robert Scott, were performing nontherapeutic abortions on women whose requests had been denied. The Supreme Court of Canada ruled in their favor upon appeal, with a 5-2 ruling in favor of decriminalizaling abortions on the grounds that the existing restrictions violated women's security of person.

Thomson, Judith Jarvis. "A Defense of Abortion." (1971). *Philosophy and Public Affairs*, 1.1: 47–66.

> Using her famous violinist example, Judith Jarvis Thomson argues in this essay that granting the fetus a right to life does not entail that abortions are impermissible. The right to life should be construed as the right to not be killed unjustly. Abortions are not an example of unjust killing because no one's right to life, including fetuses, entails the right to the use of someone else's body for continued sustenance. Thomson argues that this conclusion applies to rape cases, but also in cases where a woman engages in voluntary sexual intercourse.

United Nations. *Universal Declaration of Human Rights.* (1948). https://www.un.org/en/universal-declaration-human-rights/

> Written by representatives of countries all around the world in 1948, the document was published by the United Nations, and details basic, universally protected human rights that all countries should aspire to uphold.

Wilcox, John. "Nature as Demonic in Thomson's Defense of Abortion" in *The Ethics of Abortion*, edited by Robert Baird and Stuart Rosenbaum. (2001). Prometheus Books: 257–271.

> In this essay, John Wilcox argues against Judith Jarvis Thomson's conclusion in her article "A Defense of Abortion" by looking at various ways the case of the violinist is disanalogous with the standard cases of pregnancy and abortion. For example, he argues that a woman has special obligations to her fetus that does not exist in the violinist example because the latter is a stranger and the former is the woman's child. He also argues that, unlike the case of the violinist, a woman is morally responsible for the fetus's state of dependency given her participation in voluntary sexual intercourse. He is also critical of Thomson's examples throughout her essay, maintaining that they are all unlikely science fiction thought experiments that cannot be compared to the natural and commonplace occurrence that is pregnancy and childbirth.

Day 5

Barot, Sneha. "A Problem and Solution Mismatch: Son Preference and Sex-Selective Abortion Bans." (2012). *Guttmacher Policy Review*, 15.2. https://www.guttmacher.org/gpr/2012/05/problem-and-solution-mismatch-son-preference-and-sex-selective-abortion-bans

> Abortions due to sex-selection are prevalent in countries in East and South Asia, and possibly amongst some immigrant communities in the United States. This article explores the attempt to ban abortion on the basis of sex-selection. Sneha Barot argues that this is just another incarnation of the many attempts to undermine reproductive rights in the United States. Opponents of such laws argue that such a prohibition would do more harm than good for the intended communities to which such a law would apply. Rather than trying to curb reproductive rights, Barot argues that what should be done is to explore the underlying cause of such abortions: strong son preference and the consequent imbalance of sex ratios

in countries with such preferences. Although there have been countries that have tried to outlaw abortions on the basis of sex, such laws have largely proven to be ineffective. Attempts to pass such laws in the United States, Barot argues, are less about combatting gender discrimination and more about chipping away at reproductive rights.

Centers for Disease Control and Prevention. "Data and Statistics on Reproductive Health." (2016). https://www.cdc.gov/reproductivehealth/data_stats/index.htm

This article summarizes relevant data and statistics on issues in reproductive health in the United States. This includes abortion, but also assisted reproductive technologies, infant health, women's reproductive health, maternal health and pregnancy, teen pregnancy, tobacco use and pregnancy, and unintended pregnancy.

Christensen, Erika. "New York Forces Women Like Me to Carry Nonviable Pregnancies to Term." (2017). https://rewire.news/article/2017/05/23/new-york-forces-women-like-carry-nonviable-pregnancies-term/

In this article, Erika Christensen tells the story of her abortion at 32 weeks gestation, when her very wanted fetus was diagnosed with a condition that was incompatible with continued life. At the time, New York banned abortions after 24 weeks gestation unless the woman's life was in danger, and so Christensen and her husband traveled to Colorado to have the abortion, at a cost of over $10,000. Christensen argues in favor of New York's Reproductive Health Act, passed in 2019, which now allows for third trimester abortions in cases where the pregnancy is deemed nonviable.

Guttmacher Institute. "Later Abortions." (2019). https://www.guttmacher.org/evidence-you-can-use/later-abortion

This essay goes over state laws and policies concerning later abortions in the United States. It includes the Supreme Court's decisions on later abortions, and contradicts claims regarding fetal sentience (the ability to feel pain) during early and mid-gestation. The article also includes the reasons why women may choose later abortions, many of which are logistical reasons that render it difficult to obtain the abortion at an earlier time.

Hales, Stephen. "Abortion and Father's Rights" in *Analyzing Moral Issues*, edited by Judith Boss. (2005). McGraw Hill Press: 118–125.

Stephen Hales argues that men and women do not have equal reproductive rights. This is because women can have a "second chance" of avoiding parenthood once she is pregnant by getting an abortion. Men, however, have no such opportunity; once the woman is pregnant, whether or not he becomes a father is entirely in her hands. What is needed, Hales argues, is what he calls the "right of refusal" – a man's moral right to avoid the future duties and responsibilities, including financial ones, of parenthood should the woman not exercise her right to an abortion and the child is born. Hales's argument does not apply to men who are already supporting existing children; the right to refusal is meant to parallel a woman's right to an abortion and therefore only extends as long as she is able to exercise that right.

Hesketh, Therese, Li Lu, and Zhu Wei Xing. "The Consequences of Son Preference and Sex-Selective Abortion in China and Other Asian Countries." (2011). *Canadian Medical Association Journal*, 183.12: 1374–1477.

> The preference for male children in countries in East and South Asia, and the Middle East and North Africa, can be traced back to several factors. These countries have strong patriarchal traditions; men have, on average, higher wage-earnings than women, are often the ones who care for aging parents, and do not require a dowry for marriage. As a consequence, countries such as China, South Korea, and in parts of India, have skewed sex ratios at birth, with much more boys being born than girls. As a result, many of these countries will experience "male surplus" leaving many men without opportunities to marry and reproduce. The article outlines many of the possible consequences of this surplus, including increased male depression and the possibility of antisocial behavior.

Hursthouse, Rosalind. "Virtue Theory and Abortion." (1991). *Philosophy & Public Affairs*, 20.3: 223–246.

> In this essay, Rosalind Hursthouse first spends some time explaining the normative theory of virtue ethics, which goes as far back the writings of Plato, and, most notably, Aristotle. From a virtue ethics perspective, the morally right thing to do when facing a moral dilemma is to act in such a way that illustrates a good, or virtuous, moral character. When discussing the ethics of abortion in particular, Hursthouse argues that we must extend the conversation beyond the question of whether a woman has a moral right to an abortion. One can believe that women have such a right, and yet note that this alone says nothing about the morality of abortion from a virtue ethics perspective. Instead of focusing just on the discussion of moral rights, virtue ethicists, when it comes to abortion, are more interested in the reasons why women choose abortion, and whether that choice reflects a virtuous or vicious moral character.

Kalish, Stacey. "Hidden Male Grief." (2016). *Psychology Today*. https://www.psychologytoday.com/us/articles/200405/hidden-male-grief

> This article discusses male grief after abortions, and how men lack any socially sanctioned means of discussing or assuaging that grief. Many men do grieve after their partner's abortion, even in situations where they feel abortion was the best option, and that grief often manifests itself in psychological and behavioral ways, for example as low-self-esteem or substance abuse. Stacey Kalish points out that male grief after abortion is being taken increasingly more seriously, with organizations such as Planned Parenthood sometimes providing male-targeted counseling services.

Manninen, Bertha Alvarez. *Pro-Life, Pro-Choice: Shared Values in the Abortion Debate.* (2014). Vanderbilt University Press.

> In this book, Bertha Alvarez Manninen defends a pro-choice view on abortion ethics by supplementing Judith Jarvis Thomson's arguments in "A Defense of Abortion." She also tries to dispel many stereotypes that pro-choice advocates face, including the belief that they are "pro-abortion" and that they do not care about children, families, or motherhood. Manninen also writes about what role potential fathers should play when it comes to abortion, and she works to

highlight areas of agreement between pro-choice and pro-life advocates, with the hope that such a focus can help pave the way for fruitful dialogue between the two sides.

Manninen, Bertha Alvarez "Pleading Men and Virtuous Women: Considering the Role of the Father in the Abortion Debate." (2007). *International Journal of Applied Philosophy*, 21.1: 1–24.

In this essay, Bertha Alvarez Manninen uses the moral framework of Kantian deontology and virtue ethics in order to discuss the issue of what role men's desires and interests should play when discussing abortion rights. Manninen first argues that men should never be able to force women to gestate a mutually created fetus, even if they are against the fetus's abortion. Allowing men to force women to gestate treats women as mere means to the man's end; instrumentalizing her and ignoring her own rational will over her body. However, while men can never be given veto power over a woman's abortion decision, that does not mean that men's input should have no place when making the decision to abort. Manninen argues that a virtuous woman would sometimes take the man's interests and his care of the fetus into account when making an abortion decision. If the man is caring, sincere, may possibly be a good father, and is expressing attachment to the fetus, there may be cases where being a virtuous woman may mean that she should choose to gestate the fetus for the sake of the prospective father (but the decision must always be her choice).

McClain, Linda B. "Equality, Oppression, and Abortion: Women Who Oppose Abortion Rights in the Name of Feminism" in *Feminist Nightmares: Women at Odds: Feminism and the Problems of Sisterhood*, edited by Susan Ostrov Weisser and Jennifer Fleischner. (1994). New York University Press: 100–116.

In this essay, Linda B. McClain outlines the history of the feminist pro-life movement. Members of pro-life feminist groups consider abortion to be a consequence of the oppression of women, rather than a result of their liberation, and they deny that abortion rights are part of women's quest for social equality. Instead, they argue, feminists should harken back to the days of the first wave feminist movement, where abortions were decried. Society should be encouraged to meet pregnant women's needs and interests rather than encouraging the destruction of the fetus in order to meet the demands of a society hostile to pregnant women and mothers. McClain also highlights some areas of commonality between pro-life feminism and the modern feminist movement, including the quest for equal pay, paid family leave, quality and affordable childcare, and the prevention of unwanted pregnancies.

Oaks, Laury. "What are Pro-Life Feminists Doing on Campus?" (2009). *National Women's Studies Association Journal*. 21.1: 178–203.

In this essay, Laury Oaks outlines the history of pro-life feminism, going all the way back into the 1970s. These groups often argued that, rather than empowering women, abortion is wrong because it condones violence against women, and allows men to sexually exploit women with little consequence. Members of the Feminist for Life of America movement (FFL) often align themselves with members of the first wave feminism, emphasizing that early feminists like

Susan B. Anthony, Mary Wollstonecraft, and Elizabeth Cady Stanton all spoke out against abortion. The legalization of abortion, according to members of FFL, only serves to reinforce the view that motherhood is an impediment to being full participants in society. Oaks follows the more contemporary incarnations of the FFL movement, focusing on the group's presence on college campuses via Campus Outreach programs in the 2000s in an attempt to spread their message and gain new membership.

Parens, Erik and Adrienne Asche. "The Disability Rights Critique of Prenatal Genetic Testing: Reflections and Recommendations" in *Prenatal Testing and Disability Rights,* edited by Erik Parens and Adrienne Asche. (2007). Georgetown University Press: 3–43.

In this essay, Erik Parens and Adrienne Asche highlight some morally problematic aspects of prenatal genetic testing (PGT), which enables prospective parents to know whether their embryo or fetus may have some genetic abnormalities. Parens and Asche's main concern is that PGT, followed by abortion in cases where a disability is discovered, can potentially harm persons with disabilities by sending the message that their existence should have been prevented. There are two main arguments Parens and Asche offer in support of this claim. First, there is the expressivist argument, which states that PGT and selective abortion sends a negative and hurtful message to the disability community by screening for, and aborting, fetuses with disabling characteristics. Second, there is the parental attitude argument, which states that PGT and selective abortion conveys a problematic approach to parenthood because parenting is about loving and accepting whatever child a parent ends up receiving, not about creating the "perfect" child. Parents who opt for PGT and abortion are allowing the disabling trait to substitute for the whole child, ignoring that parenting a disabled child can still be a fulfilling and positive experience. Moreover, prenatal testing and selective abortion are based on misinformation – studies show that families with disabled children do not, on average, fare worse than families without disabled children. If disabled persons were fully integrated into our community, then disabilities would not be as much of a "handicap" as it is right now. The goal should not be the eradication of disabled persons through PGT and abortion, but rather to change and evolve society so that all people of differing abilities can thrive.

Quinones, Julian and Arijeta Lajka. "'What Kind of Society Do You Want To Live In'? Inside the Country where Down Syndrome is Disappearing." (2017). https://www.cbsnews.com/news/down-syndrome-iceland/

This article goes over Iceland's reduction of Down Syndrome children via prenatal diagnosis and abortion, where almost 100% of women choose to terminate a pregnancy after a Down Syndrome diagnosis. Other countries' numbers of termination include the United States at 67%, France at 77%, and Denmark at 98%.

Rapp, Emily. "Rick Santorum, Meet My Son." (2013). https://slate.com/human-interest/2012/02/rick-santorum-and-prenatal-testing-i-would-have-saved-my-son-from-his-suffering.html

Emily Rapp tells the story of her experiences parenting her son Ronan, who was afflicted with Tay-Sachs disease, a degenerative muscle condition. In her story, she admits that had she known Ronan had Tay-Sachs she would have opted for abortion to avoid her son living with debilitating pain and suffering before his inevitable death.

Savulescu, Julian. "Procreative Beneficence: Why We Should Select the Best Children." (2001). *Bioethics*, 15.5/6: 413–426.

In this article, Julian Savulescu argues in favor of using in vitro fertilization and pre-implantation genetic diagnoses in order to choose an embryo that, given its particular genetic constitution, is likely to lead the best possible life from all the alternative embryos. Savulescu defends what he calls "procreative beneficence" – the moral obligation to choose to have the child, out of all the possible children one can have, who is expected to lead the best possible life. Couples who have to choose between implanting a "defective" embryo and a "healthy" one should always pick the healthy embryo, since this is the embryo that is likely to have the life with the most well-being. However, while using persuasion to make such a choice is justified, the choice should never be coerced.

Sharnak, Debbie. "Raped, Pregnant, and Denied a Life-Saving Abortion–All at 10-years-old." (2015). *Amnesty International*. https://www.amnestyusa.org/raped-pregnant-and-denied-a-life-saving-abortion-all-at-10-years-old/

The article discusses the case of a 10-year-old girl in Paraguay who was raped by her step-father and whose pregnancy was discovered at 21 weeks gestation. Child pregnancies are thought to be especially dangerous, often leading to many complications and even death. The girl's mother submitted an administrative plea for an abortion but, given Paraguay's restrictive abortion laws, she was denied. Organizations like Amnesty International and the United Nations contributed to the public outcry against the decision, but to no avail. The child was transported to a center for young mothers where she gave birth to a baby girl via cesarean section.

Shimabukuro, Tom, Scott Grosse, and Catherine Rice. "Medical Expenditures for Children with an Autism Spectrum Disorder in a Privately Insured Population." (2008). *Journal of Autism and Developmental Disorder*, 38: 546–552.

This study gives an account of the medical expenditures incurred by children and adolescents diagnosed with an autism spectrum disorder (ASD) who are covered under employer-based private health insurance. The study found that a diagnosis of ASD brought with it several increased costs. For example, the median expenditures for a child with an ASD is 8.4–9.5 times higher than children without an ASD. Medical co-pays and deductibles are also higher for children with an ASD; whereas non-ASD children spend approximately $150–$200 per year in co-pays and deductibles, children with an ASD spend approximately $500–$600 per year.

Solomon, Andrew. *Far From the Tree: Parents, Children, and the Search for Identity.* (2012). Scribner Press.

In this book, Andrew Solomon explores the obstacles, complications, and rewards of parenting "unique" children, such as children with varying disabilities, child prodigies, children who become criminals, and transgender children. In the chapter relevant to this book, Solomon takes a look at women parenting children as a result of being raped, from single instances of sexual assault to repeated rapes during periods of genocide. While some women manage to find happiness and peace after their rape via their resulting children, other women struggle to accept and love these children, especially when the child reminds them so much of their rapists.

Steinbock, Bonnie. "Disability, Prenatal Testing, and Selective Abortion" in *Prenatal Testing and Disability Rights*, edited by Erik Parens and Adrienne Asche. (2007). Georgetown University Press: 108–123.

> In this essay, Bonnie Steinbock writes in defense of prenatal testing and selective abortion. If abortions are permissible at all, then they are certainly permissible in cases where a fetus, once born, faces a life full of difficulties, including pain and suffering, a shortened life-span, hospitalizations, and restricted educational and job opportunities. Steinbock agrees that persons with disabilities are often met with much societal discrimination. She also agrees that many of the "handicaps" that persons with disability contend with are socially constructed, but that is not the case for all disabilities. While some disabilities can be overcome by removing social barriers that prevent thriving, other disabilities really are intrinsically limiting. Already in society we employ means of preventing disability. Women are encouraged to take folic acid to avoid neural tube defects, they are also encouraged to avoid risky behaviors during pregnancy, such as drinking alcohol and smoking, in the interest of the fetus's future health. If preventing disabilities in these ways is morally acceptable, then prenatal screening, along with selective abortion or embryo selection, should also be regarded as a morally acceptable means of preventing disabilities.

Thomson, Judith Jarvis. "A Defense of Abortion." (1971). *Philosophy and Public Affairs*, 1.1: 47–66.

> Using her famous violinist example, Judith Jarvis Thomson argues in this essay that granting the fetus a right to life does not entail that abortions are impermissible. The right to life should be construed as the right to not be killed unjustly. Abortions are not an example of unjust killing because no one's right to life, including fetuses, entails the right to the use of someone else's body for continued sustenance. Thomson argues that this conclusion applies to rape cases, but also in cases where a woman engages in voluntary sexual intercourse.

United States Supreme Court. *Planned Parenthood v. Casey.* (1992). https://www.law.cornell.edu/supremecourt/text/505/833

> In Pennsylvania, new laws were enacted restricting abortions, including a 24-hour waiting period, requiring minors seeking an abortion to obtain the consent of at least one parent, and requiring a married woman to notify her husband of her intent to obtain an abortion. Planned Parenthood challenged these laws, and the Supreme Court, in a 5 to 4 split, upheld the new abortions laws except for the spousal notification one because it was deemed to cause an "undue burden" on pregnant women. The court also overturned the trimester framework of *Roe v. Wade*, and allowed states to impose abortion restrictions

after the onset of fetal viability regardless of when in gestation it takes place (mostly in the third trimester, but also during the latter part of the second trimester).

Ziegler, Mary. "Women's Rights on the Right: The History and Stakes of Modern Pro-life Feminism." (2013). *Berkeley Journal of Gender, Law, and Justice*, 232: 232–268.

In this article, Mary Ziegler outlines the history of the feminist pro-life movement, going all the way back to the 1970s, where the commonalities with first wave feminism, which decried abortion, were often emphasized. Feminist pro-life advocates often argued that abortion harms women, rather than advancing their rights and their quest for social equality. Ziegler also highlights their political influence, for example how pro-life feminism helped in passing bans on abortion for sex-selection in some U.S. states. Members of Feminist for Life of America (FFL) and the American Citizens Concerned for Life (ACCL) championed the view that feminists should simultaneously support women's equality while opposing abortions, which, they argued, allowed men to sexually exploit women with little consequence or responsibility. As the pro-life movement began to align itself more with the religious right (which were largely anti-feminist), pro-choice groups like the National Abortion Rights Action League (NARAL) started to maintain that the pro-life movement and the anti-feminist movement went hand-in-hand. Pro-life feminists found themselves excluded by both groups, which led to its decline in the United States as an influential political movement.

INDEX

abortion: access point in pregnancy 9; Bible prohibits 2–3; cases of rape 130–133; class presentation on 1–2; conscious beings 42–43; contraception roles 13; disposable masses of cells 56; fathers 125–126; fetal disabilities 121–122; in first trimester 4, 6; harmful to women 18–22; kills an innocent child 27–29; later abortions 118–119; legal in Japan 56; legal in United States 78; masculine element 109; men and grief 129; non-viable pregnancies 119–120; profamily support policies 110–111; relationship between rights and desires 34–35; religious diversity 55–56; security persons 78–79; selective abortion 123–125; sex education roles 13–14; sex selection 113–115; sexual exploitation of women 110; tax dollars 14–15; thalidomide scare 3–4; unintentional or intentional 56; viability and quickening 26–27; the violinist example 85–88; virtue theory 115–118
Abortion and Mental Health: Myths and Realities 24n23
American Citizens Concerned for Life (ACCL) 112
Anthony, Susan B. 111
anti-abortion laws 7

Aristotle 57, 72n5, 72n6
Asche, Adrienne 136n26, 137n27, 137n28, 137n30, 137n31, 137n32

Baird, Robert 104n3
Barot, Sneha 135n14, 135n15
Bearak, Jonathan 23n14
Beckwith, Francis 48n5
Bible prohibits abortion 2–3, 51
Biblical beliefs 2
Bland, Anthony 53, 54, 72n7
bodily autonomy arguments 78
Boonin, David 23n12, 106n13, 106n14, 106n17, 106n18, 106n20, 107n24, 107n27
Boss, Judith 137n33
Brown, Mark T. 74n29
Burgess, J.A. 50n28, 50n29

Callahan, Catherine 110
chemical thalidomide 3
Christensen, Erika 119, 136n21
class presentation on abortion, America 1–2
cognitive traits of personhood 30–31
Cohen, Susan 24n23
compelled military service 103
compensation objection 103–104
conscious awareness 45
consent objection 94–95

Davis v. Davis 16, 24n22
death harm, fetuses: bodily autonomy
    arguments 71; conscious awareness
    70; conscious life 70; psychological
    connections 71
A Defense of Abortion 23n12
Doe. v. Bolton 7, 10, 23n6, 23n11

early feminism 109
Eisenstadt v. Baird 23n7
embryos: early fetuses 33–34; fertility
    treatments 16–17
Equal Rights Amendment 112, 113
Exodus 21:22–25 2
expressivist argument, selective
    abortion: disability 123; negative and
    discriminatory attitude 123; negative
    and prejudicial attitude 124

families with disabled children 122–123
Feinberg, Joel 49n18, 50n19, 50n20,
    50n21
Feminist For Life (FFL) 110
fetal disabilities, abortion: Down
    Syndrome pregnancies 121; positive
    life aspects 121; private decision 121
fetuses, future person: accidental
    properties 64; DNA 64; essential
    properties 64; personal identity 63;
    soul at conception 64
fetus sentient 45–47
Finkbine, Sherri 3, 4
forcing women, gestate: control over
    women's bodies 129; killing the fetus
    130; woman's choice 129
Ford, Norman M. 75n34, 75n36, 76n37
Fourteenth Amendment's appeal 5, 7
future like-ours arguments: argument
    from potential 59; breaks your
    soul 57; consequence of killing
    57; contraception 58–59; kinds of
    euthanasia 58; loss of his or her future
    57; morally wrong 58; potential
    personhood 59; preventing a possible
    person 58; valuable future 59
futures of value, fetuses: mental
    connections 63; permissible to kill
    62; psychological connections 62,
    63; robust mental capacities 62; self-
    representation 62

Garrett-Bakelman, Francine E 75n35
genetic humanity 31–33

gestation: 13 weeks 4, 118; 20 weeks
    20; 23 weeks 8; 32 weeks 119; 30–35
    weeks 45
gestation fetuses 5
Goltz, Patricia 110
Griswold v. Connecticut 7
Grob, Kristina 48n1, 48n2
Grosse, Scott 136n24
*Groundwork for the Metaphysics of
    Morals* 88

Halappanavar, Savita 13
Hales, Stephen 137n33
harmful to women, abortion: mental
    health 18; post-abortion syndrome
    19; pre-existing mental conditions
    19; pro-life concerns 18; recreational
    drug use 21; religious viewpoints
    22; suicidal thoughts 19; 20 weeks
    gestation 20; unwanted pregnancies
    20
Henshaw, Stanley 23n18
Hesketh, Therese 135n13
Hursthouse, Rosalind 135n16, 135n17,
    135n18, 136n19

infants, right to life 35–36
innocence apply to embryos 28–29
interest to harm 43
in vitro fertilization (IVF) 16, 37

Kaczor, Christopher 107n23
Kalish, Stacey 138n35
Kant, Immanuel 105n8
Kant's principle of humanity 88–91;
    formula of humanity 89, 90; moral
    law 88; need for survival 89
killing abortion doctors 17–18
killing *vs.* letting die: cause of
    death 99; directly killing 98;
    disconnecting 98; method of killing
    100; murderous intentions 99; pain
    and suffering 98; traditional abortion
    99
Kim, J.H. 23n1
Koop, C. Everett 18, 24n24
Kost, Kathryn 23n18
Kuljis, Rodrigo O. 50n26

Lajka, Arijeta 136n23
later, *Eisenstadt v. Baird* 7
laws: against abortions 11–12;
    prohibiting abortion 12

legalization of abortion on demand 4–7
Li, Lu 135n13

Manninen, Bertha Alvarez 23n21, 24n26, 49n10, 77n45, 104n6, 106n16, 106n21, 138n34, 138n36, 138n37
Marquis, Don 73n15, 73n16, 73n17, 73n18, 73n19, 73n20, 73n21, 74n22, 74n23, 74n24, 74n25, 74n26, 74n27, 75n30
maternal health 10–11
Maynard, Brittany 58, 60, 61
McClain, Linda B. 134n2, 135n10
McFall, Robert 84, 91
McFall v. Shimp 85, 86, 95, 104n4, 127
McInerney, Peter K. 75n32, 75n33
McMahan, Jeff 75n31, 76n38, 76n39, 76n40, 76n41, 76n42, 76n43, 77n44
mental capacities 36
mental traits of personhood 33–34
moral law 88
morning sickness 3
Mulder, Jack 49n10, 77n45

The National Council of Jewish Women 56
negative right, right to life: freedom of religion 80; freedom of speech 80; rights of non-interference 80
newly fertilized egg: conception 65; moot point for abortion 65; primitive streak 65
Nobis, Nathan 48n1, 48n2
non-viable pregnancies: abortions of convenience 120; single parenthood 119
Noonan, John 49n15

Oaks, Laury 134n5, 135n7
objection: consent objection 94–95; relationship objection 96–98; responsibility objection 91–94
onechild policy 87

Parens, Erik 136n26, 137n27, 137n28, 137n30, 137n31, 137n32
Paul, Alice 112
personal identity: animal organism 65, 66; brain functioning 66; capacity for consciousness 68, 69; continuation of a conscious mind 67–70; continuation of mental contents 66–67; embryonic

organism 65; end and beginning of life 68; fetal organism 65; identity relationship 68; lack of brain activity 67; persistence of a human organism 65–66; pre-conscious fetuses 69, 70; pro-life view 70; rudimentary consciousness 68; Terri Schiavo case 67; vegetative state 67, 68
Personhood Amendments 15, 16, 103
PEW research center study 56
Planned Parenthood v. Casey 8–9, 23n8, 109, 134n1
positive right, right to life: right of non-interference 80; right to legal counsel 80; right to religious freedom 80
potential person: argument from 36; as embryo 38; mean 36–40; persons have same right 40–41; probabilistic sense 39
pro-choice and pro-life feminists: abortion rights 111; American Citizens Concerned for Life (ACCL) 112; anti-feminist movements 113; control fertility 111; crisis pregnancies 113; legalized abortion 111; parental leave 111; true freedom of choice 112
profamily support policies: The Family and Medical Leave Act 111; 15 weeks of *paid* leave 111; parenting 111
pro-life advocacy 108, 109, 112

Quinones, Julian 136n23

Rachels, James 107n25
rape: abortion 130–133; children of bad memories 132; emotional and psychological issues 132; save mother's life 131; the violinist example 91
Rapp, Emily 54, 55, 72n10
Reagan, Ronald 18
Regan, Donald H. 105n9, 105n10, 107n22
relationship objection 96–98; adoptive mother 97; adoptive sibling 97; biological mother 97; failed contraception 91; interpersonal experiences 97; negligent driver 92; result of negligence 93; shared genetic relationship 96; surrogate pregnancies 96; voluntary sexual intercourse 93
religious diversity: *mizuko kuyo* 56; moral value 56; public and vehement debate 56

Reproductive Health Act 9–10
responsibility objection 91–94
restricting abortion, after viability: later
  abortions 102; premature babies 101;
  right to terminate pregnancy 101;
  survives an abortion attempt 101
Rice, Catherine 136n24
right of refusal 126–129; bodily
  intrusion 127; future duties of
  parenthood 127; future responsibilities
  of parenthood 128; rights and
  responsibilities of parenthood 126
right to life: infants 35–36; negative
  right 80; positive right 80; protects
  persons from harm 42
right to privacy 7–8
Roeder, Scott 17
Roe v. Wade 1, 4, 5, 6, 7, 23n4,
  105n9, 128
Rosenbaum, Stuart 104n3
R vs. Morgentaler 78

Safe Haven laws 125
sanctity of life arguments: abortion in
  Bible 51; death penalty 52; Do Not
  Resuscitate order 55; and euthanasia
  53–55; infanticide 53; killing a
  human being 55; later abortions
  55; life sustaining treatment 53;
  modern genetic science 52; persistent
  vegetative state 53; physician assisted
  suicide 54; Promethean attitude 54;
  result of conception 52; supporter
  of slavery 53; Tay- Sachs disease 54;
  Western conception of God 51
Savulescu, Julian 136n25
Schiavo, Terri 67, 68, 70
Schnell, Lindsay 73n13, 73n14
Scialli, A.R. 23n1
Sedgh, Gilda 23n14
selective abortion: expressivist argument
  123–124; parental attitude argument
  124–125
self-motivated activity 31, 32
sentient in order to have
  interests 44
sex selection: China and India 114;
  against girl fetuses 114; restrict
  abortion choice 114
sexual assault 94
sexual exploitation 110
Sharnak, Debbie 138n38

Shimabukuro, Tom 136n24
Shimp, David 84
Singer, Peter 48n7, 48n8, 49n9, 49n12,
  49n13, 49n16
Solomon, Andrew 138n39, 138n40,
  138n41, 138n42, 138n43, 138n44,
  138n45, 138n46, 138n47
Stanton, Elizabeth Cady 111
state-sanctioned killing 1
Steinbock, Bonnie 50n22, 50n23,
  50n24, 50n25, 137n29
Stone, Jim 49n14, 49n17
strict sense *and* potential
  persons 40
Supreme Court decisions 1, 4, 5,
  7, 8, 12, 23n4, 23n11, 78,
  104n1, 134n1

Tawia, S.A. 50n28, 50n29
Terri Schiavo case 67
thalidomide 2, 3, 23n2
Thomson, Judith Jarvis 104n2, 104n3,
  105n12, 106n15, 107n26
Tooley, Michael 48n6, 48n7, 49n9

United Nation's Universal Declaration
  of Human Rights 86

A Vindication of the Rights of Women.
  111
the violinist example: abortion 85–88;
  anti-abortion argument 85; aplastic
  anemia 84; bodily autonomy
  84; continued survival 83; fetus
  personhood 85; moral obligation 82;
  need for survival 86; organ donation
  83; person's body integrity 86; pro-
  life arguments 85; rape 91; respect
  for the individual 85; right to bodily
  autonomy 86; right to life 85; right
  to use your kidneys 82; security of
  persons 86, 87;
  thought-experiment 83
virtue theory: financial hardships 117;
  freedom of speech 116; non-vicious
  reasons 118
voluntary sexual intercourse 91,
  93, 94

Warren, Mary Anne 48n3, 48n4,
  48n6, 49n9
Wells, Deanne 49n13

Wilcox, John 104n3, 105n11, 106n19
Wilson, Jeff 73n11
Wollstonecraft, Mary 111
wrongful killing 29–30
wrongness of killing: anti-poverty
  measures 61; continued existence 60;
  desire continued life 59; devoid of
  value 61; discontinuing of experiences
61; fraught of pain and suffering 60;
futures of value 61; wrong-making
feature of killing 60

Zhu, Wei Xing 135n13
Ziegler, Mary 134n3, 134n4, 135n6,
  135n8, 135n9, 135n12